Making Sense of Fatherhood

Gender, Caring and Work

As family and work demands become more complex, who is left holding the baby? Tina Miller explores men's experiences of fatherhood and provides unique insights into paternal caring, changing masculinities and men's relations to paid work. She focuses on the narratives of a group of men as they first anticipate and then experience fatherhood for the first time. Her original, longitudinal research contributes to contemporary theories of gender against a backdrop of societal and policy change. The men's journeys into fatherhood are both similar and varied, and they illuminate just how deeply gender permeates individual lives, everyday practices and societal assumptions around caring for young children. This book acts as a companion to *Making Sense of Motherhood* (Cambridge, 2005) and, together, these innovative studies reveal how gendered practices around caring become enacted.

TINA MILLER is a Reader in Sociology at Oxford Brookes University. Her research on motherhood and fatherhood has led her to be engaged as an expert advisor by the World Health Organization, to present her work at UNICEF headquarters in New York and to regularly participate in TV and radio programmes on issues related to motherhood, fatherhood and family life. She is the author of *Making Sense of Motherhood* (Cambridge, 2005).

Making Sense of Fatherhood

Gender, Caring and Work

TINA MILLER
Oxford Brookes University

CAMBRIDGE
UNIVERSITY PRESS

CAMBRIDGE UNIVERSITY PRESS
Cambridge, New York, Melbourne, Madrid, Cape Town, Singapore,
São Paulo, Delhi, Dubai, Tokyo, Mexico City

Cambridge University Press
The Edinburgh Building, Cambridge CB2 8RU, UK

Published in the United States of America by Cambridge University Press, New York

www.cambridge.org
Information on this title: www.cambridge.org/9780521743013

First published 2011

Printed in the United Kingdom at the University Press, Cambridge

A catalogue record for this publication is available from the British Library

Library of Congress Cataloguing in Publication data
Miller, Tina, 1957–
Making sense of fatherhood : gender, caring and work / Tina Miller.
    p.   cm.
Includes bibliographical references and index.
ISBN 978-0-521-51942-7 (hardback)
1. Fatherhood.   I. Title.
HQ756.M54   2010
306.874′20941 – dc22   2010035129

ISBN 978-0-521-51942-7 Hardback
ISBN 978-0-521-74301-3 Paperback

This book is dedicated to three fathers. The first two are no longer living but the legacy of their different styles of fathering is threaded through their children's and grandchildren's lives today. The first of these is my own father, Kenneth Arthur French, a wonderfully funny, intelligent and handsome man who provided a rock-solid foundation from which his four children's lives could unfold. The second is my father-in-law, John William Miller, a loving father and grandfather and great storyteller and immensely successful vegetable grower. Both of these men are missed on a daily basis. But in the here and now it is to Frank, the father of our three beautiful daughters, that this book is most centrally dedicated with love and thanks.

Contents

Acknowledgements

There are many people who have contributed in different ways to this book being written and who I want to acknowledge and thank. Although writing has enjoyably occupied many months of my time over the past two years, 'writing the book' (denoted in Joey from *Friends*' air apostrophes) has become a family euphemism to describe any activity *other than* writing a book (thanks, Kiff). I have been lucky enough to spend time working on the book whilst also enjoying encouragement and hospitality from friends in various places. These include Bettina and Volker in Switzerland, Giovanna in Milan and, closer to home, Diana and Kiff in Devon. Other writing companions to thank are Diana, Freya, Lydia and Phoebe who in their different ways kept me company on a writing trip in France. Back in the UK thanks also go to my colleagues in the department of International Relations, Politics and Sociology at Oxford Brookes University, and to Joanne Bailey and to Paula, Maria and Tin Tin at the Institute for Gender Studies at Oxford University where I spent an enjoyable and productive writing sabbatical. Thanks as always go to my three beautiful daughters, Hannah, Freya and Lydia, who are now delightful young women with exciting lives stretched before them and to Frank for endless cups of early morning tea. But final thanks go to all the men who shared their journeys into fatherhood with me. Without them this book would not have been possible.

Introduction

Recently, I was queuing in a large department store in a nearby city when I noticed that a sizeable crowd of people had gathered in a circle just beyond the checkout. When I craned my neck to see what had caused this amount of interest I was met with the sight of a father sitting on a chair bottle feeding his young baby. The crowd, mostly older women, were smiling admiringly and making enquiries as to the age of the infant, whilst I was struck by how *in*visible this activity would have been if it had been a mother sitting on the chair bottle feeding her infant: it would hardly have registered as people went about their shopping. But then fathers seem to be everywhere at the moment in the UK – in the press, in political party pledges, in policies and in public places and spaces – as visible displays of doing fathering become more common place and everyday. Ideas of more emotionally expressive men have become associated with ideals of involved, caring fatherhood as conjured up in media images of fathers such as David Beckham and Brad Pitt. Yet ideas and practices around fathering, just like mothering, have always been subject to change, and research has illuminated its diverse historical, cultural and social dimensions. But continuities, too, can be traced. For example, whilst we will see that the fathering expectations and practices of the men in this book are different to those of their own fathers, paid work remains a significant factor in all the men's lives and this is shared *across* the generations. The contemporary Western context in which fathering is experienced and fatherhood understood is, then, one of change *and* continuities *and* optimism. The optimism springs from the concurrence and overlapping of a number of shifts in societal structures and features, which appear to herald, and make possible, new opportunities for men's engagement in fathering practices in the UK.

This book is written as a companion text to an earlier work on motherhood, *Making Sense of Motherhood: A Narrative Approach* (Miller, 2005), and in response to a question regularly asked in relation to this earlier research – 'what about the fathers?'. The two studies have followed the same longitudinal trajectory capturing, this time round, men's narratives of transition to first-time fatherhood as these have unfolded. An overarching question has been to explore how men make sense of this period of transition and how this is similar to and/or different to the women becoming mothers in the earlier study. Fathering and societal ideas about fatherhood clearly exist in relation to societal ideas about mothering and motherhood. But these can be quite differently conceived and although contingent they do not exactly mirror one another: which is not to say that men lack a capacity to do the caring necessary to raise a child – as many men in a range of circumstances have demonstrated. But whilst more mothers now take up paid work outside the home this has not been matched by an equivalent number of men remaining at home taking on primary responsibility for childcare and/or domestic chores. The reasons for this are complex – and sometimes more straightforward – as will be seen across the chapters of this book. They encompass embedded gendered practices around caring responsibilities, policies related to work and family life, personal choices, and lack of choice and power. Exploring and illuminating the ways in which these areas come together and shape expectations, practices and experiences of first-time fatherhood provides a key focus in this book. The book also addresses questions which have arisen in other recent scholarship on fathering and so explores the ways in which 'the processes of women and men "doing gender" within households' become practised and how any 'gender differences are articulated and justified' by the men as new fathers (Doucet, 2006: 228; Dermott, 2008: 77). Gender, then, provides an important conceptual lens through which the men's unfolding experiences of new fatherhood are explored.

Researching and writing about men and fatherhood can be a tricky endeavour for all sorts of reasons: and there are numerous caveats I would want to place around this work whilst also celebrating the unique insights into gendered processes and practices the research makes visible. Fatherhood and its associated responsibilities and practices are not so clearly defined or morally 'policed' as motherhood. Even so, dominant and recognisable discourses of the 'good', involved contemporary father as noted earlier are now more prevalent and discernible across many Western societies (see chapters 1 and 2). These normative visions of fatherhood tend to conjure up images of men who are employed, partnered, present and intending to stay and where fatherhood fits temporally into an adult life-course so that (particularly economic) responsibilities for a child can be met. Clearly, many other ways of being a father are also possible and can be successful but these other ways are also likely to be more subject to scrutiny and/or problematised in policy (e.g., see Duncan *et al.*, 2010). The men whose experiences of becoming a father run through this book in many ways conform to the normative vision and discourse of the good, involved father outlined above. They are all employed in a wide range of skilled jobs that would mostly position them as middle-class, they are partnered (some are married) and they mostly regard becoming a father as a culturally recognisable stage in an adult life-course. They are also white (several are in ethnically mixed partnerships/marriages) and heterosexual and they are the biological fathers of their children. Their structural location and access to resources and corresponding choices are greater than those in less advantaged groups might enjoy (Miller, 2007). Yet it is because this group of men are so readily identified with normative ideals of the 'good' father and assumed practices of caring involvement that their particular experiences – and how these are understood, practised and voiced – are of interest. What do their unfolding and complex accounts of impending and actual fatherhood tell us about individual, masculinist practices of agency and caring, the contours of their involvement and how paternal identities are individually understood and managed? If the circumstances of these men's lives appear to present them with more possibilities and position them as most able to take up new initiatives such as parental and paternity leave and share caring in more equal ways, what actually happens at the everyday, household level? How is agency manifested and who is left holding the baby?

By taking a qualitative, longitudinal approach and focusing intensively on a group of seventeen men as they anticipate and then become fathers for the first time the findings from this study reveal both individual and collective practices and, most importantly, illuminate the intricacies and complexities of doing gender.[1] In turn, these findings are analysed and (in chapter 6) set alongside some of the data from the

---

[1] This was a self-selected sample resulting from a requirement set by the Oxford Brookes University research ethics committee that potential participants must opt into the study (see chapters 1 and 7 for further details).

earlier transition to motherhood study, providing compelling insights into gendered practices and narrations. This book, then, contributes to wider contemporary debates on men, fathering and masculinities by making an innovative and ultimately revealing contribution to this complex area. The findings go beyond simplified categorisations and representations of men as fathers and the fine-grained focus reveals how gender plays out in early parenting amongst this group of men in complex ways. And whilst the findings will be recognisable to many fathers (and mothers) – and have been when the data have been presented in different forums – they could not be and should not be generalised to all fathers. Similarly this book focuses upon a very particular, intense period as fatherhood and fathering relationships are anticipated and then established for the first time and it is acknowledged that these relationships will surely undergo change as children grow, other children are born and personal biographies and lives shift. Relationships will not just change over time but may also feel shaped in significant ways by the sex of the child. Other individual, couple and life circumstances will also mediate paternal relationships and practices of involvement and their possibility within lives that are lived in a wide array of social circumstances that also shift. But a notable and resilient thread running across much of the literature, and which overrides class, ethnicity and age, is many fathers' stated desire and intention of 'being there' for their child: yet as other research shows, complicated – and sometimes chaotic – lives can get in the way of this being achieved and/or sustained.

This book, as the book on motherhood before it, is written with the intention and hope of reaching a wide audience beyond the discipline of sociology from which it primarily emanates. It is anticipated that as well as being relevant to an academic and policy audience the book's focus on 'gender' (chapter 2) and subsequently how gender shapes men's (and women's) lives, choices and parenting practices, will be of use to those working in NGOs where gender mainstreaming is a prominent policy initiative, as well as to other practitioners and service providers. Importantly it is also hoped that men who are fathers or are anticipating becoming a father – or are just curious about this thing called fatherhood – will also find the rich, sometimes profound and sometimes humorous narratives of transition that are woven through the chapters both illuminating and thought-provoking. For comparative purposes the format of this book follows closely (but not exactly) that of the earlier motherhood book. The theoretical and conceptual framework is set out across the first two chapters and includes an overview of contemporary debates around fatherhood, caring, gender, paid work and masculinities. These areas are then illuminated further using the empirical data across the subsequent three chapters. As outlined above, the next chapter (chapter 6) brings together data from both transition studies. The theoretical considerations – particularly related to what the findings enable us to say about 'doing' and 'undoing gender' – are returned to in the final, concluding chapter alongside reflections on the methodological issues which have arisen during the course of the study.

Across the chapters key concepts and terms have been used and definitions of these now follow. This book, just as the motherhood book before it, is set against the backdrop of 'late modernity' (see chapter 1). This setting refers to contemporary society as a period which can be characterised by more rapid changes than in the previous period. A feature of these changes and transformations is that new possibilities are invoked – especially in relation to gender – as (some) individuals are seen to be less tethered to traditional, gendered ways of being. Contemporary fatherhoods and paternal identities are considered against this transformational backdrop (see chapters 1, 2 and 7) and specifically through the lens of 'gender' (see chapter 2). The term 'caring' features liberally throughout the chapters and is used in a generic way to refer to men's descriptions of meeting the needs of a new and growing baby through hands-on practices, activities and emotional thinking, commitment and responsibilities.[2] The term 'nurturing' is used much less because of its associations with physically breastfeeding a baby. 'Involvement' is used to refer to men's practices of caring, which range across hands-on involvement and sole responsibility for periods of caring, to their own perceptions of involvement as providing economically for their children and/ or just being physically present. Against the backdrop of late modernity, modern fatherhoods are shaped by 'discourses' and articulated in relation to these. Discourses are the societal visions of how things should be: individual lives often do not fit with these normative ideals but nevertheless dominant, gendered discourses are hard to escape as life events (becoming a father) are anticipated and everyday lives articulated in ways that

---

[2] It is recognised that 'caring' can be conceptualised in more nuanced and complex ways – for example, as components of an 'ethic of care' as in the writings of Fisher and Tronto (1990).

are culturally recognisable and socially acceptable (see chapter 1). The term 'fathering' refers to the personal individual experiences that men have as they engage in fathering practices whilst 'fatherhood' refers to the wider societal context in which fathering takes place and which is usually conjured up and reinforced through discourses – for example, the contemporary discourse of the 'good', involved father. Father-hood, then, like motherhood, is a socially constructed category which is shaped by and through an amalgam of political, social, cultural and historical antecedents and contemporary concerns. Interestingly, whilst the 'myths of motherhood' denote the ways in which individual mothering experiences so often do not resonate with the category 'motherhood', an equivalent gulf has not (so far) been articulated in relation to a misfit between individual fathering experiences and the category 'fatherhood'. Some of the men's narratives, woven across the empirical chapters of this book, provide insights into why this might be the case.

The contemporary context, then, in which men come to fatherhood could be described as more fluid than in previous times and so offering new possibilities. But it also remains deeply etched with the legacies of particular forms of masculinities alongside gendered notions of who does caring, especially for new babies and young children. Thus, seeing men engaged in some aspects of caring that has for so long been 'naturally' associated with women can still be regarded as novel and/or out of place as noted at the outset of this introduction. Yet for those men who want to take on a more hands-on caring – or even primary – responsibility for their child there can be obstacles too. As already seen, paternal identities and practices remain less distinct when set beside easily recognised – 'natural' – maternal spheres of assumed knowledge and practice: but this lack of recognition and 'natural' association can also make it easier for men to opt out. What follows, then, is a group of men's narratives of transition as they first anticipate and then set about being a new father and doing fathering. Their journeys, which are similar and varied, emotionally charged, frustrating, rewarding, depressing and ultimately (mostly) life changing, illuminate just how deeply practices of caring for our children are shaped by and through gender. But ways of doing gender differently are also optimistically glimpsed through these rich, unfolding accounts of transition.

1 | Gendered lives and caring responsibilities

An overview

I think in terms of the kind of era thing, I think, yeah, it's almost more acceptable now to be, you know, a man, a male, showing your emotions.

(Mike)

This book explores the journeys of a group of men into first-time fatherhood in the UK. It does so at a time when discussions about men and their involvement in family lives – or lack of involvement – continue to occupy political debate, newspaper column inches and of course individual and family lives too. Whilst so much around women's lives and motherhood is simplistically assumed, taken for granted and unquestioned, the relationship between men and fatherhood is seen as more problematic: requiring definition, 'claims' and other interventions in order to shape its visibility (or deny it), its dimensions and direction. The parameters of fatherhood are, then, less clearly drawn when set beside those which powerfully and morally encompass motherhood. But both are shaped by the 'choices' and constraints in which gendered lives are lived and which converge on the domains of the home and paid work. These domains provide the settings in which many of the responsibilities associated with motherhood and fatherhood – caring and providing – have been understood and practised. Yet these responsibilities and the ways in which they are understood and undertaken are not fixed but rather configured in relation to complex structural, cultural and gendered conditions in an historical moment. In discourses of modern fatherhood in the UK men's involvement in caring for their children has been positioned as (ideally) 'emotionally engaged', 'involved', 'active', 'sensitive', 'intimate' and 'positive' rather than as previously characterised more exclusively in relation to economic provision and the 'breadwinner role' or indeed absence. Such shifts correspond to more nuanced and critical understandings of masculinities and male identities together with other transformations in late modernity: but this is a complex, congested and shifting landscape. The ways in which lives are lived and men and women as mothers and fathers care for their children emanates from deeply embedded, 'durable', practices in which biological assumptions, patriarchy and power remain explicitly or implicitly woven together (McNay, 2000). Whilst shifts in discourses and policies may imply change, research findings continue to highlight entrenched and gendered practices in the division of domestic labour and paid work between the 'logic of cash and care' (Hobson, 2002). It is little wonder, then, that ambivalence and contradictory messages can characterise men's and women's experiences of caring and providing for their children. But what can an examination of the contours of modern fatherhoods and, importantly, a group of men's understandings and experiences of these tell us about how agency and gender are woven through and practised in this arena? How do choices and constraints operate alongside ideas of fathering 'responsibilities' to facilitate, restrict or deny possibilities in men's lives as they become fathers? And how are these understood in relation to motherhood? These questions form the overarching themes addressed across the book which, importantly, has at its core men's voices as they draw upon different discourses and narrate their experiences of transition through first-time fatherhood.

Researching men's lives

This book is written by a woman who is an academic, a mother and a feminist and who likes men. The research began with an optimistic belief that men can do the sort of caring for a child that we associate more usually with women as mothers in many Western societies: this is not a view shared by all feminists and/or those who wish to prioritise the mother–child relationship. The research was also undertaken at a time that seems to offer more possibilities and opportunities to men as fathers, as policies and traditional ideas are shifting, albeit in slow and uneven ways. The research involved many hours of listening to men talk about their hopes and fears as they anticipated fatherhood and subsequently engaged in early fathering for the first time. The data generated across the longitudinal research returned me to the academically theorised and familiar areas of patriarchy, equality, difference, power and contestation but in the unfamiliar position of writing about and representing men's voices. This led me to consciously prioritise the focus on men and fatherhood, avoiding the oft-felt temptation to add 'and mothers too' or 'what about women?' At times I felt unease in this experientially foreign land, aware that some might feel that I have 'sold out' and others that I have no platform from which to speak (Doucet, 2006; Dermott, 2008; Featherstone, 2009). Notwithstanding this, the research involved me in a much closer reading of the growing litera-ture on masculinities and the rich, longitudinal interview data provided more nuanced understandings of how different men in different ways make sense of, and negotiate, the terrain of modern fatherhoods. But I remain aware at all times that I am treading a difficult pathway through the highly contested areas of equality and difference in men's and women's lives around caring for our children. My overarching aim, then, was to listen closely to men's accounts through their tran-sition and to present these unfolding narratives across the chapters in this book, whilst recognising the struggles which have implicitly and explicitly circumscribed women's 'historical connection to care giving' and men's exclusion from it (Doucet, 2006: 29).

Setting the context

In recent academic and popular literature fatherhood has been descri-bed as 'in crisis' and as a 'work in progress' as men as fathers have 'become central figures on the policy agenda' amidst debate about whether this 'is a good thing' and questions around 'what father-hood is' and the 'future of fatherhood' (Hobson and Morgan, 2002; Dermott, 2008; Doucet, 2006; Featherstone, 2009; Hochschild, 1995; Lewis, 2000; Marsiglio *et al.*, 2000; Gregory and Milner, 2005; Lloyd *et al.*, 2003; Williams, 2008). Noted, too, has been an increased empha-sis on 'caring' and 'involved fatherhood' discourses, signalling an apparent 'detraditionalisation of fatherhood' – and gender more gen-erally – and emphasising the 'rising cultural importance of hands-on fathering' (Sanchez and Thomson, 1997: 750). In turn this has drawn attention to the 'competing narratives of fatherhood' that are now more apparent and available (Morgan, 2002: 278; Wall and Arnold 2007; Knijn and Selten, 2002; O'Brien, 2005; Vuori, 2009). Yet Lewis and O'Brien noted in the 1980s that 'discussion of the "new father" far outweighs evidence to demonstrate his existence' and so a concern within this book is to see how far changes have occurred in practi-cal terms (Lewis and O'Brien, 1987: 3; Williams, 2008). More recent research findings have, for example, shown that men can experience difficulties in 'being both provider and supportive partner and home builder' (Henwood, 2001; Henwood and Proctor, 2003), and that categorising resident fathers 'as either good providers or active carers fails to properly describe modern fatherhood' which is much more complex and multidimensional (Smith, 2007; Hearn *et al.*, 2006). This growing body of literature underscores the complex and contradictory landscape of contemporary fatherhood within which an assortment of father 'types' are included and appealed to, from 'biological' to 'non-resident' through 'absent', 'gay', 'adoptive', 'teenage', 'social' and 'stepfather', married, unmarried, living in 'intact families' or apart or in other configurations. These descriptions and definitions emanate from and reflect policy and legal concerns and individual practices (Collier, 2001; Duncan *et al.*, 2010). What is beyond doubt is that many men have become much more *visibly* involved in child-related activities. In this changing context, theorisations of men's lives and masculinities have also become more critically and sensitively focused upon (Connell, 2000; Connell and Messerschmidt, 2005). This has resulted in a move away from the idea of 'a single model of unified masculinity' and has precipitated consideration of aspects of men's lives as fathers and associated constructions of fatherhood (Morgan, 2002: 280; Vuori, 2009). The connections between these – masculine identities, fatherhoods and fathering practices – have been explored in relation to structural conditions – for example, employment practices and models of welfare – together with cultural, familial and individual understandings of caring responsibilities and practices (Hobson, 2002; Hearn *et al.*, 2006; Dermott, 2008; Rossi, 2006; see chapter 2). Reflecting upon these shifts, which are discernible in uneven ways across Europe, it has recently been noted that whilst 'traditional "solutions" in domestic arrangements' continue there is also a 'growing recognition of the micro-politics of fatherhood, domestic responsibilities and homework reconciliation *for at least some men*' (Hearn *et al.*, 2006: 43, emphasis added). These observations suggest that adopting a finer focus could reveal change – and the processes at work – at an individual and everyday level of practice: illuminating the 'micro-politics' and 'reconciliations' which shape, and are shaped through, individual lives and which form the focus of men's experiences of fatherhood in this book.

In this chapter the conceptual, theoretical and methodological framework for the areas explored across subsequent chapters is laid out. The first section examines how men's responsibilities as fathers have been conceptualised: what counts as 'involvement' and how have elaborations of care been understood in relation to men and workplace demands? By exploring these elaborations *over time* the interplay of individual agency and shifting structural conditions – and their gendered dimensions – becomes clearer. So, too, do the relational and unequal dimensions of the division of labour around the home and work and children – an important and well-trodden area in feminist writing across disciplines and generations (Firestone, 1971; Rich, 1977; Oakley, 1979; Chodorow, 1978; Hochschild, 1989). Contemporary understandings of fatherhoods and the practices of fathering are informed by cultural ideals woven through the discourses which shape and are shaped by political, legal, cultural and moral definitions and understandings of types of fathers. For example, the contemporary discourse of the 'good father' is based upon ideas of particular types of emotional involvement and sharing of care as well as financial provision and stands in stark contrast to ideas of the 'absent' or 'feckless' father conjured up in constructions of a 'bad father' discourse. Indeed it has been argued that trying to achieve all aspects of what a good (involved) father discourse encompasses is 'becoming more challenging' for men (Featherstone, 2003: 241). Discourses, then, thread through and inflect the relationships and corresponding behaviours that men might anticipate and eventually achieve or reject – or be denied – as fathers, workers and individuals. Discourses can be competing and can overlap and contradict, but a particular feature is their recognisable *everydayness*: their potency lying in the tendency for them to be taken as how things should be and correspondingly associated with 'truth' (Miller, 2007; Martin, 1990; Vuori, 2009). These areas – of caring practices and associated discourses – are, then, considered against the backdrop of late modernity and contemporary theorisations of agency and men's lives. Here 'rapid changes in gendered relations' characterise a less certain world in which it has been observed that 'emotional contracts between men and women are also being redrawn' as opportunities for gender displays become more relaxed (Featherstone, 2003: 244; Beck and Beck-Gernsheim, 1995). In the following section we chart the conceptualisations and associated

debates which have in different ways circumscribed men's lives, paternal caring responsibilities and everyday fathering practices, before
moving to a more detailed consideration of discourses and the contemporary context.

Caring

The division of labour in and between the home, caring for children
and the workplace have provided a fertile area of debate amongst
feminists and others for many years. These debates have ranged across
considerations of gender, biological determinism, models of welfare,
caring responsibilities and patriarchy and emanate from different
disciplinary positions. The advent of a child into this arena serves
to underscore the gendered and contested nature of these domains
and how responsibilities are conceived of and practised within them.
For example, writing in the 1990s Sanchez and Thomson argued
that 'parenthood crystallizes a gendered division of labour largely by
reshaping wives' and not husbands' routines' (1997: 747). But more
recent policy and other changes appear to provide the conditions
under which greater sharing of caring in relation to our children
and 'gender convergence' or 'gender symmetry' may be more tenable
(O'Brien, 2005; Doucet, 2006; Browne, 2007). This has included
in the UK context the introduction of 2 weeks' paid paternity leave
in April 2003 and the right for fathers to request 'flexible working'
and the 'duty' of employers to consider such requests under changes
in parental leave (O'Brien, 2005). Plans to further extend paternity
leave for some men under certain conditions are currently on hold
following the election of a new coalition government in the UK (http://
www.publications.parliament.uk/pa/cm201011/cmhansrd/cm100722/
debtext/100722-0001.htm, accessed 23 August 2010). All these
changes (which are considered further in chapter 2) remind us not just
of the permeability of constructions of motherhood and fatherhood,
but of their cultural dimensions. In contrast to the UK, a legal
entitlement to paid paternity leave was introduced in Sweden in
1974 but is still not available in some other industrialised countries –
for example, Ireland or the USA where economic fatherhood is
emphasised (Townsend, 2002). The provision made by different
policies and the models of welfare from which they emanate shape
in significant ways men's and women's caring practices in relation to

their children, home and the workplace (Ellingsaeter and Leira, 2006; Rossi, 2006). Possibilities and practices around parenthood are, then, extremely culturally specific and the impact they have on individual lives is dramatically different (Hobson, 2002). It is not just that different cultural policies and practices are discernible and confusing but in many countries they signal a continuation of workplace barriers which preclude even the possibility of more equal practices around care. But workplace structural conditions are clearly not the only factor here. Sitting somewhere in amongst all these debates, and explored later in more detail, are the more tricky and fundamental questions about men's capacities to care (Doucet, 2006; Vuori, 2009; Dermott, 2008) and so by implication whether mothers and fathers are 'interchangeable' (Holloway, 2009).

The categories 'fatherhood' and 'motherhood' are contingent and so made sense of in relation to each other and reinforced by and through 'modernist language' and 'gender dualisms' (Mac an Ghaill and Haywood, 2007: 43; see chapter 2). Ideas, then, about caring for children are shaped in relation to our notions of what fathers and mothers are and what they do – their 'obligations', 'responsibilities' and 'practices' – and these are shaped in both familial and wider social and cultural, classed and 'raced' contexts and historical epochs. The everyday experiences of fathering and mothering practices, 'being there' and the doing of childrearing and workplace activities, often do not resonate with wider societal constructions which continue to have at their core essentialist notions of who can – and should – 'naturally' care and how. The essentialist assumptions which shape women's lives and position them as maternal, whether they have children or not, continues to construct parenting in some Western societies in ways that can leave little – or at least ambivalent – spaces for men (Hearn *et al.*, 2006; T. Miller, 2009). And whilst years of debate have challenged such assumptions, emphasising the gendered contexts in which agency is understood and practised and pointing to research which has found that some women do not find mothering instinctive or natural, such ideas continue to be deeply embedded in many Western cultures (Bobel, 2002; Davis-Floyd, 1992; Hays, 1996; Hrdy, 1999; Miller, 2005, 2007). Men as new fathers, then, may find themselves looking for ways into this sphere, unsure of what their own involvement and caring practices should look like (Marsiglio *et al.*, 2000), but also be reassured by their presumption of a wife or partner's natural caring 'instincts' (see chapter 3). But this has not always been the case, as a review of historical representations of fatherhood and practices of fathering can reveal (Bailey, 2010; Gillis, 1997). For example, the idea of the remote, unemotional and disciplinarian father popular in Victorian and more recent imaginings and writing had supplanted 'the tender father' and 'nursing father' common in the eighteenth century (Bailey, forthcoming). These fatherhood types were characterised by 'hands-on' and emotionally involved 'caring' but became less fashionable as they came to be considered 'too effeminate' in the early 1800s. Whilst adopting an historical view enables us to see how ideas of 'good fatherhood' and associated ideals of masculinity have prevailed and changed over time, it also enables us to see how practices are accepted – or rejected – as displays of appropriate masculinities or femininities (Broughton and Rogers, 2007; LaRossa *et al.*, 2000).

Historians have shown that for a period in the late eighteenth and early nineteenth centuries the 'tender father' characterised the ideal of fatherhood in England (Bailey, forthcoming; Gillis, 1997). This representation of fatherhood emphasised men's devoted and 'loving engagement with children from infancy' and their participation in 'routine activities as well as play' (Bailey, forthcoming). Some two hundred years later this description of men's close emotional involvement with their children could equally well be used to describe contemporary discourses of the involved 'good father'. Yet the tender father was not regarded as being in opposition to, or eclipsing, the ideals and practices of motherhood at the time, but rather as a challenge to 'anti-patriarchal' masculinity. Indeed it is suggested that the advent of the tender father in this period 'may have been one way to maintain male ascendancy in an era in which the culture of childhood was coming to be dominated by mothers' (Bailey, forthcoming). The ways in which different fathering and/or mothering activities and caring relationships have been emphasised historically illuminates the temporal and varied dimensions of gendered practices against a backdrop of patriarchal power displays. Whilst the tender father may not have been constructed or regarded as being in opposition to 'a feminine other', in contemporary explorations, fatherhood and motherhood and their associated caring responsibilities and practices are relational. For example, a recent newspaper article titled 'Mum is the missing word' has echoes with the male ascendancy argument noted above, when it claims that 'motherhood has almost been erased from the lexicon of family policy' as mothers have been pushed into work and dad's 'encouraged' into 'fathering': it, too, alludes to changing forms of patriarchal arrangements but in the contemporary era (Roberts, 2008). The tender father, then, shows us that in previous times men *have been* involved in hands-on, emotional care of their children in ways that overlap with ideals of modern fatherhoods. This focus reveals men's capacities to care, just as a review of different cultural practices might reveal the same. But contemporary Western societies exert different pressures in relation to how economic provision and care giving are organised (Gregory and Milner, 2005; Hearn *et al.*, 2006; Hobson, 2002; Rossi, 2006; Townsend, 2002).

For many men as fathers, where, how and what caring constitutes in relation to their children is, and has been, significantly influenced by the structural condition of paid work outside the home (Lamb *et al.*, 1987; Townsend, 2002; Lewis and O'Brien, 1987). Attention has been drawn, for example, to the 'variations across generations in the ways in which men [have] expressed themselves in relation to masculinities' and their elaborations of 'fathering as *care*' (Brannen and Nilsen, 2006: 349, emphasis in original). 'Caring' and 'being there' for some men has been characterised by being a good breadwinner and providing economically for their family. For others, different understandings and practices of caring have been realised once the structural demands of paid work outside the home are removed – for example, in the case of grandfather involvement in hands-on caring for their grandchildren once they have retired from paid employment (Miller and Mann, 2008). Clearly, men's understandings and practices of caring *can* shift as circumstances – both personal and structural – change, but research suggests that often they do not. Findings from research carried out in North America have shown that 'despite significant increases in paternal involvement in recent decades, fathers still spend considerably less time in parenting activities than do mothers' and their involvement in housework remains low (Gaertner *et al.*, 2007: 962). These findings are echoed in research from the UK, other European countries, Australia and North America (Brandth and Kvande, 2003; Johansson and Klinth, 2007; O'Brien *et al.*, 2007; Ranson, 2001; Rossi, 2006; Torres *et al.*, 2007). Research has also shown that even though women are now much more active in the world of paid work, 'they still remain as primary caregivers' whilst men 'have retained a secondary role in care giving' (Doucet, 2006: 6; Plantin, 2001; Plantin *et al.*,

2003; O'Brien, 2005). This is even though there is much greater recognition of a discourse of gender equality across many Western countries (Rossi, 2006; Torres *et al.*, 2007; Vuori, 2009). Explanations for these different patterns of childcare and household involvement have included arguments about patriarchy and men's greater 'choices' and preferences around their involvement, to the discriminatory practices enshrined in policy and legislation, to the contradictions between 'the culture and conduct of fatherhood' (Wall and Arnold, 2007: 510) in which behaviours are found to be out of step with representations and discourses resulting in a 'lagged adaptation', to the powerful affects of 'maternal gate-keeping' and some mothers' reluctance to give up their 'status as primary parent' (Allen and Hawkins, 1999; Browne, 2007; Dermott, 2003, 2008; Gatrell, 2007; Gershuny *et al.*, 1994; Kimmel, *et al.*, 2005; McBride *et al.*, 2005; Sanchez and Thomson, 1997; Vuori, 2009).

However, although men's involvement in caring for their children has not changed as dramatically as structural or other changes would appear to have made more possible, some change across the course of the past 40 years is evident (Burgess, 1997). The 'slow pace of change' documented by Lynne Segal (1990) has been subsequently interrupted to some extent by some policy activity and other shifts. These have sought to tie *some* men more responsibly ('responsibly' here being largely equated with economic provision) into family life, whilst others have vociferously fought for recognition of their paternal and parental rights (for example, pressure groups such as Fathers 4 Justice in the UK: see Featherstone, 2009: 111). In policy terms in the UK, it has been claimed, there are 'two populations of fathers' – those who want to be more involved and those who are more absent (Lewis, 2002). Across these populations fatherhood research has, in more general terms, increasingly come to focus on the *quality* rather than the *quantity* of men's involvement in their children's lives (Lamb *et al.*, 1987; Marsiglio *et al.*, 2000; Marsiglio and Pleck, 2005; Gaertner *et al.*, 2007; Dermott, 2008; Stueve and Pleck, 2003). Previously, father involvement had been defined rather bluntly in terms of how much time fathers spend in activities which involve the child (Lamb *et al.*, 1987). At the same time the methodological problems of measuring or assessing men's involvement as fathers have also been noted (LaRossa, 1988; Doucet, 2006; Lewis and O'Brien, 1987; Burgess, 1997).

The consideration of the quality of men's involvement presents a complex task because of the wide variations in cultural, fathering and family circumstances and practices which can determine the parameters of quality and/or involvement. In broad terms the workplace, particular models of welfare, family dynamics and personal biographies, including learnt models of fathering, have been found to be significant determining factors in father presence and the quality of their involvement (Gregory and Milner, 2005; Masciadrelli *et al.*, 2006). But capturing the facets of men's involvement is a hard task. This is in part because the 'ambiguity and lack of specificity of the term "involvement" allows almost all fathers to be described in this way, despite their widely contrasting situations' (Dermott, 2003: 11). Also, as already noted, men's involvement as fathers has been interpreted in different ways at different historical moments and according to different and changing discourses of the 'good father' (Broughton and Rogers, 2007; Gillis, 1997). It has also included understandings and opportunities intricately compounded by class, occupation, 'race' and age. However, looking more closely at how paternal involvement is practised and narrated in men's lives may help us to better understand in more nuanced ways the change and lack of changes reported in research findings. In her UK research on fathers and work, Dermott found elements of what she has called 'intimate fathering', including 'emotional openness, communication and a close relationship to children' which can be seen as quality components in 'involved (good) fathering' (Dermott, 2003: 12). In other literature father involvement has been described as 'multidimensional' with 'direct engagement' found to be important at various developmental stages in a child's life (Gaertner *et al.*, 2007: 963). Men's positive involvement has similarly been associated with healthy outcomes for the child in terms of social and emotional wellbeing, including 'cognitive development' (Fägerskiold, 2008: 64; Plantin, 2007). Men's greater involvement in the home in dual-earner, couple households has also been reported to change 'attitudes to childcare and their parental role as a result' (Gregory and Milner 2005: 3). Recent research on dual-career couples with preschool children in the UK also reports that 'fathers demonstrated a higher level of involvement with children than might have been anticipated' given the findings of earlier parenting research (Gatrell, 2007: 360). Similarly, it has recently been reported that 'in dual-income households in particular, there is

growing evidence to show that men are taking increased responsibility
for childcare even if both men and women tend to identify the mother
as primary carer' (Williams, 2008: 490). Research indicates, then, that
more men are more aware at some level that 'good fathering' involves
emotional closeness to their children and in some cases more sharing
of caring activities as well as financial provision – in ways that are different to previous, twentieth-century generations. Yet where changes
in men's involvement have been noted – and there are significant country, cultural, group and individual differences – questions of what this
actually represents have been raised. For example, is men's involvement always a good thing and do such 'changes represent real social
"progress" or sometimes recreations of patriarchal dominance in relatively novel forms?': a question which will be revisited later in this
book (Hearn *et al.*, 2006: 124).

Whilst the quality of some men's involvement and the time spent
with their children has in real terms (at least) changed and/or increased,
'there seems to be relatively little change in fathers' *responsibility* for their children' which, it has been argued, 'remains limited'
(Gregory and Milner, 2005: 6, emphasis added; Clarke and Popay,
1998). Research has shown that there continues to be a 'tendency for
men to participate in the "fun" aspects of parenthood, while women
are in charge of the rest' (Johansson and Klinth, 2007: 19). It is to consideration of this that we now turn. In trying to tease apart and explain
men's continued secondary role in care giving, research has focused
on dimensions of involvement alongside what some have argued are
fundamental, biological differences between men and women. These
arguments in many ways converge on understandings of ontological
ways of being, thinking and doing in relation to caring for children
and how perceived differences between men and women as fathers and
mothers can be explained (Baraitser and Spigal, 2009). Contested ideas
of nature and nurture – including what, if anything, is 'unique' about
the mother–child relationship – sit at the core of these debates. Theorists in this congested domain range across a spectrum from socio-
biologists who emphasise the role of 'social selection' and instinctive and intuitive behaviours to poststructuralists for whom (almost)
everything can be reduced to discourse and 'gender displays' (Butler,
1990). Clearly, caring for a child involves at some level an overarching and all-encompassing way of thinking and doing which requires
much more than a set of practices and activities. But this orientation

and 'way of thinking' may, it is argued, be achieved through continual and repeated practice – for example, as Browne notes, '"parenting" demands a whole range of abilities . . . which, by any account, are not the sole preserve of one particular sex' (2007: 271). Yet of course if one person takes on this all-encompassing orientation and associated responsibilities then a context is created in which another parent can be – or is positioned as – secondary. A recurring question, then, has been 'can men care in this *primary* rather than secondary way?', or, put another way, 'can men mother?' (Doucet, 2006).

Masculinist constructions of mothering have, according to some commentators, focused exclusively on women's biological, and therefore assumed natural, instinctive capacities to take the primary caring role. This, then, implicitly and explicitly shapes the relational category 'fatherhood' and assumptions about men's activities and abilities as fathers. Yet in contrast, other feminist writers have sought to explain and illuminate the ways in which 'maternal practice' sits at the core of caring (Ruddick, 1989) and that a loving relationship may be developed over time and through practice but not experienced as natural, instinctual or instant (Miller, 2005, 2007). Similarly, others have emphasised the ways in which 'emotional labour', strategies and 'layers upon layers of socially constructed elaborations' have come to shape caring responsibilities in gendered ways (Hays, 1996: 13; Bobel, 2002; Hochschild, 1989; Hrdy, 1999). As Ruddick observes, 'care is not tied in any way to particular activities of female bodies, as mothering is often mistakenly taken to be' (1989: 46). Other explanations have drawn upon theories of psychosexual development to show the ways in which the organisation of childrearing *reproduces* mothering and associated ideas about caring capacities. This, it is argued, is because children are brought up by their mother which leads female children to eventually want to mother, but male children to seek relationships with women like their mother and so these behaviours are reproduced (Chodorow, 1978). In other philosophically informed work, Gilligan has used ideas of 'moral reasoning' to explain women's and men's different orientations in relation to caring and commitment. Here women have been associated with an 'ethic of care' or 'care voice', whilst men have been more closely associated with an 'ethic of rights' (Gilligan, 1982). More recently there has been a call to 'retheorize the fundamental importance of mothering to ethics, wellbeing [and] the "good society"' (Holloway, 2009: 2). This is in order to wrest the distinctive terms 'mothering' and 'fathering' from conflation within the term 'parenting' which can erase lines of gendered practices or be assumed to imply 'mothering'. The interplay between theorisations of gender, caring, mothering and fathering will be returned to in chapters 2 and 6. For now it is sufficient to note that attempts to explain men's and women's different types of engagement in childcare have ranged from biological imperative to unconscious 'intersubjective dynamics', philosophical ethics to social construction and psychosexual reproduction. Laid bare, such explanations can be seen to either exclude men from possessing the capacities to engage in care in more than just a supportive and secondary way, or, conversely, they powerfully underscore the ways in which caring responsibilities in relation to our children are socially, culturally and historically constructed *and* so permeable and changeable.

But what are we talking about when we move away from theoretical explanations of how caring work has tended to be divided in the West to focus on men's capacities to be proficient and capable carers? (Doucet, 2006). What are their obligations, duties and responsibilities – and abilities – within domestic, caring and work spheres as work outside the home becomes a more dominant feature of women's lives? Teasing apart responsibilities associated with caring, domestic work and paid workplace demands is complex and has been the subject of years of debate for many of the reasons already outlined above. In her thought-provoking book *Do Men Mother?*, Doucet draws attention to a range of literature to show how components of '*responsibility* in relation to the care of children' have been examined (2006: 34, emphasis in original). She cites, for example, the influential American research of Lamb *et al.* from the 1980s in which men's responsibilities as fathers are conceptualised and disaggregated into the spheres of 'engagement', 'accessibility' and 'responsibility' (1987). But the effective measurement and assessment – and indeed understanding – of these different facets of caring responsibilities are clearly problematic. This is also evident because much research has shown that structural conditions (e.g., workplace demands, employment structures, household types, models of welfare) affect the ways in which these responsibilities of caring are, or can be, practised in everyday life – and individual biographies will shape how these are construed. For example, in more recent research in the USA Townsend has noted the centrality of work in men's lives as part of what he calls the 'package deal'. This includes putting 'together a "package deal" of work, marriage, home and children' (Townsend, 2002: 30). Part of this 'package deal' involves recognition of 'successful' fatherhood as including 'emotional closeness, provision, protection, and endowment' and where financial provision for their children is seen as the most important of these facets of fatherhood (53). Even in countries where the 'nurturing man' has been acknowledged for many years (e.g., Finland) it is noted that men do not tend to 'raise questions of child care and family leaves at their workplaces' (Vuori, 2009: 17). Clearly, then, individual practices of agency and men's 'engagement', 'accessibility' and 'responsibility', shaped in relation to powerful ideals about providing for their children, are (currently) shaped in different ways to those of women as mothers. As women continue to be positioned as primary carers this affords men other choices and opportunities in a context where motherhood can be viewed 'as a societal duty and fatherhood as personal and elective' (Vuori, 2009: 1). Writing in the USA over twenty years ago Lamb *et al.* concluded that 'fathers are unlikely to change their life-styles radically so as to become more involved in child-care unless they feel that the changes are desirable and beneficial for themselves' (1987: 116). Other researchers, too, have noted that the demands of labour markets 'do not fit easily with the ideologies of caring fathers' (Knijn and Selten, 2002: 171) – or indeed mothers (Hochschild, 1989) or parents (Browne, 2007). And this appears to be the case even where men express a desire to be more involved (Brandth and Kvande, 2003). Fathering responsibilities have, then, been (re)conceptualised and (re)configured over time and across generations: their changing contours are woven through the 'powerful societal discourses which fathers are both subject to and invest in' (Featherstone, 2003: 241). Yet gendered dimensions of power remain an obdurate thread in the discourses which shape and inscribe ideas of modern fatherhoods, and practices of agency, and to which we now turn.

Discourses

It was noted earlier that more men have become more visibly involved in hands-on caring for their children. This visibility is apparent on many streets in many towns and cities across the Western world. Of course, sharing childrearing amongst extended family members has long been a feature of boys' and (some) men's lives in other parts of the developing world. This increased visibility resonates with cultural shifts in ideas of father involvement and the 'nurturing man' and 'new care-oriented masculinity' which can be traced through changing discourses of gender equality and rights and obligations emerging in policies, laws and (some) practices from the late 1980s in the UK, but earlier across other northern European countries (Johansson and Klinth, 2007: 2; Browne, 2007; Bjornberg, 1998; Gregory and Milner, 2005; Hearn *et al.*, 2006; Lewis and O'Brien, 1987; Vuori, 2009). But redefinitions and re-imaginings of contemporary fatherhood have been differently interpreted and enabled, or at least recognised, in policies and practices across different European countries (Johansson and Klinth, 2007; Brandth and Kvande, 2003; Hobson, 2002; Hearn *et al.*, 2006; Plantin *et al.*, 2003). For example, the introduction of the 'daddy quota/month' in parental leave legislation in the 1990s across Finland, Sweden and Norway clearly signalled a shift which highlighted and supported 'the care responsibilities of fathers' and elements of discourses emphasising 'equality' and 'shared parenting' (Knijn and Selten, 2002: 196; Bjornberg, 1998; Johansson and Klinth, 2007: 2; Vuori, 2009). But in contrast, whilst fathers' caring responsibilities have also been increasingly emphasised in the UK, their economic obligations to their families have also continued to be a pervasive feature (e.g., child support) (Lewis, 2002; Lewis and O'Brien, 1987; Williams, 2008).

The significance, then, of different models of welfare and policies and practices in powerfully shaping particular strands of discourse – and so normative ways of thinking about men's lives and fatherhood – should be noted. So too should the ways in which gender and social class continue to underscore and permeate this complex area (Plantin *et al.*, 2003; Walkerdine and Lucey, 1989; Gillies, 2007). Discourses are therefore culturally recognisable societal visions of how things are or should be (Miller, 2007). They are 'linguistic expressions' that we can feel compelled to draw upon, even when our actual experiences may not be reflected within them, such is their normative power (Vuori, 2009; Johansson and Klinth, 2007; Bjornberg, 2004). Through discourses, moral views are transmitted, which in implicit and powerful ways privilege certain meanings over others. So whilst strands of dominant discourses may have shifted in the European context emphasising men's caring responsibilities, it is important to acknowledge again both the diversity in types of fathers and family variability and, at the same time, the power of discourses to promote particular ideas of expected and accepted father behaviours (Bjornberg and Kollind, 2005; Barclay and Lupton, 1999; Dienhart, 1998; Duncan *et al.*, 2010; Featherstone, 2009; Kaganas and Day Sclater, 2004; Lupton and Barclay, 1997). For example, as Morgan has pointed out, 'most discourses around fatherhood privilege hetero-sexual identities' (2002: 275). Although it is clear that fathers are not a homogeneous group it is still hard to escape powerful discourses and their normative cultural meanings which 'play a key role in defin-ing the boundaries of the plausible, the possible, and the acceptable' in relation to modern fatherhoods (Hearn *et al.*, 2006; Featherstone, 2003; Wall and Arnold, 2007: 509).

Discourses, then, provide a powerful 'societal vision' of how things should be: but everyday individual experiences reveal how they really are (Johansson and Klinth, 2007: 2; Bjornberg, 2004; Morgan, 2002). At the core of this book sit the everyday experiences of a small group of men as they become fathers for the first time. Their accounts were collected in a study which repeated and complements an earlier piece of research on transition to first-time motherhood (Miller, 2005, 2007). But it is important to recognise that the discourses which inflect father-hood are both different *and* similar to those which circumscribe moth-erhood: their orientations are differently focused and presume/assume different types of engagement. For example, the 'moral minefield' of motherhood conjures up different demands and expectations when set beside those of fatherhood in the UK currently. So even though we can recognise cultural shifts in which fathers are now expected to be more nurturing, emotionally involved and sharing in care giving, choices and constraints continue to operate in ways that can impede realisation of these practices (Wall and Arnold, 2007: 509; Brandth and Kvande, 2003; Plantin *et al.*, 2003). The legacy of deeply embed-ded gendered and contradictory discourses, together with practices of patriarchy and other structural conditions, perpetuates and rein-forces divisions (Bradley, 2007). So policies and even attitudes may change but everyday practices do not necessarily follow. For exam-ple, in Sweden surveys since the 1980s have shown that whilst men have 'positive attitudes toward parental leave', the statistics and their actions can tell a different story of disappointing take-up (Johansson and Klinth, 2007: 2; Hearn *et al.*, 2006). A disjunction between changed societal attitudes and actual practices has been reported more

widely across Europe (Torres *et al.*, 2007). Exploring the interplay
between discourses, expectations, experiences and discursive practices
can, then, provide important insights into how different individuals understand and experience fatherhood and engage in fathering
practices (or continue not to) in a shifting context. These emerge from
and are reinforced by an amalgam of policies, legislation, popular culture and understandings of hierarchies of masculinities (Collier, 2001;
Connell, 1995; Johansson and Klinth, 2007; Kimmel *et al.*, 2005).
They can also be contradictory and experienced in ambivalent ways
and thus lead to the production of 'counter discourses' (Brannen and
Moss, 1991), 'counter narratives' (Miller, 2005) and dynamic discursive activity (Miller, 2007). For example, in the UK contemporary,
normative ideas about good fathers emphasise ideas of involved fatherhood *and* simultaneously the economically productive male worker.
Similarly, discourses around parenthood in which family continuity is
envisaged are at odds with those in which intimate relationships are
seen to be more transitory and increasingly at risk of breakdown and
divorce in more fluid social worlds (Bergnéhr, 2007: 1). The changes in
ideas which run through reframed discourses of modern fatherhoods
can be seen to echo wider societal changes which are claimed to be
features of late modernity and it is to consideration of this changing,
contemporary context that we now turn.

The contemporary setting

Change has always been a feature of all societies. More recently, however, social theorists have drawn attention to the more rapid transformations which have come to characterise what has been termed late-
or post-modernity. These transformations have led to a fundamental
questioning of established ways of doing, thinking, caring and being
as social life has become increasingly characterised by ambivalence,
insecurity, disorder and changes in time and space. The 'certainties' of
previous times – for example, the nature and pattern of working life,
'gender fates', family life and men's and women's traditional roles –
have been shaken up and can no longer be assumed. In this increasingly uncertain world, it is argued, intimate relationships and ways of
doing family have become more fluid and less tethered in traditional
patterns, resulting in increased fragmentation of social and cultural
life *and* greater individual choice (Beck *et al.*, 2003; Sheller and Urry,
2003); albeit that 'choice' will be shaped and exercised in the context

of particular individual, structural, material, gendered and cultural circumstances. The contemporary context, then, becomes one in which 'the normal family, the normal career and the normal life history are all suddenly called into question and have to be renegotiated' (Beck *et al.*, 2003: 4; Williams, 2008). Part of this 'renegotiation' calls for greater reflexivity on the part of the individual who must negotiate, and make sense of, a life in circumstances that are argued to be less embedded in traditional patterns or shaped by the experiences of previous generations. For example, although men's own fathers' involvement (or lack of) in their childhoods can inform their own fathering intentions, traditional practices can also be seen as outdated in the context of contemporary discourses of the 'new man' and emotionally involved fathering (Bjornberg, 1998; Johansson and Klinth, 2007; Masciadrelli *et al.*, 2006). It is not surprising, then, in this changing landscape that there is greater 'uncertainty' in relation to 'men's place in the home and as fathers a growing recognition of ambivalence' (Hearn *et al.*, 2006: 43).

The contemporary context is also one in which a 'complex project of self daily living' can characterise individual lives and practices (Holstein and Gubrium, 2000). It is argued that increased possibilities as well as uncertainties require that 'ontological security' or well-being is maintained in this more complex time through reflexivity and self-monitoring (Birch and Miller, 2000; Giddens, 1991, 1994; Miller, 2005; Lash, 1994; Lupton, 1999). These practices emerge as a response to the detraditionalisation of areas of social life and an increasing emphasis on individual subjectivity, agency and reflexivity (Giddens, 1991, 1994). Practices of agency and reflexivity and corresponding understandings of embodied selves can help to illuminate the ways in which individual social actors make sense of, and negotiate, events in a life in this more fluid and less certain world. But the concepts of reflexivity and so individualisation are not unproblematic and it is important to consider the assumptions which underpin them. All individuals possess a capacity to be reflexive but not all life circumstances either facilitate reflexivity and a project of self or render it a concern (Miller, 2005: chapter 1; Lash, 1994; Adkins, 2002). Similarly, it has been argued that some ideas of reflexivity and individualisation have been premised on masculinist assumptions which have neglected real, fleshy bodies, focusing instead on an 'overly rationalistic understanding of the late modern self and human action' (Adkins, 2002: 36; Bradley, 2007; Sevenhuijsen, 2000; Bjornberg, 2004). Issues related to gender identity in connection with subjectivity, embodiment and reflexivity had, then, been ignored in earlier theorisations of reflexivity and individualisation (Adkins, 2002; McNay, 2000; Jamieson, 1999). So too had proper consideration of the affects of structural conditions and its classed and 'raced' dimensions (Lash, 1994). As daily living has become entwined with notions of individuals' (working on) 'projects of the self' there is a danger that these are always assumed to be emancipatory or implicitly teleological, yet sometimes life is just about getting by and surviving. However, notwithstanding these important critiques, a focus on reflexivity together with understandings of selves and individualisation have usefully oriented thinking, further critique and new, more nuanced theorisations of selves and agency (Adkins, 2002; McNay, 2000; Miller, 2005). In this contemporary setting, then, 'we are never simply selves, but gendered selves' who make sense of the world, and operationalise agency, from classed and 'raced' positions circumscribed by gendered assumptions (Coole, 1995: 123). These in turn are shaped through the legacy of traditional (sometimes regarded as outdated), 'durable' practices and interwoven with new elaborations and possibilities (McNay, 2000: 2). In this less certain context a focus on how individuals reflexively make sense of life events and narrate their gendered selves has become one way of producing more nuanced theorisations of everyday lives (for a more detailed account see Miller, 2005: chapter 1; Frank, 1995).

Narratives

It has been argued that through narrative construction individual 'life is given unity and coherence' as 'discrete actions which lead nowhere' are given order or rendered coherent by the individual (MacIntyre, 1981: 199; Miller, 2005). At some level, then, we are all storytellers who bring meaning to our actions through the stories we tell – our narrations of our lives and selves which as social actors we present to others (Plummer, 1995). Clearly, being able to produce coherent and culturally recognisable and acceptable accounts of events is an important feature of the storied human life in late modernity (Miller, 2005). But just as the associated practices of reflexivity are subject to particular conditions which can either facilitate its practice or override its relevance, so too actively engaging in producing acceptable narrative accounts may be heightened when set amongst particular life events – for example, where understandings of selves and identities are challenged by significant change or transitions (Miller, 2005). Similarly, other research has shown that if experiences do not match expectations or coincide with intentions then an individual's ability to produce or sustain a coherent, culturally recognisable and socially acceptable narrative may be compromised (Frank, 1995; Miller, 2005). Whilst for women becoming mothers this can lead them to work hard to produce what they feel to be acceptable narratives of early mothering, only *retrospectively* feeling able to risk revealing how it really was, is this the same for men? Do the morally inflected responsibilities and obligations embedded in the discourses which circumscribe motherhood and ideas of how things should be, similarly emanate from the discourses and experiences which shape men's lives on journeys into first-time fatherhood? Are men so compelled to narrate their experiences in these ways? Taking a longitudinal focus to explore paternal subjectivities through transition will illuminate how a particular group of men make sense of past experiences, present and future hopes and expectations: how selves and identities are understood, practised and narrated *over time* in what is for them the subjectively uncharted territory of new, early fathering.

In anticipating, making sense of, and narrating experiences of fatherhood individuals are faced with a range of 'competing narratives' (Morgan, 2002: 278; Miller, 2007; Vuori, 2009). Yet although experiences of fatherhood may be different to how they have been imagined, the 'limited repertoire of story lines' which it has been argued are available to women as mothers may not be so drawn for men (Miller, 2005: 160). Dominant and 'counter' discourses reinforced by gendered practices of socialisation, and played out across the structural features of Western societies, can present choices *and* constraints to men as fathers that are different to those available to women as mothers (Brannen and Moss, 1991; Lupton and Barclay, 1997; Doucet, 2006; see chapters 2 and 6 of this book). But this is not to suggest that men's pathways into, and experiences of, fathering are less confounding than for women as mothers, but rather that more, and different, choices and options are open to them. Indeed the apparent range of possibilities in men's lives can facilitate or deny different elaborations of fathering involvement. Whilst ideas about women as mothers are too readily assumed, men as fathers do not conjure up such universal – albeit erroneous – visions. It is not surprising, then, that terms such as 'ambivalence' and 'uncertainty' have been used to describe men's experiences of agency and their production of 'new self-narratives' in relation to contemporary fatherhoods (Featherstone, 2003; Hearn *et al.*, 2006). This is because whilst dominant – hegemonic – discourses and other experiences provide ideas about how things *should be* the lived reality of everyday life is always more complex and lived as things are. Men as fathers of course 'have many different standpoints and many different stories to tell about their lives and experiences' (Morgan, 2002: 286) and this book focuses on what can be seen as the 'stories' of a more privileged group of men (employed and part-nered) as they embark on what could be called 'optimistic journeys' into fatherhood (pregnancies are proceeded with positively, even if not necessarily planned). In many ways they appear to conform to an unspoken but nevertheless recognisable (and so normative) 'ideal model of fatherhood' conjured up and conveyed in discourses of the 'good, involved father': they mostly self-identify as middle-class, they are white and heterosexual and will not be seen to have embarked on fatherhood at too young an age. They, too, appear to have accepted 'dominant cultural images of masculinity' (Townsend, 2002; Doucet, 2006). Yet this does not mean that we should dismiss or not 'lis-ten carefully and critically' to their experiences (Morgan, 2002: 286). Rather, it is important to do so specifically in order to 'develop a more nuanced picture than that invoked in stereotypes' which have been premised on men such as these (Featherstone, 2003: 241). Indeed, as will be seen their experiences turn out to be diverse, complex, per-plexing and rewarding and they challenge the dominant discourse of involved fatherhood whilst illuminating in dramatic ways the gendered dimensions of agency, selves and reflexivity.

Methodology

The data which sit at the core of this book were generated by fol-lowing a group of seventeen men through a period in which they became fathers for the first time, replicating the earlier motherhood study (Miller, 2005, 2007) and producing comparative data.[1] The study was UK based and the data collection period ran from 2005 to

---

[1] See the introduction (pp. 2–3) for further details of the sample and caveats.

2009.[2] As noted in the introduction to this book the data from the study add to wider contemporary debates on men, fathering and masculinities by making a small but innovative, timely and ultimately revealing contribution to this complex and unfolding area. More importantly, the findings go beyond simplified categorisations and representations of men as fathers and the fine-grained and longitudinal focus used reveals how gender plays out in complex ways, and is articulated, across early parenting. These findings contribute to more nuanced theorisations of how gender is 'done' amongst a group of men (and their wives/partners) who at the outset appear to largely conform to normative ideals of the good, involved father. The study design involved taking a qualitative approach with a specific emphasis on how individuals make sense of transition and personal change through a longitudinal focus on narrative construction. Importantly, transition here is seen as a *process* rather than an event. As with other research using qualitative methods this approach produced 'intensive evidence' on individual-level experiences and processes which are not captured in complementary large-scale quantitative approaches (Duncan *et al.*, 2010: 16).

The design, analysis and theorisations within the fatherhood research were informed by the earlier study on transition to motherhood and some comparisons between the data sets are included specifically in chapter 6. The contingent and relational dimensions of the categories 'fatherhood' and 'motherhood' were continually apparent in the ways in which discourses were drawn and narratives constructed and presented. The intensive and iterative longitudinal research design involved in-depth interviewing of the participants on up to four occasions before and following the birth of their first child(ren). In this way the design addressed the need to study men's 'pre- and postnatal experiences' which has been acknowledged as lacking in other research (Marsiglio *et al.*, 2000: 1179). The first interview was timed to take place around 7–8 months into the pregnancy and the subsequent interviews scheduled to take place at 6–8 weeks following the birth, and then at 9–10 months after the birth. The timings of the first three interviews followed those in the motherhood study. In addition a fourth interview was carried out with some of the fathers at around

---

[2] At the time of the study the participants were geographically located in the southern half of the UK – from the South West across to London.

the time of their child's second birthday, thus providing a longer view of their experiences. This detailed, iterative research approach, which also included email 'conversations' between interviews and an end-of-study questionnaire,[3] generated compelling, complex and contemporary accounts of these men's experiences of transition to first-time fatherhood.[4]

Recruiting men into a study to talk about their selves and fatherhood during the period before the birth of their first child was not without challenge (Dermott, 2003). Research has shown that men can feel detached and peripheral to the (embodied) processes of pregnancy that their wives/partners are going through (Draper, 2002a, 2002b; Locock and Alexander, 2006). Other research has noted the (potential) difficulties of getting men to talk in unstructured/semi-structured qualitative research and university ethics approval had also required that potential participants must 'opt into' the study. Given these less than ideal conditions, a range of recruitment strategies was employed to try to attract a diverse sample of potential participants. This included posters and leaflets (containing opt-in details and a returnable postcard) being displayed in a large car manufacturing plant, a city bus depot, a sports centre and a high street store selling baby equipment. Subsequently, 'snowballing' was also used successfully. Over the course of several months and following initial enquiries which did not translate into participants, an eventual sample of seventeen men 'consented' to participate in the study. All the men were white, heterosexual and living with their wife or partner at the time of the study and all were the biological father of the expected child(ren). The mean age of the participants was 33.7 years at the time of the first interview; ages ranged from 24 to 39. In the UK average paternal age is on the increase and the mean age of fathers in England and Wales had increased to 32.1 years

---

[3] The end-of-study questionnaire was sent out following the third interview as had happened in the motherhood study. It was designed to collect data on age, education, etc., and to ask participants to assign themselves to a social class. In addition participants were asked about their experiences of being in the longitudinal study and whether there was anything they had felt unable to talk about in the interviews, in response to which one participant wrote: 'I'm glad you didn't ask about sex.'

[4] Although the findings have been recognisable to many fathers (and mothers) when they have been presented in different academic and practitioner forums they are not and could not be generalised to all fathers. The findings are theory-generating and illuminating, in detailed ways of personal experiences, rather than generalisable.

in 2003 (Bray *et al.*, 2006) although trends are complicated by some differences in births occurring outside marriage (*Social Trends*, 2006). All but one of the participants were UK citizens; the one who was not was a North American professional studying in the UK at the time the research was undertaken.[5]

Interview guides which closely resembled those used in the earlier motherhood study were used in each of the in-depth interviews and covered areas such as expectations, practices and perceived individual and societal change, which were revisited in subsequent interviews in order to explore shifts. In addition, newspaper cuttings of topical events involving fathers (e.g., Fathers 4 Justice) were taken along to the first interviews as an extra 'prompt' if needed: but these were never used. The longitudinal component of the research both captured the fluidity of a transitional life process (becoming a father) and invited a more relaxed research relationship to become established as participants came to feel more comfortable and familiar with the interview process. The majority of interviews took place at the home of the participant but some were carried out in workplace locations, my university office and on one occasion a motorway service station. The interviews were mostly carried out in the evenings or weekends, reflecting the way these men's lives continue to be patterned by employment following the birth of their child(ren), in ways that in the early months the new mothers' lives were not. The men's competing home and workplace demands also made it difficult to get back to do follow-up interviews according to the time frame followed in the earlier motherhood study. And at times I felt that the fine line between coercion and persistence was trampled as I made repeated attempts to arrange interviews. I was also aware once again of the problematic nature of gaining informed consent in longitudinal research in which participation can be agreed to in circumstances, and at a time, when the course of transition cannot be known, only anticipated (see Miller and Boulton, 2007 for more details). But in almost all cases the original three interviews were eventually carried out – only three individual interviews being missed, in two cases because of work demands requiring participants to travel overseas.[6] The fifty-seven interviews which

---

[5] This participant was not available for the third interview as he was by then working overseas. His North American background was continually reflected upon during the analysis of the data from his interviews.

[6] See chapter 5.

lasted between 1 and 3 hours were tape recorded and transcribed
verbatim. At the end of the study transcripts from the interviews were
copied and bound and sent to those participants who had confirmed
they wanted to receive a copy. This action was taken as a token of
thanks rather than for transcript checking purposes.

   In the earlier study on motherhood, data analysis involved examining the ways in which multilayered narratives were strategically produced by participants in order to demonstrate conformity to – or
later challenge – dominant discourses and societal visions of being a
'good mother': this rigorous technique was repeated here focusing on
constructions of masculinities and fatherhoods (Miller, 2005, 2007).
Initially the interview data were thematically and narratively analysed
as individual, separate episodes in which themes were identified; also
considered were how selves were positioned and the language used.
The next step involved putting the individual's interviews together,
thus providing a longer, unfolding overview of their transition. The
individual episodes were also analysed alongside those of the other participants (see the thematic organisation of the empirical chapters in this
book) and finally the participant's individual narratives were collectively analysed and compared. Over the course of the research the men
embarked on narrative trajectories in which the types of accounts produced changed as structural realities (e.g., paid work) and the demands
of caring for a new baby/young child came together. Yet what seemed
apparent at the outset and became much clearer as the men's journeys unfolded was the much greater availability of ways of position-
ing the self as a good father and/or worker. This range of positions
was made possible because of different constructions of masculinities
and strands of discourse in which experiences could be located and
agency accordingly operationalised. As the men's journeys into fatherhood and narrative trajectories unfolded, significant involvement and
(sometimes equal) sharing of caring for the children was optimistically
envisaged: but the practices over time came to reveal a different and
more complex story.

Conclusions

It is clear that elaborations of care giving and the practices and
associated responsibilities of caring change over time. Conventional
assumptions about women's lives have included an expectation of them

'being there for others' (Adkins, 2002). But more recently contemporary understandings of care-oriented masculinities and discourses of 'involved fatherhood' have led to a greater emphasis on men, too, 'being there' for their children in more emotional ways which have been previously more closely associated with women. At the same time policy shifts have been put in place that appear to offer some opportunities for *some* men to realise greater hands-on involvement in caring for their children. Whilst the amount of time fathers spend on childcare has increased in more recent years this increase emanates from a low starting point (*Social Trends*, 2006; O'Brien, 2005). So, whilst women's participation in paid work in the UK has increased dramatically men's contribution more generally in the domestic sphere has not. The greater involvement in childcare noted in some research does not often involve men taking *primary* responsibility for their child but rather spending more time engaged in specific tasks and activities with them. But these are often mediated through their wife/partner who continues to be positioned as having primary responsibility (Townsend, 2002). The question of whether or not men possess the capacity to plan, schedule, remember, feel, think and take action in relation to their children must also be understood in relation to the social and cultural contexts in which lives are shaped and in which choices, 'preferences' and constraints are experienced. Whilst it is recognised that capturing paternal responsibility is a complex task (Dermott, 2008; O'Brien, 2005) and that there may be some 'discrepancy between what men say and what they do' (Johansson and Klinth, 2007: 2) the fine-focus, longitudinal approach taken in this book will illuminate what men say, and do, as they embark on personal journeys of transition to fatherhood. What in the context of modern fatherhoods does men's caring for their children look like? And can more critical and contemporary theorisations of gender and masculinities illuminate further the ways in which choices and constraints operate in men's (and so, women's) lives as they become fathers? In the next chapter contemporary debates around gender, masculinities and the division of labour are explored.

2 | *Gendered discourses*

Men, masculinities and fatherhood

We do very briefly speak about child related...I don't think the conversations necessarily become feminised, I think the behaviour is going that way.

(Gareth)

What is gender? In many areas of life the term 'gender' is used liberally and often incorrectly as a shorthand reference to women's lives and issues of equality. But gender is equally about men's lives. In its simplest form 'gender' refers to what it is to be 'masculine' or 'feminine' at any given time in particular social and cultural contexts. It is a fluid concept which can help us to understand how expectations, behaviours, assumptions and practices are socially and culturally shaped and varied and change over time. Importantly, it is different to the term 'sex' which refers to biological differences in and between men's and women's bodies: aspects which are usually taken to be (more or less) fixed. But these simple definitions belie the highly contested dimensions of these terms and the debates which have ensued, ranging across theoretical, empirical, legal and policy terrains. These debates have focused upon whether, and how far, it is possible to disentangle 'gender' from 'sex', whether these two ways of thinking about individuals and bodies are sufficient or proficient and the implications of such conceptualisations. New theorisations, prompted by changes in the ways lives are (or can be) lived in contemporary society, together with advances in biological sciences and more nuanced understandings of masculinities and femininities, have led to both greater recognition of gendered practices across a myriad of social arenas *and* a more critical interrogation of the concept. Theorising gender has, then, become more complex and less certain. In practice, the much greater recognition of how societies are organised in gendered ways – and the displays of power which can underpin these – has led to a preoccupation with women's lives, patriarchy and questions of equality and difference. If biology patterns lives in what are currently limited, and more specific, ways, gender offers all sorts of possibilities as 'a social category' which includes men too (Scott, 1988). It is an error, then, to think of gender as something just associated with women. But it is not surprising that this has been the case given the structures and practices of (what is now termed) 'patriarchy' which have historically patterned women's lives in unequal, limiting and sometimes violent and abusive ways (Walby, 1990; Seidler, 2006). Given this legacy it is also not surprising to find that much research continues to reveal men's domination in a range of areas of the social world (Hearn *et al.*, 2006). However, the arena of reproduction and the associated practices and responsibilities of childcare are one setting in which women have historically been much more closely associated, tied in through erroneous and overriding assumptions of essentialism and women's biology being their destiny. But such ideas have left little space for consideration of men as involved actors in this arena – misplaced assumptions about their biology largely locating them in activities outside domestic caring domains. More recently such omissions and assumptions have been increasingly challenged as more critical understandings of the inter-actions between gender and masculinities and their variations have been explored alongside recognition of different types of patriarchy (Browne, 2007; Connell, 1995; Peterson, 2003; Hearn *et al.*, 2006; Hobson and Morgan, 2002; Seidler, 2006; Walby, 1990). In order to illuminate these areas, this chapter will examine further the contested concept of gender, providing an introduction and overview to some of the debates, before moving to consider the growing literature on 'mas-culinities' and the implications of both these areas on men's lives more generally and the practices of modern fatherhoods in particular. This focus on gender will also provide a platform for examining changing political and policy contexts across Europe, before focusing on the UK where the research discussed in subsequent chapters is set.

Gender

The term 'gender' gained impetus in the social sciences in the 1970s and 1980s as a way to classify 'individuals socially rather than just biologically' (Browne, 2007: 1; Jackson and Scott, 2002). This was as a result of the growth of academic activities in women's studies and feminist movements and challenges to a social system premised on male dominance (Bradley, 2007; Oakley, 1972; Jackson and Scott, 2002). It was argued that if 'gender was a cultural phenomenon' and so gendered behaviours were learned, they could also 'be unlearned' (Bradley, 2007: 17). Such a position challenged many taken-for-granted aspects of how the social world was structured and how women's and men's lives were organised within it in unequal ways. Until this time differences between men and women had been more accepted – or at least tacitly understood – as consequences of biology and genital and genetic differences, which 'naturally' predisposed women to emotional, caring, 'expressive' behaviours and men to 'rational', emotionally detached actions. The debates around inequalities between men and women and the role of biological differences, which characterised this period, drew upon the conceptualisations and theoretical frameworks of 'patriarchy' and 'essentialism'. Patriarchy, albeit configured in different ways, refers to 'a social system of male dominance' in which men have more power, access to resources and corresponding choices than are available to women as a result of the ways in which societies are organised (Bradley, 2007: 16; Walby, 1990). 'Essentialism' is the term which is used to describe and explain inequalities between men and women as naturally occurring, 'essential' differences. For example, up until the early 1970s explanations of the division of labour around caring, paid work, parenting and childrearing drew heavily upon naturalistic and essentialist assumptions about women's lives: explanations reinforced by the 'evidence' provided by other arrangements (e.g., men's paid work outside the home), and taken to be the 'natural order' of how things should be (Stanley, 2002). But such explanations neglected the socially and culturally produced and reinforced character of this 'natural base' (and even the term itself) along with implicit power dynamics which had led women to be positioned as primary carers (Hays, 1996). Explaining women's oppression through the lens of gender analysis characterised much of the groundbreaking work undertaken by feminists in the early 1970s (Bradley, 2007; Rich, 1977; Segal, 1990; Oakley, 1974). In the intervening years, debates around the gendered dimensions of men's and women's lives have intensified as philosophical and theoretical developments have led to more critical concerns, questions and contestation.

Whilst contemporary debates around gender relations have continued to share a concern with unjust inequalities, these are now considered across a broader philosophical, theoretical and contextual canvas using 'a variety of analytical and methodological tools and approaches' (Hearn *et al.*, 2006: 5). These developments have drawn attention to the fluidities and increasing complexities of individual lives lived in contexts where claims about 'a weakening of the determining character of gender' imply new possibilities and raise new challenges (Morgan, 2002: 278; Deutsch, 2007). Developments in studies of sexualities, biology and medicine have led to previous distinctions between 'sex' and 'gender' being revised as more permeable dimensions of bodies and boundaries have been acknowledged (Shilling, 2003). Similarly, the ways in which class, 'race' and sexual orientation 'intersect with' gender and so 'break down the dichotomous notion of gender' have also been noted (Deutsch, 2007: 117). These shifts away from a focus on fixed and immutable categories, together with an increased rejection of dichotomous thinking, arise in part from theoretical shifts associated with poststructuralism and postmodernism (Bradley, 2007; Peterson, 2003; Seidler, 2006). One of the most notable contributions to emerge from this latter theoretical paradigm has been the work of Judith Butler. Butler argues for an alternative way of thinking about and 'doing' gender which is achieved by deconstructing the binary categories of 'sex' and 'gender'. In her work, gender is argued to be a construction and an 'imitation' without an original which is enacted through 'imitative performances' (Butler, 1990). For Butler, then, gender is seen to imply a core which does not exist and where 'the production of self and gender [are] a discursive effect' (Elliott, 2001: 117). But whilst Butler's work has been thought-provoking it has also been critiqued by some for not taking sufficient account of real bodies and the management of embodied selves and structural histories. Others, however, have claimed that through her work 'Butler outlines the significance of the body as a medium through which the discursive signs of gender are given corporeal significance' (Nayak and Kehily, 2006: 468). But gender is also experienced in contexts that are materially diverse and enacted in circumstances where choices and power inflect and shape agency. So whilst gender is something we *do* (West and Zimmerman, 1987) it is practised and understood from embodied and diverse positions in the social world and in relation to – and at times inseparably from – the binary category 'sex' (Messerschmidt, 2009).

Understanding the social world in the context of binary classifications – for example, 'woman' and 'man' or 'mother' and 'father' – orientates gendered meanings, discourses and (potentially) corresponding behaviours in particular ways (Kagansas and Day Sclater, 2004). It also implies 'biological determinism, essentialism' and heteronormativity, all of which are dominant motifs running through the literature on maternal studies and, differently oriented but also dominant, in much of the literature on men and fatherhoods (Peterson, 2003: 55). For example, using language premised on the 'gendered dualism of female homemaker' and 'male breadwinner' underlines and universalises particular ways of thinking about and doing mothering and fathering (Mac an Ghaill and Haywood, 2007: 43). This is because it implies, and so reinforces, essentialist and bio-logically determinist ideas of differences between women and men and their associated responsibilities, thus explaining particular gendered activities. Yet individual experiences are not universal as evidenced by research which has repeatedly revealed women's varied, ambiva-lent and sometimes baffling experiences of mothering and mother-hood within and across cultures (Bobel, 2002; Davis-Floyd, 1992; Hrdy, 1999; Hays, 1996; Oakley, 1979; Rich, 1977; Miller, 2005). At the same time, within the growing body of literature on masculinities and fatherhood, some men's capacities to be 'proficient care-givers' has also been documented alongside commentary on absent, 'feck-less' and 'fragile' fathers (Gaertner *et al.*, 2007: 962; Doucet, 2006; Johansson and Klinth, 2007; Dermott, 2008; Duncan *et al.*, 2010; Brannen and Nilsen, 2006). Developments in studies of gender have, then, led to timely calls for 'a more reflexive use of categories and con-cepts' rather than 'unhelpful dichotomies' and a 'corrective insistence' through recognising and paying attention to 'complexity and multiplic-ity' (Bradley, 2007: 71; Seidler, 2006: 33; Peterson, 2003: 55). One of the consequences of this has been a shift in academic attention to focus on theorisations of masculinities and fathering engagement and practices – the doing of fathering – which are explored in more detail later.

To recap, then, the intention of this overview of gender has been to introduce some of the key debates which have shaped ideas around the concept of gender and also to emphasise its changing and contested character. This aspect includes more recent calls to 'ask how we can undo gender' and the need for greater attention to be paid to exam-ples of 'undoing gender' or 'genderless' behaviours in gender research (Deutsch, 2007: 106; Risman, 2009: 81). For example, Risman has recently noted that 'as marital norms become more egalitarian, we need to be able to differentiate when husbands and wives are doing gender traditionally and when they are undoing it – or at least trying to undo it' (2009: 82). Indeed could it be that the increased involvement in caring practices by some men is evidence of 'undoing gender' or just doing gender differently rather than 'traditionally'? Does 'undoing gender' mean 'genderless'? And how do issues of power and choice operate in these negotiations? These important questions will be returned to as men's accounts of new fatherhood unfold across subsequent chapters of this book. Questions about the 'efficacy' of the concept of gender itself have also arisen more recently amidst concerns that it can obscure what in practice are 'discriminatory practices' based on 'sex' whilst appealing to 'stereotypical assumptions' based on gender (Browne, 2007: 272). Similarly, questions have been raised about 'what kind of change is actually *desired*' and whether even '"gender equality" is in fact a desired goal' (Sullivan, 2000: 438, emphasis in the original). It is no surprise, then, that studies 'have shown that people, including researchers, have different ideas about the meaning of gender equality' (Bjornberg, 2004: 34). Yet the outcome of these ongoing academic debates and developments has, importantly, resulted in a much greater sensitivity to, and knowledge about, the everyday gendered social world and a greater understanding of pragmatic responses to its affects. These debates have highlighted socially and culturally constructed inequalities and injustices between and within women and men's lives in different and varied contexts. Informed by this work, responses have included policies, legal directives and frameworks of action at local, national and international levels, some of which are considered later (Hearn *et al.*, 2006; O'Brien *et al.*, 2007). Prominent amongst these has been the policy and practice of 'gender mainstreaming' within international organisations (e.g., the European Union and World Health Organization). This initiative aims in theory to address, across all areas of policy, gendered inequalities which continue to pattern access – still too often women's – to resources, 'choices' and justice (Woodward, 2008; Hafner-Burton and Pollack, 2002). But this has been a contested undertaking leading to questions of the effectiveness of state mechanisms in mainstreaming activities and the inherent, associated tensions that can arise. However, notwithstanding these challenges, concerns with gender equality and difference remain vital. This is because it is through the close and vigilant examination of how 'sex/gender' distinctions are drawn and experienced and through which gender meanings and power relations emerge that the *relational* dimensions of the social world and individual subjectivities are revealed and can be challenged and/or supported in more appropriate ways.

It is clear, then, that individual agency, embodiment and subjectivity are experienced in contexts where 'gender is a central organising strategy' and through which discourses, understandings and practices are inflected (Lupton and Barclay, 1997: 12). At the same time (re)conceptualisations of gendered identities have 'prompted a rethinking of agency in terms of the inherent instability of gender norms and the consequent possibilities for resistance, subversion and the emancipatory remodelling of identity' (McNay, 2000: 2). In compelling and permeable ways, then, gender is both agency and structure as evidenced through a myriad of social science research findings and theorisations (Bradley, 2007; Connell, 2000; Kimmel *et al.*, 2005; Seidler, 2006; Jackson and Scott, 2002). Whilst these research foci have ranged across (all) domains of the social world, the division of (domestic) labour, reproduction and the 'gendered costs of caring' have provided a particularly rich and resonant sphere through which to explore gender (Doucet, 2006: 6). It is here that sex ('nature') and gender ('nurture') distinctions are most often drawn upon to claim, deny, exclude, explain and/or critically challenge arrangements, actions, responsibilities and identities. It is also here that attention has increasingly turned to focus upon men, masculinities and the 'gendering of fathers' and it is to consideration of these that we now turn (Morgan, 2002: 274).

Masculinities and fatherhoods

As has been shown, one of the most significant developments in gender theories, emerging largely as a consequence of feminist critique, has been the acknowledgement of difference, ambivalence and hierarchies within and around categories (Connell, 2005; Seidler, 2006). But whilst 'there is no single mode of being a man or being a woman' we have seen that culturally dominant stereotypes of femininity and masculinity powerfully reinforce ideas of how we should be (Jackson and Scott, 2002: 27). In recognition of the fluidity of gendered identities and the multiple ways of expressing masculinity and/or femininity, the plural terms 'masculinities' and 'femininities' are now more widely recognised and used. This has led to greater sensitivity in understandings – for example, around 'paternity and familial masculinity' – but also acknowledgement that not all masculinities are 'equally persuasive or dominant' or fathering a homogeneous undertaking (Morgan, 2002: 280; Mac an Ghaill and Haywood, 2007). Certainly it is the case that culturally dominant modes of being continue to powerfully pattern familial and reproductive domains – in which motherhood remains a central feature. This backdrop must be borne in mind as questions around 'gender equality', 'undoing gender', 'caring' and 'fatherhoods' are considered throughout this book as the men's experiences unfold. Also to be borne in mind is the feminist caution with regard to 'the ways that we understand the voices of one gender against a landscape designed by the other', especially as we set out to explore men's experiences in what have been 'female-dominated domains of social life' (Doucet, 2006: 28; Seidler, 2006). What, then, are the implications of more nuanced understandings of masculinities and associated ideas of 'good fatherhood' for both configurations and men's practices of modern fatherhoods (Hobson and Morgan, 2002; Vuori, 2009; Williams, 2008)?

Debates on the gendering of men and masculinities have grown as gender studies and theory continued to develop through the 1980s onwards. But early work on men and masculinity was found to either 'ignore fatherhood altogether or mention it only briefly', thus emphasising ideas of men's 'natural' absence from care giving and more emotional aspects of family lives (Lupton and Barclay, 1997: 3). Men's absence was also reinforced by naïve ideas of gender as being just about women. In the intervening years, however, this position has been addressed through a 'burgeoning' of research and writing on fatherhood *and* masculinities (Doucet, 2006: 8). This has been significantly influenced by masculinity studies, responses to feminisms and 'other forces for change' including 'gay movements, queer politics' and advances in new reproductive technologies and possibilities (Hearn *et al.*, 2006; Gregory and Milner, 2005). What it means, then, to be a 'man' and/or a father is understood through cultural ideas and ideals of (types of) masculinities: although, interestingly, they are not conflated in the ways 'woman' and 'mother' so often are. These not only 'vary enormously from one culture to another' but in significant ways within cultures, groups and across individual subjective experiences and identities in schemas of self-understanding (Kimmel *et al.*, 2005: 58; Lawler, 2000: 58; Seidler, 2006). Importantly, then, individual subjectivity is understood in relation to, and patterned by, multiple masculine positions which exist within hegemonic – dominant – hierarchies of masculinity as both agency and structure and reproduced through normative discourse (Connell, 2005; Vuori, 2009). This focus has, however, been criticised for not taking account of and confronting 'the emotional and personal' in men's lives which in turn becomes 'legitimated by the very discourse of hegemonic masculinities' (Seidler, 2006: 30). As noted earlier, then, all masculinities are not perceived as equal, but are rather defined in relation to prevailing ideal types, subordinated others and differential power: but in the 'gender order' they are (usually) perceived to be superior to women. The structure and agency dimensions of masculinities in particular cultural and classed contexts can be seen in men's engagement in the world of paid work (structure) and subjective identification with economic provision and being a breadwinner (agency). Other ways of being – for example, involvement in unpaid nurturing and childcare – could be perceived, or experienced, as threatening to, or weakening, a sense of self-identity that is contingent on and understood within a framework of hierarchies of masculinities where paid work is often a central, and highly valued, feature and emotion work is absent. As Wall and Arnold have noted, 'involved fathering, especially of young children, continues to clash with hegemonic cultural ideals of masculinity' (2007: 520). At the same time men may feel excluded (or indeed be excluded) from a domain that has been intimately associated with women and their 'natural' capacities to care; at the same time care is undervalued, regarded as easy (because it's 'natural') and so not real work, and in this domain men may feel they lack the 'natural' skills or competencies to participate competently or 'appropriately'. Clearly, the landscape is complex: littered both with more fluid notions of masculinities against a pervasive backdrop of power relations and structures emanating from hegemonic forms of masculinities, including essentialist assumptions about women's and men's lives *and* the economic demands of labour markets (Knijn and Selten, 2002). These competing and sometimes contradictory demands are revisited later.

As noted in the preceding chapter, although there has been a dramatic increase in women's employment outside the home in the UK this has not been matched by a dramatic increase in men's domestic labour or childcare-related activities. There are of course different patterns across Europe and these will be discussed in more detail later. But one explanation for differences between different European countries (especially in relation to the Nordic countries) may be the increasing coexistence and greater acceptance – in practices and policies – of different masculinities. Across the literature two arguments prevail: the first is that 'involved fathering' is more a recognisable cultural representation and ideal than a material reality; the second is that more involved fathering and changes in the rights and responsibilities of men in relation to their children potentially signals 'recreations of patriarchal dominance' in new guises amidst 'male fears about the erosion of masculine authority' (Hearn *et al.*, 2006: 124; Gatrell, 2007: 369; Ranson, 2001; Wall and Arnold, 2007). Clearly, there are contradictions here and whilst the slow pace of change may just reflect change occurring at different rates in different country contexts, claims around new forms of patriarchy are of more concern. In the UK, some southern European countries and North America explanations for what has been a 'slow process of change in fathering roles and men's general contribution to domestic work' have largely focused on hegemonic ideals, patriarchal arrangements and men's power within these (Gregory and Milner, 2005: 8; Collier, 2001; Ranson, 2001; Gatrell, 2007). For example, ideas that paid work outside the home is a 'choice for women but not for men' underpin and continue to reinforce patriarchal arrangements whilst ignoring both a long history of working mothers, a continued gender pay gap and the lack of genuine opportunities for men to take a primary role in caring for their children (Wall and Arnold, 2007: 520; Hill Collins, 1994; Browne, 2007). But notwithstanding this, the problem of men's power – and so their choices – is also impossible to ignore.

As already seen, research focusing on fathers' involvement and time spent in childcare practices continues to report that men are more likely to participate in its more enjoyable aspects, 'choosing to leave the more mundane activities to women' (Bradley, 2007: 119; Johansson and Klinth, 2007). These findings are not a surprise when so much research identifies women as *continuing* to have primary responsibility for children. They could also reflect the fewer opportunities for men to undertake caring in a less task-activity-based way because of expectations and practices of full-time work commitments. But this does not explain how women who also work full-time often continue to have primary responsibility for their children in addition to their paid-work commitments. As observed in chapter 1, there have been a number of explanations – biological, psychodynamic, social and cultural – for these different practices. Explanations have also focused on the personal *preferences* that it has been claimed women express through the choices they make around 'combinations of family work and paid employment' (Hakim, 2000, 2002; McRae, 2003; Crompton, 2007). In preference-theory explanations of the division of labour, gender becomes 'redundant' as a way of 'explaining the pay gap' and the focus shifts instead to considerations of men's and women's *preferred* 'social roles' (Browne, 2007: 12; Hakim, 2000, 2002). Not surprisingly there have been numerous critiques of preference-based theories because of the assumptions about choice and behaviours implicit within the value-laden term 'preference'. For example, as McRae has noted, understanding women's paid-work choices following childbirth 'depends as much on understanding the *constraints* that differentially affect women as it does on understanding their personal preferences' (2003: 317, emphasis added). But it is also apparent that (most) men do have greater freedom to express choices than women in the arenas of work and caring: their agency bolstered by the dominance of the male breadwinner identity, hegemonic masculinities and the 'privileges' that men have been able to 'take for granted in their relationships with women' (Seidler, 2006: 34). These have for so many years emphasised economic provision as a measure of (a relatively fixed) masculine identity and, correspondingly, a defining feature of 'good fathering'. The hard and largely externally unrecognised and undervalued work of nurturing and raising a child can – and often does – come as a shock to anyone becoming a parent for the first time (Miller, 2005; Rich, 1977). Perhaps in regard to this it is men's ability 'to pick and *choose* a suitable parental role', to operationalise a preference, that 'is the most significant expression of their power position' (Johansson and Klinth, 2007: 19, emphasis added; Collier, 2001). So, even though it is clear that there are many different types of fathers (see chapter 1) and that 'more caring and more distant fathering may coexist' and change across a life-course, it is also evident that amongst many groups of men, choices about their involvement in the domestic sphere and nurturing exist in ways not available to women as mothers (Lewis, 2002: 127). Even with the increasing scrutiny on men's fathering practices (or absence of these) and recognition of father diversity in social, cultural, political and legal arenas, 'men's power as fathers and in fatherhood remains pervasive' (Hearn, 2002: 271). This situation is further underpinned, some have argued, through the 'rights' and 'responsibilities' emphasised in more recent policy and legal frameworks and debates 'about fatherhood which conceptualizes social change in a superficial way' (Collier, 2001: 543; Gregory and Milner, 2005; Hearn, 2002).

So where does all this leave us in moving towards 'gender convergence' and/or equality and/or 'genderless' behaviours in the arena of caring for children and are these desirable and should they be an aim? Does the very action of focusing on gender only continue to highlight and reinforce differences between men and women – for example, through focusing on 'fatherhood' and 'motherhood' categories and practices rather than focusing on 'parenting' which, it has been argued, can be 'genderless' (Deutsch, 2007)? What are the losses and gains of using more neutral language? In his study on marriage, work and fatherhood in the USA Townsend found that the men he interviewed 'frequently spoke about "parenting" in a way that linguistically erased gender lines' (2002: 91). Other research has also suggested that at the level of individual couples 'equally shared parenting' can be achieved through creating 'a genderless model [by] taking turns and equalizing all aspects of parenting' (Deutsch, 2007: 117; Dienhart, 1998). But in practical and pragmatic terms, as already noted in this chapter, men as fathers are often more able to choose the dimensions of their parenting because they are not naturally positioned as the primary carer. Similarly, in many contexts 'parenting' continues to imply and conjure up or be conflated with 'mothering' (Scourfield and Drakeford, 2002). So, whilst large-scale 'genderless parenting' may be the 'holy grail' – located metaphorically beyond hopes of gender equality or convergence and requisite structural changes – getting anywhere close will surely only be achieved through continually observing, interrupting and resisting taken-for-granted 'gendered' behaviours; and thinking in new ways. But this is a complex – and some might argue a utopian – undertaking given that gender has patterned in such intricate and, at times, imperceptible ways lives, discourses, practices and taken-for-granted ideas of how things should be. Such a focus may also obscure 'unsettling questions' – which become overlooked in debates on changing discourses of fatherhood, parenting and gender convergence – such as 'issues of power and material interest' and men's greater access to these (Collier, 2001: 542). It also overrides practices of maternal gate-keeping (Featherstone, 2009). But notwithstanding this, gender remains an important analytical category even in the context of more recent calls to try to 'undo' gender through paying attention to the 'less-gendered' aspects of everyday interactions rather than continually focusing on difference (Deutsch, 2007: 114). This may be especially important when even debates around 'difference' and the *'quality of equality'* have been 'framed in male terms' (Doucet, 2006: 27, emphasis in original; Seidler, 2006). It is clearly necessary, then, to be vigilant about our own gendered locations – and their effects. For me as a woman and mother researching men's experiences of fatherhood this involves resisting 'the impulse to measure, judge and evaluate' men's experiences through the maternal gaze of my own experiences (Doucet, 2006: 28). But whilst acknowledging different gendered locations and experiences is necessary, it also risks reinforcing dichotomies and obscuring the fact that men, too, can feel limited by the power of patriarchal structures and associated expectations. This for some in the Western world has increasingly involved 'the state and its networks of power, in the definition, construction and control of fathers and fatherhood' (Hearn, 2002: 270).

Policies and practices

It is across the sites of production and reproduction that divisions of labour and gendering practices can be seen: enmeshed in contingent and reinforcing ways. Men's 'responsibilities' in the workplace and in relation to family life have been framed in discourses which simultaneously emphasise deeply rooted traditional practices and new possibilities. But the 'demands of the labour market' can sit uneasily alongside discourses of the 'new man' and 'involved fatherhood' where the 'good provider is necessarily a good worker too' (Knijn and Selten, 2002: 171; Ranson, 2001: 6–7; Williams, 2008). Similarly there are sometimes dramatic country differences in men's identification with, and self-fulfilment through, work and a breadwinner status. For example, in Sweden some have argued that traditional constructions of the male breadwinner role have been eroded whilst in the USA it continues to be an important cultural expression of being a provider and 'successful father' (Bjornberg and Kollind, 1996; Bjornberg, 2002; Townsend, 2002). Comparisons between countries are of course often problematic because 'the extent of inequality, and gender labour market patterns, set distinctive gender contexts for men's and women's relations to children' (Hearn and Pringle, 2006: 371; Hearn *et al.*, 2006). But what can be said is that across a number of European countries a range of different parental leave policies has in more recent years been put in place (Ray, 2008; Moss and Wall, 2007). Each of these has been framed within particular social, cultural and political contexts but shares a 'universal goal' to at some level 'help families balance or reconcile work and family responsibilities' (Marshall, 2008: 5). Moss and Wall (2007) have identified 'six main leave policy models' across Europe which in different ways and to different degrees attempt to address this 'reconciliation' of work and family life. Within these different models the traditional 'male breadwinner role' plays out in different ways, from being 'eroded' – for example, in Denmark, Sweden and Iceland – to remaining dominant in its traditional form in Italy, Greece and Spain and modified in others. As Wall has noted, 'male breadwinning is important [in these countries] in couples with and without children' (2007: 11). Across all the different leave models constructions of motherhood – and so fatherhood – are clear and once again emphasise the contingent nature of these categories. Where paternity leave models embrace at some level notions of gender equality, they include a range of incentives aimed at enabling, encouraging or coercing men into taking responsibility in both caring (sometimes as primary carer for a period of time) and economic ways for their children. But even where policies and initiatives are in place to support men's participation in caring, a 'decision to use' them still has to be taken: changes in behaviour and practices do not automatically follow policy implementation (Deutsch, 2007: 119).

Efforts to disrupt more traditional patterns and practices of care clearly require more than policy changes and 'family friendly' workplace initiatives: it is more fundamental shifts that seem necessary. Clearly, the legacies of patterns of care in which ideas about 'natural roles' and 'natural orders' have been prominent, have helped to create gendered schemas of self-understanding in which individual choice, control, self-fulfilment, financial reward and power are much more readily identified with facets of a working male identity. Although it is clear that these terms do not describe all men's experiences across a hierarchy of masculinities and types of employment or unemployment, it is also clear that they are not terms readily conjured up when describing caring for children. And even where men may want to take up parental leave and/or request flexible working, or leave paid employment in order to care for their children, they may encounter negative responses from employers, work colleagues and others (Brandth and Kvande, 2003; Doucet, 2006). Indeed the 'uneasy relationship' between work and family responsibilities for men and women is perplexing and continues to be confounding (Ranson, 2001: 24). Furthermore, the need to reconcile work and family life often implies or assumes that this is something mothers need to be concerned with, but not men. This continued association between 'successful' masculine identities and paid work, even alongside the dramatic increase in working mothers, has been drawn upon to explain why in the USA 'the revolution in family life has stalled' (Townsend, 2002: 195). And even though there is evidence of pockets of 'revolution in family life' in some (mostly northern) European contexts, it still seems timely to ask of working men who are fathers a question much more often asked of women who are working mothers, which is how 'family responsibilities affect their working lives' (Ranson, 2001: 4).

Research has shown, then, that across Europe 'work cultures in different social contexts can be more or less sensitive to parenting' (Hobson and Morgan, 2002: 7; Hearn *et al.*, 2006; Plantin *et al.*, 2003; Rossi, 2006; Torres *et al.*, 2007; Equality and Human Rights Commission, 2009). Those that are more sensitive include the Nordic countries (Norway, Sweden, Denmark, Finland and Iceland), where models of welfare and policies to support families and work can enable both parents to exercise choices around childcare not available in other countries (Moss and Wall, 2007; O'Brien *et al.*, 2007). It was during the 1970s that campaigns for paternity leave emerged in northern European countries, leading subsequently to paternity leave entitlements and parental leave quotas. This movement reflected a growing recognition of the need for change in how family 'responsibilities' and practices around 'cash and care' had been organised (Hobson and Morgan, 2002). The impetus for change occurred alongside, and in response to, wider social, cultural and political transformations that have since come to be accepted as features of late modernity (see chapter 1). Yet the need for change was interpreted and responded to in radically different ways across the different countries of Europe (Moss and Wall, 2007). For example, caring for children has come to be regarded as a universal and social right for parents in the Nordic countries, including the 'daddy month(s)', alongside other initiatives put in place to emphasise and anticipate paternal involvement in childcare responsibilities; whereas in other European countries men's financial obligations to their families have continued to be prioritised and dominate. But slowly more generic shifts have been discernible across Europe and in 1996, some twenty years after the campaigns for paternal leave emerged in Sweden, a European Union (EU) directive to member states was passed. This directive set minimum standards in 'legislation pertaining to maternity and paternity leave, as well as workplace protections for pregnant and nursing employees' (Ray, 2008: 3). It also reflected the EU's broad agenda and commitment to 'strong legal and policy emphases on equality and gender equality' yet was not signed up to by the UK government (Hearn and Pringle, 2006: 372). Since then different countries within the EU have interpreted, resisted and/or put in place different levels of support and provision with regard to maternal, paternal and parental leave. In the UK this has more recently involved 'substantially' and 'significantly' revising 'public policy regarding fathers and care' and the introduction of 2 weeks' paid paternity leave under the Employment Act of 2002 (Lewis, 2002: 148; O'Brien, 2006; Featherstone, 2003, 2009; Plantin *et al.*, 2003; Scourfield and Drakeford, 2002; Williams, 2008).

Supporting parents in the UK: Paid work and caring

In the UK a statutory right to take time out from paid employment to prepare and care for a child was initially provided to qualifying women through (paid) maternity leave introduced in 1976. Practices of being a 'good' father at the time involved economic provision and support for the family but nothing that would disrupt a working life. But ideas of clearly defined – and largely separate – maternal and paternal responsibilities and practices (and spheres) have undergone significant change since this time. This has been in part through policy responses to some men's 'failure' to maintain and provide for their children in circumstances of more complex intimate relationships, family formations and individual lives. For example, during the 1980s and 1990s a key policy concern 'regarding men centred on how to tie them into families, enforcing parental responsibilities' (Lewis, 2002: 130; Williams, 1998). This was in the context of evidence which suggested that 'both more caring and more distant fathering may co-exist' (Lewis, 2002: 127). Resulting policy shifts have included a statutory right introduced in 1999 allowing fathers as well as mothers to 'access up to 13 weeks of statutory unpaid parental leave' if they have children under five years of age and a right to request flexible working (O'Brien, 2006: 1). The government is also currently undergoing a period of consultation on changes to paternity leave which would allow mothers 'to transfer the last 6 months of their maternity leave to the father, with 3 months paid' (http://nds. coi.gov.uk; http://publications.dcsf.gov.uk/eOrderingDownload/CM-7787.pdf). Men's entitlement to paid paternity leave and parental leave has, then, arisen against a backdrop of both policy concern about men's commitment to family lives and political rhetoric. The latter has signalled, in theory at least, recognition of the need for 'work–life balance', 'family-friendly policies' and 'flexible working patterns' (Hobson and Morgan, 2002). Through these, it has been argued, men have been provided with the 'discursive resources' with which 'to make claims upon their employers' (Hobson and Morgan, 2002: 14). But in the UK as in other European countries, levels of take-up of paternity and parental leave amongst those men who have a statutory entitlement has so far tended to be disappointing (O'Brien, 2006; www. fatherhoodinstitute.org; Johansson and Klinth, 2007). Explanations for low take-up have included perceived and actual job (in)security, levels of pay during paternity leave, 'the availability of alternative income sources' together with the broader recognition of the 'inadequate provisions' within policies 'to facilitate complementarities in parenting and in its combination with paid work' (Ranson, 2001: 22; Browne, 2007: 266; Joshi *et al.*, 2007). At the same time men in the UK continue to work some of the longest hours in Europe and men who are fathers may work even longer hours: perhaps not surprising when 'Britain still offers some of the lowest specific parenting benefits in Europe' (Browne, 2007: 265; Dermott, 2008).

Clearly, household arrangements and family relationships together with employment opportunities and income sources will have significant impacts on caring/working arrangements and 'negotiations' around the care of children. But given these caveats, what 'constructions of fathers' are implied through, and emerge from, recent policy initiatives and changes in the UK and what possibilities and opportunities for men do they invite? (Featherstone, 2003: 247). As noted in chapter 1 the term 'involved father' is now widely used and understood to mean a more emotionally involved, caring and 'hands-on' father. But this conceptualisation has been critiqued for assuming too simplistically a shift from one typology of fatherhood (and associated behaviours) to another. In such constructions 'the counterpoising of "new" and "traditional" ... to "involved" versus "breadwinner"' implies 'that involvement is something distinct from the role of economic provisioning' (Dermott, 2003: 3). At the same time economic and emotional facets of fathering have been drawn upon in policy as fathers have been recognised as 'actual or potential resources for their children' (Featherstone, 2003: 239). Fatherhood is, then, 'increasingly becoming a site of complex structural and personal responsibilities' (Williams, 2008: 494). In practice, and as noted earlier, there are many different types of men who engage in fathering practices in a range of ways – economic and emotional or either or neither – which, importantly, will also change over their life-course and that of their children. But in contrast to this diversity the discourses which have more recently come to inflect ideas of modern fatherhoods in the UK context have become more distinct. These emphasise men's emotional investment in their children's lives but are underpinned by some level of economic responsibility and this of course shapes possibilities and opportunities in particular ways. As Browne (2007) has noted in her analysis of equality treatment, gender and the 'Principle of Equal Treatment' adopted by the EU, various parental leave directives continue to rely 'upon an a priori notion of what the division of responsibility between parents should be, i.e. that only mothers should be primary carers' and so such positions continue to be reinforced as other possibilities are blocked (267). So in the contemporary UK we find a complex situation in which more men may 'express egalitarian views' and anticipate being more emotionally or intimately involved in caring for their child, actively seeking ways to realise this, against a social, cultural and legislative backdrop which continues to prioritise women's primary connection to children and men's to the workplace (Equality and Human Rights Commission, 2009).

Conclusions

Viewing the social world through the lens of gender is a revelatory endeavour in which few (if any) areas are left untouched. But some areas have come under closer scrutiny than others as sites for exploring socially constructed, gendered practices. Not surprisingly reproductive and caring arenas have provided a rich terrain for exploration. Importantly, contemporary debates here are grappling with *how* progressive apparent shifts in discourses around fatherhood and associated opportunities, possibilities and practices are, and what any behavioural shifts may actually represent. Notions of gender equality and convergence, or indeed evidence of practices which undo gender and herald *genderless* arrangements – for example, in parenting where care is equally divided – have been heralded as progressive and timely (Deutsch, 2007; Risman, 2009). Yet other interpretations have explained men's practices in relation to this domain as representing new forms of patriarchal power. Clearly, ideas about hegemonic masculinities inform this latter view and in turn it seems reasonable to suggest that they will inform how men make sense of and narrate their experiences of transition to first-time fatherhood. For example, are men's experiences of agency less constrained in relation to anticipating, preparing, performing and narrating fathering practices and fatherhood experiences? In what ways are narratives through transition to fatherhood inflected by gendered expectations, orientations and language: what can and cannot be said and how? Is this different to the ways women can narrate their transition to motherhood experiences? (Miller, 2005, 2007).

Across the following three chapters men's rich accounts of experiences of transition to fatherhood will be set out in order that aspects of the 'micro-politics of fatherhood' and individual 'negotiations' and 'reconciliations' be explored (Hearn *et al.*, 2006: 43). The framework which has informed the analysis of the data adopts a micro-level focus on the ways in which men anticipate, present and position their unfolding experiences: both appealing to and rejecting strands of discourses which have in recognisable ways shaped societal attitudes of what men as fathers do. In this way the negotiations, reconciliations and justifications for particular practices and behaviours are discernible. These chapters – echoing the format of the earlier companion book on motherhood – will in chapter 3 capture the men's expectations and preparations in the antenatal period as they anticipate becoming a father. The themes identified here will be carried through the subsequent substantive chapters in order to explore the interplay and fluidity of gender, discourse, agency and structure through this period of significant personal transition. Chapter 4 will follow the men's accounts of their early fathering experiences as they (try to) come to terms with the realities of fathering and managing life with a new baby. In chapter 5 a more practised account of fathering is explored using data from two later interview points: at approximately 10 months following the birth and in the child's second year. Following this focus on men's experiences chapter 6 will uniquely bring together and juxtapose data from the earlier motherhood study with the fatherhood data in order to tease apart and illuminate dimensions of gendered practices and presentations around fatherhood and motherhood. For example, do/can men and women talk in similar ways about their responsibilities in relation to their child? What facets of their lives do men and women prioritise (and prize) and how are these understood, made sense of and presented? Through this longitudinal focus on gender as a key determinant in men's and women's narrations, anticipations and everyday practices around transition to fatherhood (and motherhood) it is hoped that the 'lack of fit between theory and practice' encountered in policy and other 'normative prescriptions' of generic parenting will be overcome (Browne, 2007: 251). But first and foremost, what sits at the core of this book are men's profound accounts of their hopes, fears, expectations and experiences as they set out on uncertain but optimistic journeys into first-time fatherhood.

3 | Anticipating fatherhood

'Being there'

I've no vision of what type of father I want to be . . . I just want to be there.

(James)

Transition to first-time fatherhood involves men embarking on uncertain personal journeys which are characterised by less clear trajectories than for women becoming mothers. This in part results from their physical bodies outwardly remaining unchanged through the antenatal period and so the signals and markers of pregnancy which shape women's transition, and others' responses, are absent. The term 'expectant mother' is instantly recognisable and conjures up visual images associated with pregnant female bodies but 'expectant father' is more obscure and clear images and associations are not readily evoked by these words. This confusion can symbolise men's own experiences of the antenatal period as they prepare to become fathers: both seeking ways to demonstrate 'appropriate' support and engagement and also feeling detached and at times excluded. In this chapter – and the three which follow – the empirical data are prioritized as the focus turns to men's own accounts of transition to first-time fatherhood. The themes identified here will be traced through subsequent chapters so that the interplay and fluidity of gender, discourses, agency and structure can be followed through transition. Using the categories employed in the empirical chapters in the earlier motherhood book (Miller, 2005) this chapter will examine the ways in which men's experiences of anticipation and associated behaviours are narrated and organised around the interrelated categories of preparing appropriately, anticipating the birth, shifting selves, and being a father and fatherhood. A further category focusing on men 'fitting' fathering in to working lives and 'being there' has been added in order to reflect the ways in which paid work outside the home figured in men's accounts. Whilst the chapter is arranged in this way in order to facilitate comparisons between the

earlier study (and reflects the use of a very similar interview schedule) it should also be noted that the amount and kinds of data which
emerged around these themes vary significantly – and not surprisingly –
between the men's and women's accounts as they look ahead to new
fatherhood and motherhood. Importantly, then, in this and the following chapters we see the different ways in which this group of
men reflexively position, perform and narrate their transition to first-
time fatherhood in what is highly gendered and, initially, unfamiliar
terrain.[1]

In chapters 1 and 2 it was noted that a discourse of involved fatherhood is now more discernible in contemporary Western societies alongside more sensitive understandings of masculinities and changing discourses of gender equality and rights (Vuori, 2009; Plantin *et al.*,
2003). It was also recognised that discourses can provide powerful
societal visions of how things should be and this is clearly echoed
across the men's anticipatory fatherhood narratives. But how things
should be for men anticipating and preparing for fatherhood in this
study can be seen to be largely mediated by others and in particular
through and in relation to wives or partners. For example, the men are
often prompted by their wives/partners about what to do and what to
read. They follow the unfolding pregnancy through prompts provided
by others ('she has tried to involve me in as much as possible. I've read
the magazines, read the books, watched the DVDs'). Antenatally, the
men are also involved in performing appropriate preparation in terms
of attending scans ('I've seen the baby through the scans, so I'm pretty
involved in the day to day') and antenatal classes ('I've made time to
go to all the actual antenatal classes'). In addition, other friends who
are already fathers, together with their own fathers (even where they
may have been absent), feature in the men's anticipatory accounts ('he
always had the time for you, so I'd like to replicate that'). The tendency
for men to construct their embryonic 'paternal identity' in relation to,
rather than independent of, the child's mother has been noted by others
in research on fathering (Pleck and Levine, 2002). But it is interesting
to note that this seeking of a paternal identity can commence as soon
as the antenatal period begins to unfold, as 'ways in' are sought ('I'm
trying to find ways to get in and share it and things like that'). The data

---

[1] All the participants have been given pseudonyms and any other significant
identifying features have been changed to protect their anonymity.

also reveal that men can experience feelings of 'disconnection', 'detach-ment', 'denial' and 'jealousy' but at the same time position themselves as willing to learn the skills (from wives/partners and other experts) necessary to be a good, involved father. Interestingly, in contrast to women there is no expectation at this stage that these capacities might be innate. Indeed, the men take comfort from their own assumptions about their wives'/partners' capacities to instinctively know how to mother ('I've seen the way she is with children anyway so for me it's very reassuring').

In all sorts of ways the men's accounts of transition to fatherhood are underpinned by and through gendered behaviours *and* biological assumptions of what fathers and mothers (naturally) do – and how these can be articulated. Yet new fatherhood is also envisioned as an opportunity to 'be there' for their child(ren) in emotionally and practi-cally involved ways that are qualitatively different to their own expe-riences of being fathered. A major thread running across the antenatal accounts concerns 'fitting' fathering and work together in ways they acknowledge their own fathers' generation were not able (or willing) to do. Once again drawing upon recognisable elements of contempo-rary 'good fatherhood' discourse the men talk about 'sharing care', 'caring', 'supporting', 'hoping to reduce work hours' and striking 'a decent balance' between being involved in caring and the demands of paid work. 'Being there' and reconciling family life and work is something that for these men appears attainable through the promise and apparent possibilities of flexible working arrangements which are initially signalled by 2 weeks' statutory paternity leave. Other shifts – including greater sensitivity to the fluidities of gendered selves (and so understandings of masculinities) and identities – have also provided a context of possibilities around fathering not so apparent in previous generations. But even as the categories 'fatherhood' and 'motherhood' are more readily recognised to be fluid and contingent, making possi-ble, in theory at least, new ways of organising caring responsibilities, deeply inscribed gendered expectations and practices remain and can be easily ('naturally') invoked.

Preparing appropriately

As noted earlier, men do not carry the outwardly visible signs of bod-ily change which signals pregnancy in women. At some level they are onlookers who can express feelings of personal change ('I feel older, people probably don't think I act any differently but I certainly feel ... the responsibility') as a result of the pregnancy but who in other circumstances could deny their involvement (or have it denied) and walk away. This indistinct relationship leads those who are positively anticipating fatherhood (albeit sometimes after the 'shock' of the news) to demonstrate and express their own appropriate preparation and involvement in ways that make it visible. As well as displaying clear ideas of what constitutes being a 'good father' in their interviews the men are also strident in describing what constitutes a 'bad father'. Key amongst the attributes of a 'bad father' are 'not being there', 'not being involved' and 'being absent'. In the antenatal interviews the men work hard to position and present themselves as preparing appropriately as fathers who will 'be there' and who are doing the right things (Draper, 2002a). But this remains a less clearly defined anticipatory period in which it is also easy to forget about the pregnancy. Whilst there are societal expectations that women will engage with a range of antenatal services and 'experts' during their pregnancy, men are expected to attend the birth and, where work permits, attend scans and perhaps a preparation class or two. From the outset the different messages conveyed through the practices and associated responsibilities surrounding pregnancy in the antenatal period begin to mark out societal expectations – and so constructions – of what fathers and mothers do.

In the study all but two of the pregnancies are described as 'planned'. But responses to the news of impending fatherhood still draw expressions of contradictory emotions including 'shock', 'massively shocked', 'happiness', 'fear', 'excitement' and being 'quietly elated' as the enormity of the news is assimilated. As Joe describes:

The first thing I felt was just nerves, just, like, really nervous first of all, my heart started racing and it was sort of nerves and I just thought 'Jesus'. So, yes, just really nervous, scared, happy but mainly nerves really, that it hit home that I'm going to be a dad because even though we were trying and obviously it's great news but nerves was the first thing ... I think like it just hit home, because we had talked obviously about wanting kids, but just the responsibility of it really. So I think, yeah, the responsibility and it's going to be, like, a child that I'm going to raise and obviously have a massive impact on its life ... and it's just the responsibility, I thought 'oh my goodness'. I was just sort of, like, 5 minutes of sort of the classic pacing around and Jane was, like, 'are you okay?' and I was, like, 'yeah, I'm fine don't worry'. It was, like, 'bang', loads to take in really.

Interestingly 'responsibility' is immediately associated with the news of impending fatherhood. Here responsibility is understood as a commitment that will involve having a 'massive impact' on a child's life in ways that appear to be more than just economic but emotional too. Whilst the other fathers respond in similar ways, Gareth speaks of his 'shock', 'horror' and 'excitement' at the news of an unplanned pregnancy:

Shock, horror, excitement, yeah, loads actually. Shock and horror was obviously the first one because there was absolutely no planning it whatsoever, zero planning. In fact it couldn't have come at a worse time to be perfectly honest but, yeah, so it was all that as well . . . but no, as time has gone on it's probably, yeah, it's a good thing.

But what is interesting here is that Gareth ends by asserting that 'as time has gone on' he sees the pregnancy as 'a good thing', clearly drawing upon a recognisable strand of discourse (in a pronatalist society) which acknowledges the unborn child (especially in couple relationships) as a wanted child. With the news of the pregnancy and their impending fatherhood the participants set about demonstrating their commitment and involvement in the pregnancy (and so to the unborn child) – especially to their wives/partners – whilst also feeling at times 'detachment'. The men, then, position themselves as willing learners in this arena where they are free from assumptions that they should possess pre-existent paternal instincts or knowledge. As Stephen says:

I mean it's such a new world for me. I know that, you know, if I go to the antenatal classes I'll be in good hands and they're going to teach me whatever there is to learn.

For all the men, preparation for fatherhood involves accessing information from 'books', 'DVDs', 'TV', 'attendance at scans', the 'internet', talking to friends who are already fathers and attendance at (some) antenatal preparation classes. All the participants talk about gleaning information from these sources – to a greater or lesser extent ('I've flicked through books'). Dean talks of the 'appropriate' information sources he and his wife have accessed:

I mean, we've done the appropriate reading, subscribed to the appropriate magazines and asked the doctor when we think there's something we need to know.

In the following extract Ben talks about his preparations:

We were thinking of going to this active birth type [class] but we brought a book instead, it was cheaper. There has been a massive pile of books that we have made our way through. That is quite good because you realise that . . . I don't know, it is quite empowering for the bloke to read the books about that stuff. You don't really know what is going on and what is going to happen so it is quite good to have an idea . . . have a sense of what is just happening at all the stages.

But he adds later:

You can imagine without having had that involvement with the scans or reading about you can almost put it to the back of your mind, you don't know anything about what is going on.

Although the participants talk of a range of sources of information they either know about or have accessed, they also acknowledge their wife's or partner's role in either orchestrating this and/or being disappointed at the level of their engagement. As Ben and Chris acknowledge:

I suppose [my wife] bought books. She has been reading books all the way through and, you know, 'look, that is what it looks like', 'look at the pictures' sort of thing and . . . when we went to the ante-natal classes I didn't feel huge sort of drive to read books . . . but I just thought it was really interesting. (Ben)

I've not been that good to be honest with you, I've been kind of leaving it to Susan a little bit, she's read hundreds of books and I've just been sort of, generally just talking to people I know who have been through the experience. I mean, I have read small amounts but nothing that much. (Chris)

Joe, too, recognises that he may not be doing all that his wife would wish:

I think she would probably really, really like it if I sort of went out and sort of read loads and loads of stuff and watched the baby channel, I know she would really like that but I just, it's not really me.

But for Joe this is 'not really me', it does not coincide with his sense of self. William, too, says that his knowledge about 'newborn stuff' is 'partial' in comparison to his wife's:

Sophie has done all the talking to other people who've had kids, she's found out what's required, what the list of newborn stuff is that we need and I haven't really got involved in that...I could have made up a list which would have been so not comprehensive. It would have been such a partial list, you know, obvious stuff like a pram and a cot I would have got...but muslin cloths would have passed me by. How do I know about muslin cloths?

Men negotiating the antenatal period position themselves in different ways which simultaneously demonstrate 'appropriate' preparation and detachment and uncertainty: as men, they are not expected to know this 'stuff'. But their narratives also reveal greater involvement in this antenatal period than their own fathers' and earlier generations of fathers' involvement. One public demonstration of involvement is through attendance at antenatal preparation classes and the men's experiences of these vary. Exceptionally James, whose wife is from Eastern Europe, says he has no knowledge of these:

I've not heard about them...not read up on them, not searched them out and to be honest with you I'm not really too worried...I sound awful...If you want advice there's, you know, my brother...you know, we're surrounded by babies next door and all down the street.

But James also recognises that not knowing about these may 'sound bad' and points to other sources of 'advice' he has around him. All the other fathers have either attended or intend to go along to some form of preparation class. Gareth has been to his first antenatal class on the day we meet for his first interview and he describes what has been covered in the class:

It was basically the normal birth, the normal labour and the normal birth, the preceding events. Time scales of when this should happen and that should happen – well, as normal as you can get with things like that – and the general progression of labour really and you should expect this, you should expect that and birth plans, know your rights...It was just lots of to-ing and fro-ing really. The three guys, there were about fifteen women and three guys, there were three guys, thank goodness, not that any of us said anything, the whole time we just sat there open mouthed. A few things came up, what was the thing that made me...? Oh, it was 'the showing' and if it's black or green or this, that and the other and you're, like, oh my goodness, I really don't want to know about this! I guess that's all part and parcel of it.

Gareth's relief that 'three guys' had also attended the class along with the 'fifteen women' is palpable. So too is his sense of being out of place and privy to things he did not want to hear or know about – but also accepting that this is 'part and parcel of it'. Stephen also talks of attending classes:

I've made time to go to all the actual antenatal classes and scans and things like that. I mean, just sharing that time together makes you feel involved anyway and it just sort of reinforces what's there.

But this in part results from him having 'not felt involved' – but excluded – during the middle part of the pregnancy:

There was a point sort of halfway through sort of the second trimester where I felt that I wasn't involved at all, it was a very personal thing to Claire and that was quite horrible. Trying to find ways to get in and share it and things like that. But now we've had a few discussions about... and I feel totally part of it, it's a shared thing between us... I think it's since we've started getting the nursery ready that I've felt as if I can sort of contribute a lot more as well, go out and get things and build things like the cot and put all that sort of thing together. So, yeah, definitely through that respect I'm very involved.

What is also of interest here – and because it is replicated across many of the men's accounts – is a sense of involvement brought about through the physical (and gendered) acts of building and preparation – for example, 'getting the nursery ready' – and this will be returned to later. Other expressions of involvement are manifested as the men talk about supporting their wife/partner which is seen as an important part of what they can do during this antenatal period. As Mike says, 'I suppose my main job has been to support her emotionally.'

Frank, whose wife is expecting twins, also talks of providing support and understanding:

I haven't missed a trick, I've been to everything... I've got to be as supportive as I can be, you know, I want to be as prepared as I can be, understand it from Gill's side, what she'll be going through, so I can support her as much as I can...

But he also recognises the limitations in what he is able to do:

I've tried to be involved as much as possible, but there's only so much you can do, you know, you can fluff the pillows and make her comfortable, you know, try and take on more round the house, but when it comes to, at the end of the day she's carrying them, she's going to have the aches and pains that go with it, and there's nothing I can do about it, so I'm totally frustrated, but I can only do what you can do, sort of thing... but, er, yes, I've said a few times, 'I just wish I could carry them for you so you could have a break from it...'

Across the men's accounts limitations on their involvement are recognised and in some cases these lead to feelings of frustration. As Nick observes:

But the emotional response of actually carrying the baby I don't experience and I think that's been hard for both of us, because she often talks about the feeling that she's got and I can't experience the feeling. I get frustrated and I think she gets frustrated that I don't pay attention to the feelings.

The men also acknowledge that their lives have – so far – changed very little (if at all) when compared to their pregnant partner/wife. There may have been some minor changes in behaviours such as limiting 'trips to the pub' and 'not drinking as much as I would have before'. But as Joe says, his life hasn't really changed yet:

I think for me at the minute, obviously I know I'm going to have a child in 2 months but it hasn't really probably hit home. My life probably hasn't really changed in the last 7 months at all really... it hasn't really changed a lot to what I was doing the year before, whereas with Jane obviously it has... and just carrying it inside of her, she's obviously protective of [baby]. So her life has sort of changed. I think when the child is born... it's going to be, I'm going to be a lot more in shock than what Jane will be, I think, because it sort of hasn't really sort of hit home at the minute.

The men's tentative forays into the paternal/parental arena are, then, largely mediated by their wife/partner with regard to information accessed and read and classes attended (Vuori, 2009). But one aspect of preparation which produces a tangible sense of their having an uncontested and recognisable role is the physical preparation of a room for the baby. Here, gendered acts more traditionally associated with 'masculine' traits of physical strength – 'building', 'painting', 'decorating', DIY and preparing the house and 'having a hand in the big stuff' – are described in comfortable and familiar ways by the men. In the following extracts Nick, Chris and Mike describe these physical activities in preparing for the arrival of the baby:

It probably took a couple of months to really sink in . . . I was thrilled because I'd wanted kids for ages and I was desperate to start planning and telling people and buying things. Yes. The cot arrived today and I've just put the cot up in the nursery and now the nursery has got everything, whereas up to yesterday it was a room with lots of stuff in it, it's now got everything in it. Yeah, it could be any time. (Nick)

I suppose I've been trying to prepare the house. We've been buying and building baby things . . . trying to get rid of our junk, we've got a lot of it and we've only got a little house . . . so just going through those sorts of things. (Chris)

I have been decorating and doing a lot more DIY. In the past it was 'oh, dad, can I borrow your drill or whatever?'; he's, like 'oh leave it out and tell me where you want it and I'll put it up', that sort of thing. But now I think, no, I need to start taking stock of things like that, start putting up blinds and start painting and decorating and stuff like that. And now with the advent of junior then we can actually start painting the room in relevant colours and brightening the whole place up really and making it a nice homely environment for it to come to once it's out of the hospital . . . over the last few months we've been buying bits and pieces and I've got a cot that I sort of lived in, so to speak, and I've just sanded it down and painted it and that kind of thing and you sort of sit there thinking, blimey, this is for our future. (Mike)

Physical, hands-on involvement in such activities is both familiar and demonstrates 'appropriate' preparation. It signals a sense of maturity ('I need to start taking stock of things like that') and the promise of an emotional, caring and protective relationship ('making it a nice homely environment for it to come to') and symbolises a future and connection to the unborn baby ('blimey, this is for our future'). But the men's activities also denote a masculine connection to the home, a place of physical things to be worked upon – 'to build and rebuild' – in contrast to it being a domestic and so, by association, a 'maternal space' (Doucet, 2006: 196). The men's actions, then, of physical preparation denote attempts to find more recognisably masculine and so familiar ways into this domain.

Anticipating the birth

One of the main changes that is routinely used as evidence of men's
increased involvement in fatherhood is their attendance at the birth
of their children (Dermott, 2003; Mander, 2004). The timing of the
antenatal interviews in this study (at between 7 and 8 months into the
pregnancy) meant that the expected date of delivery could be counted
in days and weeks and all the participants spoke of their intention to
be at the birth. Once again their involvement in this event would be
as an onlooker, supporting their wife/partner through the physical act
of giving birth. It is no surprise, then, that whilst in the motherhood
study hopes, fears and plans for the birth were a dominant feature
of the women's antenatal narratives they are much less an aspect of
the men's narratives. The hospital is seen by most to be the 'safest'
place to give birth – there are two home births contemplated and one
that materialises. Like the women in the earlier motherhood study,
the men also draw on a discourse of nature and birth as 'natural' – 'I
hope it will be natural' (Chris), 'we are going to try it as naturally as
possible' (Frank) – as well as acknowledging that they will 'support
anything she wants' (Dean). The ways in which the men anticipate
their role at the birth is as a 'go-between' as they act as an 'interpreter' between their wife/partner and the medical staff. It will be their
job to make sure 'birth plans' are followed and health professionals
are managed: but they also recognise this could be a tricky middle
ground to occupy. As Ben observes, 'You will have to get her through,
and so . . . oh shit!' Interactions with health professionals up to the
point of the birth are, not surprisingly, much less frequent for the
men than for their wives/partners and evoke mixed responses. From
disdainful – 'the midwife just talks nonsense: not read the medical
notes' (James) – to, more often, expressions of confidence in their
expertise.

In the following extract Ian admits that he hasn't yet given the birth
'a lot of thought':

I haven't really given that one a lot of thought, but I assume I will be there. I
don't think I've heard of any other people recently who haven't been there,
I think that's the presumption there is around. I think my wife will need me
there really so I'll be there.

Ian acknowledges the 'presumption' that now exists around men attending the birth and Graham confirms this 'modern convention'. He also anticipates that it could be 'pretty stressful':

Yes, I think it's a modern convention really, isn't it, the father to be there at the birth and I think we always assumed that I would be. We have talked about my role and it was a key part of the class and reassuring and if necessary being a bit of an interpreter and standing up for Rebecca to the professionals on her behalf and that sort of thing. I imagine it's going to be a pretty stressful experience because obviously she will go through a lot of pain and worry and I sort of have to go through it [laughs] precariously with her.

Stephen, too, is concerned about aspects of the birth but also reassured that they will be 'in really good hands in the hospital':

I'm not a big fan of all the blood and guts and the gore and all that sort of thing. But as it's progressed, you know, I understand that it's going to be some moments of that, there might not be but you just don't know. But if things do go wrong I know we're in really good hands in the hospital and they will only do what they need to do, they won't do anything silly basically . . . I think you just accept it; I mean, she's got to do all the work and I'm just there to support her and make her life easier if possible.

Others are worried about how they will manage the competing demands that they feel will be placed upon them as they 'support' their wives/partners during the birth. As Joe reflects,

She sort of says 'if I ask for pain relief or whatever don't . . . make sure they don't give me this' . . . So, really difficult because, like, she's said 'I don't want it, so if I ask for it you've got to be really strict' and I'm, like, 'well, that's fine, but at what point do I know whether . . . ' You've got to take some responsibility yourself because I'm going to look really bad . . . so hopefully it won't get to that point.

The men are drawn (by their wives and partners) into making plans for the birth and are expected to attend the now fairly routine prebirth visit to the hospital as part of their preparation. In the following extract Ben, in contrast to his wife, appears impressed at the available hospital facilities:

I didn't quite know what to expect, I just, I mean, I think Hannah was quite freaked out by some of the equipment in the room but it didn't seem that overly medical to me and it certainly didn't seem like a (hospital) theatre at all so it seemed all quite comfortable. You could turn the lights up and down and stuff.

The very different encounters with birth which men and women antic-ipate (and experience) are encapsulated in this extract. Whilst Ben's wife is 'quite freaked out by some of the equipment in the room' he interprets it as 'quite comfortable' and seems impressed that 'you could turn the lights up and down'. As well as visiting the hospital, prepara-tion for the birth for most involves helping to write – or think about – the 'birth plan' which then becomes a shared resource for the birth. Again this is a distinct change from their perceptions of their own fathers' involvement. In the following extract Gareth contemplates the production of a birth plan:

I mean, we've discussed it, I mean, we've got, we thought we better write a birth plan about a week ago, we thought we're getting a bit close now. Now we've packed the bags and everything is ready to go. And we've discussed some funny things like music and lighting and all this palaver. She wants to have as natural a birth as possible, but then as I said to her 'you've just got to tell me when you think it's . . . obviously you are going to be quite vocal anyway, you will probably be screaming for something or other as and when you feel'. We are very kind of 'just don't put anything in stone', because we've had friends who have said 'oh, we are going to do it this way, that way' and it's completely gone out of the window as soon as they have maybe gone into hospital. We've just said we'll go with it and you know there are certain things that we don't want.

Dean, too, thinks that 'putting things in stone' could lead to disap-pointment and recognises that birth might 'hurt' and involve 'pain'. He is forthright in his assessment of the birth process:

We think that having expectations is probably the worst way to go about it so [we] both think if it hurts, [my wife] should get something to stop it from hurting. I'm not one who believes in pain for the sake of pain and she doesn't believe in pain for the sake of pain and as for people who have these birth plans and everything, we think they are crazy . . . I mean, I don't think it's beautiful or anything . . . God seems to have done a nasty trick in terms of design, there seems to be some design flaws in the whole . . . [so] I support anything she wants to do. I feel, like, the decisions on the actual process of birthing, aren't mine, they're hers.

But most important for the participants is what the birth promises: the arrival of their first child. The men look to the birth as providing a turning point: 'a big sudden change' (Sean) that will mark the beginning of their physical, 'hands-on' involvement with their children. As James says:

to be honest with you I'm expecting – as soon as you actually can see it, feel it, touch it that's when I think the bonding starts but until then it's – for the guy's . . . I feel a bit disconnected to be honest to you.

The men talk of 'looking forward to meeting, seeing, holding the baby' (Nick), and being 'glad when I can actually see it and hopefully they will say it is alright' (Chris), but also of anxiously waiting for the birth to start. As Frank describes in the extract below, this has turned him into 'a big cissy':

I can't concentrate at work, the phone rings and I am getting jittery with it, I'm quite a level-headed person, take everything in my stride, but I'm just a nervous wreck, I just can't concentrate on things at work, it's kind of . . . a little bit disconcerting that, you think 'come on, you big cissy, just get on with it . . .

What is interesting here is the effeminate language used by Frank ('big cissy') which conjures up negative masculine ideals to describe what he regards as inappropriate behaviour for the workplace where he is normally 'quite a level-headed person' and by implication in control of himself and less emotional. The birth and anticipation of the birth have implications, then, for how the men see their selves and their shifting identities as they move closer to being a father and it is to consideration of this that we now turn.

Shifting selves

A discernible strand running through the narratives during the ante-natal period involves the men envisioning themselves as fathers. This centres on their changing perceptions of a self now imagined as a father – being mature, having new responsibilities and interacting with the baby/child – and the affect of this on how they think about other areas of their lives and, most significantly, work. Once again it is noticeable that the men are less constrained in how they think about and present their selves in this period when compared to women

anticipating motherhood (Miller, 2005). Whereas women are concerned to present their changing pregnant selves in ways recognisably
consistent with the ideal of the 'good mother', other possibilities exist
for men. Not surprisingly, then, paid work is a dominant feature both
in how men talk about their (changing) sense of self and in preparing for and doing fathering as it, too, is identifiable as a dimension of
appropriate fatherhood. Interwoven across the narratives are recognisable, gendered patterns and associations between men's lives and paid
work, responsibilities and economic provision: but also more optimistic and different ways of 'being there'. Most of the men speak of
always thinking that at some point in their lives they will become a
father. Confirmation of this news is greeted as having 'kind of proved
your virility' and it being 'part of the life plan' (William) leading some
to talk of feeling 'quite grown up' (Ben) and others of the need to 'grow
up' (Joe) and 'life becoming more serious' (Dylan). In the following
extracts Gareth reflects on the changes he has experienced in himself
as he anticipates fatherhood:

I feel older, people probably don't think I act any differently but I certainly
feel, maybe that's just the responsibility and the pressure and everything else,
but I certainly feel, yeah... No, I definitely view myself differently now, I
have to be a lot more patient. I haven't been historically a very patient
person, that is another thing I've had to work on as well, consciously on
a minute by minute basis, you know, plenty of deep breaths. So just being
able to deal with the stresses and the pressures.

He goes on to comment on what the most significant change has been:

My attitude to work really, I think. Apart from the realisation that I'm not
going to have the social life that I had previously or the freedom, just the
freedom of being able to go off and do whatever you want when you want.
Yeah, my motivations at work, I'm kind of thinking, I'm thinking more long
term now as opposed to next week, next month... So I think the fact that
my attention and motivation have shifted now... So, yeah, it's that shift
between selfish short term to, yeah, long term I guess... Basically, yeah,
and it's a serious conscious effort because as I say, you know, yeah, I have
travelled a lot of the world, I went to university, I've done all these single
type things, so, yeah, to change what comes naturally is probably harder
actually than most things, not being able to do what I want all the time.

Here Gareth speaks for many of the fathers as he reflects back and forth
over how things have been and how they are changing. 'Motivations at
work' have shifted and he talks of the 'responsibility' and 'pressure' he

has experienced whilst horizons move from short to long term. Implicit within the narrative is a curtailing of individual 'freedom', 'single type things' and 'selfish' spontaneity as he must now focus his attention on others. Joe, too, talks of having to change his behaviour:

Yeah, just like at the back of my mind I know that I'm going to be a dad and I do feel a little bit more responsible even though the baby is not born yet, if that makes sense. So even though the baby is not born I'm a little bit more worldly or wiser, I've got to be a bit more responsible and that sort of stuff and I can't just stagger back [from the pus] at whatever time of night...

But he also wonders what other men do, trying to gauge how 'normal' his responses to anticipating fatherhood have been:

But I don't know what most dads do, whether sort of most dads as soon as they find out, sort of change their life straightaway. It hasn't really been like that to be honest, I don't know if that's normal or not?

Earlier Joe had confided:

Yeah, I've got to be honest, I don't have many in-depth chats about the pregnancy with my friends – no.

Joe, like others in the study, alludes here to some of the differences between men's and women's experiences of the antenatal period. For Joe the pregnancy has not yet changed his life and it isn't a major topic of conversation amongst his friends. He confides at the end of the interview that it has 'been good to talk like this', alluding to men not having the same opportunities as women to talk openly and at length about what might be seen as more emotional 'women's stuff'.
    In the following extract Dylan, too, reflects on his need for 'support':

I am feeling a little bit unsupported so I have got to find extra support for [my wife] but I am not sure where it is coming from me for me. I suppose that is just me getting around to talking to people, to other dads but men don't chatter as much... underlying this pride is sheer fear.

Here Dylan poignantly encapsulates feeling caught between providing support and feeling unsupported, wanting to find support through talking to other men – 'but men don't chatter as much' – and wanting to present himself as a proud father-to-be but actually feeling 'fear'. This extract lays bare how particular understandings of masculinity can shape men's behaviour – they should be strong and proud as they anticipate fatherhood and it would imply weakness (being a 'cissy' as Frank said earlier) to admit to anything else. This contrasts with Gareth's observations, as his friends who are already fathers phoned him in order to offer him the opportunity to chat:

[They were] saying, oh, I just want to say congratulations, if ever you want to chat and all this sort of stuff . . . It was almost more maternalistic than paternalistic.

Pregnancy, then, may be a confusing time for men, an in-between time where nothing physical is actually happening to them but they may feel a sense of change or that they should change and/or feel impending significant change in their lives. They are travelling through unknown territory as they prepare for fatherhood and the ways in which particular masculine selves are understood in this emotionally laden arena is sometimes contradictory and confusing. As Frank says:

all the talk is baby, everything is baby – we have two sets of friends, one's just had their second, one their first, so everything is baby orientated, so I'm quite glad to escape every so often, and get off to watch rugby and just be a bloke for a couple of hours [laughs].

Just being 'a bloke' and engaging in an activity more clearly associated with men and masculine ways of being is much more familiar and less uncertain: here Frank can be his 'normal' self for a 'couple of hours'. But implicit across Frank's and other participants' narratives is that life will change ('massively', 'hugely') once the baby is born. As Stephen says, 'I've got to be responsible for somebody at the end of the day.' This looming responsibility is dominant across the men's narratives and is linked to refocusing 'priorities' in relation to work and home as the costs involved in providing are contemplated alongside feelings of 'pride' and a sense of achievement.

Anticipating fatherhood/being a father

As noted earlier, for comparative purposes the empirical chapters in this book largely follow those in the earlier companion study on motherhood (Miller, 2005). But it is noteworthy that this section on 'anticipating fatherhood/being a father' generated much more data than in the comparative study and so an additional section will follow. This will specifically focus upon another dominant strand in the men's narratives: how men envisage 'fitting fathering in' and achieving a

'work–life balance'. For women becoming mothers, (hopeful) anticipation of instincts and innate capacities influence their ideas of what
mothering/motherhood will be like, but for men there are not the same
storylines available, although they, too, talk in hopeful ways of their
'instincts' coming to the fore and 'bonding' once the baby is born –
'hopefully all the instincts, urges and so on kick in' (Dylan) and
'just trying to bond' (Mike). Yet again men are less constrained than
women: they are not expected to be (naturally) knowledgeable in this
reproductive domain. But they are clearly aware of societal visions
(and have personal experiences) of what constitutes 'good' and 'bad'
fathers and corresponding constructions of masculinities and types of
fatherhoods are implicit throughout their unfolding accounts.

The 'enormity' of becoming a father ('it's the biggest thing in the
world having a baby') is also recognised as being 'for life' (Joe). But
the enormity of the event can be offset to some extent by assumptions
that their wife/partner will 'naturally' know what to do, that a *small*
thing like a baby ('a little mite') can't be that much work and should
be controllable. This is a common misperception and miscalculation
between size and control which was shared by the women in the earlier
motherhood study too. As William says:

I'm looking forward to that very early stage when it's just a little mite and
you can carry it and look after it very easily and it squeals and stuff but it's
not too demanding.

But at the same time there are apprehensions too about *doing* fathering.
In the following extract Frank, whose wife is expecting twins, expresses
his concerns, which resonate with those of other participants:

and handling a small baby, as I say, you know, how did I get selected to be a
father, what qualifications have I got to be a father? You know . . . And yet
I'm going to be able to bring little things home from the hospital without
supervision. That's a big responsibility there. You know, you get selected to
do your job on a skill base or your character – father, you can become a
father quite easily, it's frightening how easy it is . . . erm . . . it's just the . . . you
know, 'Am I up to it? Will I be able to cope with it?' I don't know.

In other accounts there is a clear trajectory where an older baby is
envisaged as more robust and less dependent. Nick, like some other
men, talks about getting through the first '18 months':

Most of what I'm looking forward to is actually when our baby hits
18 months or so. I feel far more anxious and nervous about the first

18 months. I want a baby who can start, who can hold their own head, and can crawl and start learning how to walk and stuff like that and those are the bits I'm looking forward to far more than sort of the helpless baby who's so dependent on parents.

Dean, too, has his concerns about 'the first two years of vomiting and sleepless nights' and Sean says he is 'not looking forward particularly to no sleep and everything being covered in vomit'. But irrespective of their various concerns about different aspects of fathering, the narratives the men produce as they anticipate being a father are optimistic and full of hope.[2] Their sentiments are captured by Sean:

you know, it's that fantastic bond and the positive things I have been told, kind of everything else becomes unimportant and it's such a kind of fantastic feeling and the parent love thing, there's kind of such a bond, such a love and I'm kind of looking forward to that.

One result of inviting men to think about being a father is that they – not surprisingly – reflect on their own experiences of being fathered. Across their narratives it is striking just how important their relationships with their biological and/or social father (stepfather) or other male relatives has been in shaping their own fathering intentions: just how important having a male figure in a life has been for these men.[3] Even where a biological father has been absent this may still be significant in either shaping aspects of their own impending fathering and/or providing them with an opportunity to correct what they regard as previous (unhappy) family patterns. For some, loving relationships are maintained with both their absent biological father and their long-term stepfather. Some stepfathers have been 'fantastic' and some resident biological fathers more remote and in one case 'austere' and there are hopes that the birth of a grandchild may help repair difficult relationships. Uncles, brothers and male friends with children are also referred to as paternal influences. The increasing fluidity of family formations and corresponding relationships is apparent in the lives of those in this study. But this has not deflected them from wanting children or wanting to be fathers themselves or hoping to provide consistency and

[2] This may well be a product of a sample who were self-selected.
[3] Their mothers, too, were an influence on how they anticipated parenting (rather than fathering) but because this appeared to be assumed and taken for granted it was also largely implied rather than spoken.

to 'be there' for their children. Exploring the ways in which earlier generations of men have influenced these participants' ideas also provides an opportunity to begin to see generational shifts in relation to constructions of contemporary fatherhood ideals and practices.

Nick thinks about his own relationship with his father and acknowledges:

there are bits that I think are great and I'd like to do like that but there are certain aspects that I strongly, strongly don't want to be like.

For Chris, too, there are some aspects of his own father he would like to reproduce but he also describes him in this way:

quite old fashioned in many of his views . . . ever since he's left [his job] he's still quite old fashioned in some ways so I don't think I would be like that. Well, I hope I wouldn't be like that, but there are lots of good sides to him.

Gareth says that his father, who left the family when he was 4 years old and was 'always letting us down', has provided him with 'a blueprint of how not to do it'. His own impending fatherhood is anticipated as an opportunity to 'stop the chain of events' as 'the history in my family isn't particularly good'. But, even so, there are still aspects of what his father did that he, too, would like to do:

like, whatever he was I would like to be the opposite, not the . . . because in some ways he was very good, but, yeah, in a lot of ways, more emotionally, I would like to be better emotionally than he was. I mean, he was great, I mean, he took us on holiday and introduced us to sport and things . . . But, again, I would just like to do more of the stuff, the stuff that he did do, I'd just like to do more of it basically. And, again, just be there from the emotional side of things because as I say . . . not having . . . it's good to have two parents around, I think.

According to Joe, when he was growing up his father 'wasn't a sort of stereotypical good dad':

When my mum and dad split up when I was sixteen, that is when I got really close, that is when really probably my dad started to become a dad to me really. Before then you just sort of take it for granted he's your dad but I never really spent quality time with him. Then my mum and dad split up and then from then really, sort of, he made a massive effort, I saw him once or twice a week and it was then, like, we did special things, whereas before we didn't really do that . . . I never had with my dad growing up, but over the last ten years or so, my dad has been great to me and my brother . . . I love my dad to bits and we have a great relationship with him, he's one of my best friends.

In the following extract Sean contemplates impending fatherhood and reflects on his own situation:

I guess the natural thing is you always think about your own, but my dad left years ago and had no contact. The replacement for that was my stepfather and he's just been fantastic, so . . . with my stepdad when I was growing up, he was, I had a very good relationship with him, but he was always working and it's like going back to when my brother, who takes his day off a week [to do childcare] and I like that thought of having that time. It is just wanting to be involved, wanting to be there when they're growing up, to see things.

Across all these and the other accounts the significance of men as figures in the participants' lives is clear. Even where their own fathers or stepfathers have been absent, inconsistent or always working or just there, they have at some level and, in significant ways, influenced the men. Interestingly, when particular events are recalled these are almost always activity based – for example, holidays, sports events or just 'quality time' (Doucet, 2006). These activity-based forms of engagement illuminate gendered differences in how fathering and mothering practices have traditionally been divided and these differences recur across subsequent chapters. But the men in the study also talk of wanting to be more involved, emotionally and in hands-on ways, in their children's lives than their fathers are in theirs. *Every* father in the study uses the words 'being there' to describe how they want to father.[4] This resonates with more contemporary ideas of 'caring masculinities' (Johansson and Klinth, 2007) and more fluid constructions of gender and caring practices (Doucet, 2006; Dermott, 2008; Featherstone, 2009). All the men are very clear about what constitutes a 'good father' ('a responsible person', 'family orientated', 'a provider', 'protecting them from the big, bad world', 'being able to help your child develop and teach them', 'being there for them whatever, whenever', 'consistent', 'responsible', 'supportive', 'approachable', 'provider of emotional as well as materialistic things', 'loving' and 'fun') and a

---

[4] In a small pilot study undertaken alongside this research four teenage fathers-to-be were interviewed and all also expressed their desire and intention of 'being there' as a dad.

'bad father' ('absent', 'inconsistent' and 'unreliable'). But how will their hopes and optimistic plans of involved fatherhood be accommodated into their working lives?

Like other participants, Nick thinks that fathering has changed significantly when he compares it to his own father's generation and recognises that men are no longer just expected to be the 'breadwinner':

I think it's changed hugely. I think there is far more emphasis on fathers to be involved, fathers to be a primary carer rather than a breadwinner, for fathers to actually understand what's happening throughout the pregnancy. I think the advent of fathers' support groups and stuff like that, the amount of textbooks that are for fathers or have a chapter for the father, I think it's hugely, hugely different. I think when, I know when my mum was pregnant with me, my father's role was to make sure that we had enough income to get whatever and to every now and then stamp down an authority.

Yet, interestingly, Nick goes on to talk about now having to provide for 'a child' – 'there hasn't been a need for us to provide for each other and now I have to provide for someone else, a child' – using language more associated with traditional ideals of the breadwinner-as-provider fatherhood discourse. In contrast to previous generations the participants all talk of contemporary fatherhood as a wide-ranging amalgam of responsibilities which are emotional as well as physical *and* economic and in which fathers and mothers (sometimes equally) can *share*. In principle, then, these ways of organising caring for children are not so caught up in gendered assumptions and/or traditional divisions which have shaped patterns of working and home life. Indeed, all the participants use the terms 'sharing' and 'caring', and sometimes 'sharing care', 'equally sharing', 'partnership' and 'teamwork', to describe their involvement in caring for their child(ren): but what do they actually envisage when they draw upon this language and position themselves in this way?

Work–life balance: 'Fitting fathering in'

A dominant theme woven through the participants' narratives relates to paid work. The men are employed in occupations ranging from building, catering, farming and IT to teaching, the arts, office-based jobs, medicine and the armed forces. Three of the participants are self-employed. The participants also live in households that are almost all dual earner.[5] All the men anticipate being significantly involved in sharing caring for their unborn child(ren) but only three of the seventeen speak of actively making plans to change the number of days they work in order to achieve this. Most say they have flexibility in their working hours which they hope will mean they can accommodate sharing care. Mike, for example, speaks of his work being 'quite flexible so I expect to be rolling my sleeves up'. Others speak optimistically of perhaps being able to work more flexibly, but for most their involvement will have to be fitted in around (inflexible) work commitments.

Joe is the only participant to say he would like to become the parent who stays at home:

I think I'll find it really difficult first of all once the baby is born when I go back to work after 2 weeks, because I'm going to be at work all day and Jane is going to be at home, I think I'm going to feel that I'm missing out. If it's up to me I would love to have the year at home with the baby and bring it up myself. But, yeah, I definitely want to make a massive . . . and, like I say, it would be nice if I could spend time with just me and the baby as well. It's going to be really scary when Jane goes out for the first time and leaves us alone together . . . Obviously 95 per cent of the time it's going to be us three but I do want to spend time with just me and the baby to take it round the park and that sort of stuff.

What is interesting in this extract is Joe's desire to stay home for the first year alongside his acknowledgement that it will be 'really scary' when he is first left alone with the baby. Like several of the other participants he wants opportunities to spend time with the baby alone to do different activities. Later he talks again of his wish that he could be the parent who stays at home but implies his wife has a greater claim:

I sort of said I'd like to and she was sort of, like, 'no, I'd like to', so it was never really a massive discussion, it was always going to be that Jane was going to stay at home.

[5] In three cases the wives were not in employment at the time of the pregnancy. This was as a result of recent immigration to the country, chronic illness and full-time study.

Nick also talks about the antenatal period enabling him to 'prepare for that primary role':

Yeah, I've enjoyed looking after [my wife] and I think there's something about preparing for that primary care role . . . I think there's something there about preparing myself for that primary care, that actually it's going to be up to me to prepare a bottle or a meal or a feed or whatever for our child.

What is interesting here is what 'primary role' actually means. It is not that Nick anticipates taking *primary responsibility* for the baby once it arrives, as the term might imply, but rather primary responsibility is related to particular tasks – preparing 'a bottle or a meal or a feed'. What emerges from the men's accounts of anticipating caring and involvement is how differently responsibilities of caring for a child are constructed and understood in relation to fathers and mothers. Nick can only describe his caring involvement in the way he does in the extract above *because* his wife is already assumed to have primary responsibility, which then enables task- and activity-based – intermittent – caring practices. This style of caring is only possible when someone else is engaged in the all-encompassing, primary caring/thinking responsibility that one parent (or someone) must assume. Others, too, envisage their involvement in similar ways to Nick. In the following extract Graham, who intends to change his working days by working the same hours but across 4 days, ponders how the 'childcare type stuff' will work out:

But I think as far as other childcare type stuff like bathing and nappy changing we will probably share that which I think is a good thing. I imagine I'll quite enjoy that, at least while it's a novelty; once it becomes a bit of a chore [laughs] . . . And I think for the first few weeks I think we will try and share those evenly . . . when I go back to work [my wife] can do more of those sort of things and I'll just do it on my one day a week when I'm at home and perhaps we can share it at the weekend. I don't think we've quite tied the details up.

Again, tasks such as 'bathing' and 'nappy changing' are drawn upon as examples of 'childcare type stuff' and indeed they are important facets, but they do not conjure up an overarching sense of equally shared responsibility. Sharing a sense of responsibility is something that Ben grapples with in the following extract as he acknowledges a lack of things being 'equal':

Well, obviously it is not equal because at first Hannah is going to have to take responsibility for feeding if that all pans out well. There is a sort of sense of shared, a very shared or a quality of kind of share in that responsibility so I will expect to be up in the night as well and just being there for them both and hopefully doing my bit, doing whatever I can.

For others, fathering involvement is something that, following paternity leave, will take place during 'evenings', 'nights', 'weekends' and 'holidays'. It will involve 'assisting', 'supporting' and 'helping' their wife/partner in 'lots of tasks'. These include: 'feeding', 'changing nappies', 'bathing', 'dressing', 'putting it to bed' and 'getting up in the night and seeing what's wrong'. Whilst the men talk about sharing care and 'home–life balance', in reality their availability is limited by their (continued) work commitments. In practice, fathering will for most be 'task' and 'activity' focused and something to be 'fitted in'. As Dylan says:

But right from the start I would like to negotiate work so that I have, you know, sort of a day off work a week to be a father and to do childcare and to be involved and I would really like to be able to maintain that throughout my working life if possible.

What is interesting here is the way in which Dylan talks about taking 'a day off work a week to be a father', suggesting that the identity 'father' is not all consuming or conflated in the ways it is understood in relation to women as mothers. For men, a sense of self as 'worker' remains important both personally and as a dominant strand of hegemonic masculinities (see chapter 2). It remains acceptable for men to talk of 'fitting fathering in' and for work to remain important: but this means it may also be difficult for men who want to assume the primary caring role and to stay at home as full-time carer. In practice, then, although the men position themselves as involved fathers and want to be 'more involved in doing tasks that would have been associated with a female role' (Mike), they are also caught up in deeply embedded gendered expectations and practices. Discourses of fatherhood also continue to assume men's economic provision for their children and the fathers recognise this. As William says:

What I'm trying to say is when I'm around the house I think I'll be quite sort of hands-on, but there'll be lots of time because of my job that I won't be around the house. I'll be making the money to kind of look after them.

Graham, too, recognises that his involvement with his child will occur mostly outside his working hours in the evening:

Just having a little part of the family, you know, something in the house which you're going to love and playing around with it and spending time, you know, quality in the evening.

All the men plan to take time off work following the birth. This is either through the 2 weeks' statutory paternity leave and/or saved annual holiday and there is some discussion about whether employers really 'believe in' paternity leave and how work colleagues without children will view it. In some ways it is the knowledge that they will have this allotted time at home following the birth of the baby that seems to herald the possibility of a qualitatively different type of involvement when compared to previous generations. Some anticipate that returning to work will 'be a hard separation' (Nick). Frank says his 'biggest fear' is that he 'will become too attached [because] I still need to provide'. But Gareth has been told by other fathers that he may feel differently:

But, then again, I think from the guys I've spoken to, I think I'm probably going to be glad to go back to work.

All the men expect to be the primary, economic provider for the family in the initial months/years. They talk about 'flexible working', 'flexi-time', 'work–home balance', 'getting the balance right' and possibly changing jobs as work 'priorities' shift, and all are clearly aware that different opportunities are available to them through new policies and legislation (Hobson and Morgan, 2002). But they also recognise that this is untrodden terrain. For example, as Chris acknowledges:

I'm hoping to reduce my hours by one day and Susan is going to do the same and then the other 3 days I think it will have to go to nursery...hope so, yes, [employers] are supposed to be quite flexible...I don't think there are any other men who do it so it will be interesting to see.

As noted in chapter 2, the very fact of introducing new policies – for example, in relation to a parent's right to request flexible working – does not mean that it will be taken up.

The complexities and contemporary contradictions in and around 'paternal' and masculine-worker identities are discernible across the men's narratives as they describe their working/caring intentions

(Vuori, 2009; Plantin *et al.*, 2003). Reconciliation between work and home for the men involves at some level recognising what they feel to be acceptable to their own sense of self as involved father, worker, provider and so on. Graham captures this when he says:

The idea of flexible working is acceptable and I think the idea that if things crop up then managers are supportive about the idea of staff having to deal with domestic issues. But I suppose I'm thinking about, I suppose, more what I find acceptable in myself... at the end of the year you think about what you've achieved and not so much what the rest of the things I've had to put up with, because in a way that's irrelevant to the work context.

The way in which Graham tentatively talks about himself at work illuminates several things. It demonstrates how important work is to him and implies that having to request 'flexible working' to deal with 'domestic issues' could affect what gets achieved in the 'work context'. Implicit, also, is the sense that what is 'achieved' at work is different to what goes on in the home, and achieving at work (which requires commitment) is more highly prized (certainly in wider society). Graham's view of paid work and the importance of the work context is not perhaps surprising given the multiple ways in which masculine (and so gendered) identities are continually conflated with work and economic production – and, as a father, economic provision. These particular, hegemonic constructions of worker identity as a prized dimension of masculinity and achievement sit at odds with constructions of more involved, emotional fatherhood that the men have also envisaged, which apparently herald new possibilities. Indeed, Nick inadvertently alludes to these alternative possibilities when asked how he thinks he will be involved in caring for his child:

At this stage I want a say in everything, I want to take the baby round [the supermarket] and do the weekly shop, I want to be doing the bath and staying at home so that Shelley can go out and all that. I want everything to be divided down the middle. How much of that is a fantasy and in 6 months' time I might be very grateful that I'm the one who is going out to work.

Clearly, then, paid work continues to be perceived as a major responsibility for these men – and (potentially) a culturally acceptable, at some level, 'escape route'. Work shapes the ways in which the men think about their selves, providing and caring for their children (and wives/partners) and, not surprisingly, features in plans for their futures. As Stephen says, as he thinks about the future:

It means . . . it has quite a big financial sort of meaning for me. Definitely providing for the child and Claire and, you know, just doing things like saving for a big house, really, so that the child has got a nice sort of background for when it gets older and just being together.

There is a paradox, then, that providing for a family necessarily demands a commitment not just to work but to work longer and harder in order to provide and make provision for the future. For Stephen, this involves 'a big house', which is envisioned more than just materially but also as part of creating and providing a 'nice sort of background' for his as yet unborn child.

Conclusions

There are distinct threads running across the men's anticipatory narratives explored in this chapter, which underscore their desire and intention to be significantly involved in their child's life. Involvement is articulated through associations with a recognisable discourse of 'good' fatherhood which prioritises 'being there' in emotional and hands-on ways. But work and economic provision are also dominant threads both in the men's narratives and in popular discourses of involved – and so 'good' – fatherhood. And it is apparent that men can weave together in different ways these potentially contradictory positions whilst women may feel much more constrained by the more morally inflected discourses which shape motherhood (see chapter 6). What emerges are the contingent, uneasy and confounding dimensions of fatherhood and motherhood as recognisable *and* fluid categories and potential experiences. The data suggest that some men may feel inhibited by the powerful gendered expectations which continue to position them as economic providers and 'modified breadwinners' (O'Brien, 2005) but at the same time anticipate, assume (and may welcome) this role.

Yet, in what other ways could the men think about and express 'being there'? What other discourses could be drawn upon that would be culturally recognisable and acceptable as masculine displays of caring and emotion? The men's reflections on generational shifts make

clearer and more visible how they understand contemporary responsibilities and the practices of fatherhood. It also implicitly signals a
sense of a developing paternal identity, which in turn is informed by,
but different to, their own experiences of being fathered. Whilst the
men may voice some concerns in relation to caring for a new baby
and may sanction themselves ('I sound bad, don't I?' says Joe as he
talks about the continued importance of football in his life) they do
not encounter the same 'policing' of their intentions and preparations
as women anticipating motherhood. At some level, just by envisioning being involved and 'being there' – regardless of the quality of the
involvement or how it will be fitted in around work – men are seen
to be conforming to the ideals of 'good' fatherhood and so preparing
appropriately.

4 | *Making sense of early fathering experiences*

We had a really nice time at the start but it does feel like reality has kicked in and now you are just trying to manage between you and juggle it.

(Ben)

The birth of a baby signals, and enables, men's involvement in a child's life in ways that could only previously be imagined, and lives and selves can be changed forever. Whilst the embodied physicality of pregnancy experienced by women can leave men feeling marginal and detached from the process of becoming a parent, the act of birth can change everything. Birth experiences, which are often different to what has been planned for and expected, set the scene for the early weeks and months of new fatherhood as men come to terms with what, in practice, 'being there', sharing care and doing fathering will involve. But all these experiences are shaped implicitly, explicitly and powerfully by and through gendered and societal expectations that men's lives continue to be largely understood in relation to paid work outside the home and little altered by parenthood. This provides a particular backdrop against which fatherhood and fathering practices are made sense of and which is significantly different to those that underpin expectations around motherhood and mothering practices (see chapter 6). For all the contemporary shifts which can be documented around men's lives – and so masculinities – their continued association with paid work and provision limits not just the possible parameters of their involvement but also how involvement can be conceived of and articulated. In this chapter the men's narratives of transition continue to unfold as they navigate and make sense of this new landscape. A dominant motif running across the men's anticipatory narratives is of 'being there' for their child and implicitly for their wife/partner too. This is conveyed as a central feature of involved fatherhood and conjured up in ways which suggest much more than just financial provision.

'Being there' is multifaceted. It is about sharing care and is also linked to establishing a relationship with the new baby, which is described in terms of 'bonding', 'instincts' and 'love'. Being there as a father is also described in terms of 'time' and being 'consistent' and creating 'stability'. At the same time it is described in more traditional ways, as in 'financial provision' and being a 'role model' for the child to look up to. Indeed these more contemporary understandings of 'being there' sound very like mothering (Doucet, 2006). So how does 'being there' take shape in practice? Where and how is it realised in caring and other ways and what are the individual 'negotiations' and 'reconciliations' that characterise it in everyday lives: what do the everyday practices of fatherhood look like as first encountered and initially practised? (Hearn *et al.*, 2006: 43).

Unlike in the earlier study of motherhood, concerns about 'coping' with a new baby are not a dominant thread across the men's anticipatory narratives. This is because there is a sense that their wives/partners will instinctively know what to do, reinforced by reading and preparation during the pregnancy. 'Coping' for the women is also associated with a sense of being seen to perform mothering in culturally recognisable and morally acceptable ways. But are men's experiences of transition to first-time fatherhood similarly fraught and precarious? How do gendered assumptions about men's lives – what they do, what they are expected to do and how such things can be voiced – encountered in relation to early experiences of fathering and fatherhood? How are emotions, selves and deeply embedded ideas of hegemonic masculinity associated with work, managed, performed and/or rejected in this new and uncertain arena? Clearly, the assumptions of essentialism and biological determinism which take for granted maternal identities – and so capacities – are not readily identified with paternal identities. For the men, then, involvement at the birth, being there and providing support, heralds a very real opportunity for their active involvement. Whilst feelings of both detachment and ambivalence through the process of pregnancy were expressed earlier, the birth provides a critical turning point as the men *become* fathers.

The interviews which provide the data for this chapter were designed to coincide with the timing of the early postnatal interviews in the companion study on motherhood at 6–8 weeks following the birth. At this time the new mothers were at home trying to get to grips with early mothering practices and experiences in the privacy of their homes and so access was unproblematic, but the men in the fatherhood study were back at work. This meant in practice that the timing for these interviews was extended up to 12 weeks in order to accommodate men's work, new family commitments and so their more limited availability.[1] In several of the interviews (which took place mostly in the evenings or at weekends around work schedules) the men sat with their new babies on their laps or asleep nearby – performing fatherhood – as the interviews ensued. The term 'emotional rollercoaster' was used by many of the men to describe the period leading up to the birth, the birth and the early weeks. Seeing and holding their child(ren) for the first time was a profound experience and (for most) is narrated at length in highly detailed, emotional and tender terms.[2] More generally in these interviews, in contrast to the antenatal interviews, the men are now more expert and comfortable with the language associated with reproductive bodies and the processes of very early childcare. They speak at times authoritatively and sometimes tentatively in language not normally associated with hegemonic masculinities of 'dilation', 'cervix', 'meconium', 'waters breaking', 'episiotomies' and 'expressing milk'. Here they demonstrate that they have (mostly) acquired the appropriate 'discursive resources' for narrating and navigating childbirth and early caring (Hobson and Morgan, 2002).

In the following extract Chris, describing the birth, draws upon this language, whilst seeking confirmation from me and so underscoring his relatively novice status:

Apparently it was quite, what do they call it, it seems like a long time ago now, the cervix that was quite thin... We went into a monitoring room when we arrived and they kind of left us for a bit and then we were given, do they call them maternity suites?

The period leading up to the birth involves some of the men 'working really crazy hours' trying to meet deadlines at work before taking

---

[1] I asked one participant (who had been particularly difficult to tie down to a day and time for his second interview, although verbally willing to participate) if he thought the problems of setting up second interviews with some of the participants might be a result of the new demands they had on their time with work and a new baby – but he swept this explanation aside, saying he just thought 'men were lazy'.

[2] The seventeen pregnancies resulted in the live births of six female and thirteen male babies (including two sets of male twins).

paternity leave. Others continue to do 'practical things to prepare the house' whilst also trying to enjoy 'the last few days of normality and sleep and things like that'. As the birth approaches, preparation for the event can seem more necessary. Richard describes attending an active birth class:

I had been, we had both gone to an active birth partner's workshop, which was the best thing I went to . . . which were very, very useful because . . . it was actually quite good to be told 'actually, you just stand there and massage her back', that's all you can do.

Richard appears reassured by the instructions provided in the class about the extent of his active involvement – 'you just stand there and massage her back'. The uncertainty of when the birth will start and what the signs of the commencement of birth might be also make this a tentative time: between 'normal' everyday life and the onset of a highly significant, life-changing event. In the following extract Joe conveys this sense of the everyday and normal (work and the pub on a Friday night) coming up against imminent change:

It was on a Friday and I had obviously been at work all day and like most Fridays, really, I would finish work and just go down the pub for a couple of drinks with the people I worked with . . . and I got a call . . . from Jane, saying 'you better get back, I think I've gone into labour' and she said 'don't have any more drink' . . . I got home, Jane wasn't in too much discomfort but she was having contractions or sort of thought they were contractions but obviously we didn't know because we had never gone through this process before.

Joe goes on to describe seeking confirmation of the onset of Jane's labour:

That night one of my friends from work was meant to come round just for a couple of drinks and a chat and I sort of thought, well, I don't know what to do and it sounds really, really . . . so [my friend] came around and personally I wanted him to be there because I thought he'd have a good idea, yes or no, if it was labour or not. So he came round and stayed for about half an hour and obviously he said 'yeah, she's in labour' and by then [the contractions had] started getting stronger.

What is interesting here is the authoritative confirmation 'yeah, she's in labour' that Joe's male friend provides. This could suggest that men are more involved in this area than is assumed and so it is not 'seen' because it is not expected. The signs of the onset of labour are not a type of knowledge that is readily associated with men. The point at which paternity leave should commence provides another type of uncertainty and, as Nick says, he does not want to use up his 'paternity leave for contractions'. Graham describes this waiting period as 'an odd time sort of waiting for a phone call, really, to sort of be home for childbirth'. Eventually the waiting is over ('we'd waited so long for this to actually kick off and finally it came') and the process of birth begins.

The birth

All the births are different in some way to what has been planned, from 'text book' and 'no big dramas' to 'emergency caesarean', and the term 'surreal' is used by many of the men to describe the events around the birth ('looking back now, it's almost like it wasn't me, that I was there, you know', Gareth). The embodiment of pregnancy means that men have often felt 'onlookers' through the antenatal period. During the birth they continue to be onlookers, but alongside a more distinct role as an 'interpreter' and as a 'go-between' (see chapter 3). This, it is anticipated, will involve ensuring that birth plans (where written) are followed, health professionals are managed if necessary and, importantly, 'being there' to provide support to their wife/partner. But men's role at birth is still ambiguous: its lack of clarity underscores men's historical absence from this area traditionally construed as a singularly maternal space. From the health care side, men are now encouraged to demonstrate their involvement through, in the antenatal phase, sharing in the writing of birth plans and attending preparation classes, and at the birth helpfully supporting their wife/partner, keeping out of the way ('they gave me a pillow to hold because I was so nervous') and cutting the baby's umbilical cord on delivery. The men's experiences of performing these roles at the birth are varied. The births, too, are varied and include five caesareans (three of which are performed as emergencies) and several others involve the use of forceps, leading to live births but, in one case, the baby's collar bone being broken ('12 hours afterwards we found out she's broken her collar bone as well'). Just as in the earlier motherhood study, most of the births are not perceived to have been 'natural' or 'easy'.

All the births except one (planned) home birth take place in the hospital.[3] Gus talks of his attempts to make the hospital room more 'homely':

I tried to make it look homely, but it just so wasn't happening, and I felt like a bit of a... I'm, like, 'Oh, I don't know what to do'... because this is... there was nothing I could do.

This sense of not knowing or having anything to do is expressed by other participants ('I was kind of stood there not really knowing exactly what to do'). Richard describes putting into practice what he has been told to do by the National Childbirth Trust (NCT) class he has attended, but still feeling 'irrelevant' and 'useless':

My role was rather irrelevant I think, that is the thing I kind of remember thinking, of feeling quite useless actually, which is the other thing, the NCT don't say that. They don't say 'you will be standing there and you'll feel really useless'. They tell you all these ways in which you are supposed to be helpful. The one thing I did which I think was vaguely helpful, Ros just had a sponge in her bag and so I just spent two and a half hours or so sponging the back of her neck and trying to do the massage thing on the bottom of the back, which may or may not have been helpful... So that was, like, so it was kind of rather, it was just a very weird experience to witness this thing and sort of clearly to understand that it's quite important for me to be there, but actually just to be there. There's nothing for me to really do.

Others describe their role at the birth as 'supporting', trying to provide comfort and giving encouragement ('even though I thought everything was going horribly wrong, I had to try to pretend that it was alright', Chris).

In the antenatal interviews the men expressed some trepidation in being expected by their wives/partners to keep things on track according to the birth plans that have been (hopefully) drawn up. In the event, this proves challenging and leads some of the men to feel 'guilty' that they have failed at this task. Most of the plans involve limiting the use of pain relief during the birth and this is to be 'enforced' by the

[3] Dylan, who along with his wife, planned and, indeed, had a home birth was the only participant not to be interviewed during the early postnatal phase of the research (see chapter 7). He returned to the study for the later, postnatal interview (see chapter 5).

men. In the following extract Ian describes his wife's birth plan and the subsequent events:

Polly had written a birth plan, which I have to say I thought at one point it was a bit too detailed, but the intention was for it to be as natural a birth as possible because we both believe that having a more natural birth is better for everyone concerned, you know, where possible. But medical intervention is fantastic when you need it, which we did . . . But Polly did decide to have the [pain relief] because it was more painful than she expected and I couldn't really, you know, I sort of felt that that kind of time, was the kind of time that I could have made a difference, but I went along with it . . . eventually it was a forceps delivery.

Like others, Joe also finds it hard to see his wife in pain and to continue to try to follow the birth plan:

The hardest thing for me was during the process, I don't think it was the pain as much, because each individual contraction you can obviously deal with that, but when it keeps coming and you can't see an end to it, it was so demoralising . . . that was the worst point and then for about an hour or two I sort of managed to say 'look, you don't want any pain relief' and in the end she had an epidural.

Most of the men express a mixture of unease and difficulty and admiration at being the onlooker whilst their wife/partner is clearly in pain. As Stephen says, 'I found it really hard just to see Claire go through all this pain and know it wasn't going to stop.' Gus, too, describes feeling helpless:

it was horrible, knowing that there's nothing . . . you normally, if she's in pain, I would comfort her, stroke her hair, hold her, but she didn't obviously want me to touch her . . .

Births, then, unfold in unforeseen and unpredictable ways. When their role as interpreter does not translate as planned the men can experience guilt and helplessness. But even in this foreign arena they can assert authority – propelled by a combination of guilt and helplessness and also fear. Nick describes his role in a very difficult birth that involves his wife being moved to a different hospital:

and in the end I got a bit arsy with them and said 'look, either we are transferring or we're not, but we can't be sitting waiting, . . . So I just said 'get an ambulance, we're going to the [larger hospital], I'll make the decision'.

Eventually all the labours end in the birth of healthy infants (including two sets of twins) and the men *become* fathers ('it just opens up a whole new world, it's a miracle', James). The 'brute force' and 'goriness' of some births is shocking for the men, whilst others are described as 'amazing'. Some of the men perform the relatively new act of cutting the umbilical cord ('that was just like a real kind of amazing experience', Mike) but responses are mixed. Gus says that he has been told by other 'blokes' that he 'ought to cut the cord, it's a great thing' but he describes it as 'horrible' and that he 'won't do it again' and Ian recounts the expectation of the midwife that he would want to perform this act (supposedly, this is what fathers do):

And that was very funny, the one thing they tell fathers that, the fathers are sort of expected to want to do these days, is cut the cord, for some bizarre reason and they did ask me this about three times during the day and there was just no chance at all that I would cut the cord.

But seeing their baby for the first time is for all of them an emotional event ('it was very moving to have a baby suddenly and to feel that you're a father', Graham), and this is expressed in a range of ways. Overtly emotional expression is not readily associated with ideas of controlled, dispassionate, hegemonic masculinities and the men's descriptions are narrated, and selves positioned and presented, in ways which implicitly acknowledge this. In the following extracts the men present their emotional responses, and so their selves, on the birth of their child:

I wasn't brought to tears, I wouldn't say I was brought to tears. The whole thing had been so traumatic, I was just bloody pleased that it was over. (Nick)

So I'm not really sure what I felt like, I can remember the welling up and thinking 'oh, I'm going to cry, should I cry?' and sort of thinking, no, nobody else is. I also think that actually the welling up thing was not necessarily at the birth of my baby, it was just, like, relief at the fact, not relief that the baby was born, but the relief that it was over, particularly for [my wife]. (Richard)

We both cried. I know everybody says they cry and I was like 'yeah, I probably won't cry' but I cried too. (Dean)

It was literally 15 minutes later they'd done [the caesarean] and [the baby] came out and I was sobbing with tears of joy, nobody could just console me at all, you know, the best and worst day of my life, it was amazing, absolutely amazing...I just couldn't stop crying, literally, I was just a mess, a blubbering mess [laughs], it was amazing...because I'm not a teary person, I don't cry that much, in fact I don't think I've cried for a long, long time. Yeah, just a total gibbering wreck. (Stephen)

I was quite emotional. I mean, I didn't cry as such, not that I disagree with it or anything, but I just generally don't, but, no, I definitely had a physical manifestation which was the lump in the throat and tears in your eyes...it's quite an intensive thing. I was quite emotional. (Gareth)

What is of interest here are the ways in which these different extracts illuminate what are taken to be socially acceptable and culturally appropriate responses to the birth of their child, by men. Of all events, the birth of a child might be one where unbridled emotion may be displayed and articulated and whilst this is evident in some of the narratives, self-monitoring and/or justifications are also present (Seidler, 2006). Only Stephen implies that he was out of control in some way ('nobody could just console me') but even he adds that he is 'not a teary person'. Being a 'teary person' could imply a sense of weakness – even femininity – which is not readily identified with strength and being masculine. In contrast to Stephen, Gareth says that he did not 'cry as such' and then describes a set of physical symptoms which sound very close to crying. But he also asserts that he doesn't 'disagree' with men crying, just that he is not a man who does this. Even Dean, who is employed in an occupation strongly associated with hegemonic and heteronormative masculinity, aspects of which run dominantly through his narrative of transition, admits, 'I cried.' Whilst the men's responses can be seen as gendered – that is, they position their selves and describe their reactions in relation to what they recognise as societal norms of masculine behaviours – expressing an immediate attachment or bond draws upon a discourse of essentialism: which is much more associated with women and expectations of maternal instincts and identities. Interestingly, some – but not all – of the men also talk of their sense of an *immediate* ('overwhelming') attachment, bond or feeling of love:

But, yeah, I suppose I had quite a strong attachment to him, I suppose right from the start and I suppose it did grow over time. (Graham)

I knew, obviously, that your child's going to be born, and you know that you're going to love it, but I don't think...You're not quite prepared for the strength of that...when you hold him in your arms, just this immense feeling. I wasn't, you know, I wasn't prepared for it to be that strong, it was just like 'wow, this is . . . very overwhelming', you can't, you can't quite believe that you can love something that much. (Gus)

Yeah, I just found it really, really, because I think I said to you before, one of my worries or concerns was I'd really never had any great affection before she was born whilst Jane was pregnant. Jane was, like, really the one pushing reading the books and getting everything and I would obviously go with her to do that but I never . . . it wasn't the same for me. But as soon as she was born it was sort of instant love and bond. (Joe)

Debates around fathering, masculinities, gender and essentialism will be revisited in later chapters (see chapter 6 and 7) and continue to be traced across the empirical data. But what is of interest here is how the men's relationships unfold as babies are taken home and practices of 'involved' fathering begin. How do their plans for 'being there' and 'caring' and 'sharing care' translate into everyday practices?

Hospital to home

The birth of a child can change lives in all sorts of ways. Becoming a father is described by many of the participants in terms of feeling 'grown up' and having a greater sense of maturity and responsibility. Gareth captures the sense of the enormity of the transition in the following extract:

We went into hospital as Pam and Gareth living on our own for four years or whatever and came out, yeah, a mum and dad, so . . . we both sat there and went 'God, we are completely different people now.'

Taking wives/partners home from hospital signals life returning to 'normal' as paternity or holiday leave is taken and soon ends, and patterns of caring around paid work are established. For some, complicated births necessarily delay this phase of transition and whilst Frank waits to be able to bring his wife and twins home from hospital he returns to work in order to save his valuable (2 weeks') paternity leave. In the following extract he describes this unexpected situation:

So I went back to work for 3 days and . . . it was worse than I imagined really, I just didn't want to be there. They were all in hospital where, again, I know they are being looked after well but, you know, the father instinct kicks in when you are trying to protect your family, sort of thing, and I couldn't do that from where I was. So I just wasn't at work really, I was there but I just wasn't, you know, I was just in a trance really. If people asked me to do anything, I would probably have just grunted and probably not done it but... It was a horrible feeling where, I know there was nothing I could do, so being I couldn't do anything, there was no point in being at the hospital but that is where I wanted to be, to be with them, even though I couldn't do anything. It was difficult dragging myself out of bed in the morning to go to work, especially having gone through everything. It was quite an emotional time, you know, being strong with your wife and children, but you sort of come back into your house and your four walls and you sort of let it all out, sort of thing, and then have to go to work and put a pretence of a face on when you are at work, trying to put that professional image out but, yeah, it wasn't pleasant.

What is interesting here is the ways in which Frank, in describing this difficult and unexpected period, draws upon different discourses. He talks of a 'father instinct' that has kicked in, leading him to want to *protect* his family. Whilst this invokes strands of essentialism it also engages with more traditional patriarchal and gendered ideas of father-hood and protection and 'being strong'. He must continue to manage his 'professional image' and perform in the work sphere in appropri-ately non-emotional (masculine) ways, but the privacy and security of home allows him to 'let it all out'. The gendered expectations, and so constraints on emotional displays – especially those that could be out of place and so potentially uncomfortable and/or disruptive – are clearly demonstrated here.

For the other new fathers the initial days at home are described in various ways from being like a 'baby honeymoon' to regretting not having 'gone to parenting classes'. Others expect to feel 'nervous' but 'didn't find it that terrifying at all really' whilst others speak of being at home with the baby and 'not knowing what to do' and 'feeling inadequate': it is striking but not surprising that men are able to talk of 'not knowing' in ways which women as mothers would mostly feel unable to risk. Babies are driven around in cars at night in desperate attempts by tired parents to get them to go to sleep and all are struck by the enormity of the impact of such a small person(s). As Gus says:

One of the biggest things I've noticed is, it's just this little baby, but... how much time it will take up, that was... yeh, that's the most phenomenal thing, we just weren't prepared for that.

All the men talk of their feelings of pride at becoming a father – and a family – and having their 'family' home. They all take time off work during the initial weeks either through statutory paternity leave and/or saved holiday or unpaid leave. But their involvement is framed in relation to paid work outside the home and the expectation that their transition to fatherhood marks only a very temporary period of disruption to their working life. Not all can afford to take up statutory paternity leave ('I didn't because they don't pay you enough... it's disgusting, it's about £107 but you get taxed on that') and so saved holiday is used by some. By combining paternity leave, saved holiday, unpaid leave, bank holidays and returning to work part time the men are able to take between 2 and 7 weeks off work. Some employers are found to be more understanding and supportive through this period than others ('he just didn't understand', James).

In these early weeks, patterns of involvement begin to take shape and it is paternity leave and/or holiday leave which facilitates this. As Sean says, 'I didn't think it would be as important, but having that time, it just kind of felt like I became far more involved.' In this early period both parents are at home and in the following extract Gareth talks about the 'similar' responses he and his wife have around their baby twins:

I just couldn't stop holding them, looking at them, you know, cooing, ah, you just can't take your eyes off them, well, I couldn't anyway. Well, we were both the same, we are quite similar in the way we are with them... and the first few days as well, it's just getting used to the noises and every little noise for the first week, every noise during the night I was awake at anyway – what's that, what's that, what's that, what are they doing?

Other fathers describe what their involvement actually entails in these early weeks:

Anyway, we finally got the instructions, sort of thing [they spoke to a midwife] and I think we got the hang of cleaning him, bathing him, and changing the nappy and that sort of thing. So I think on the practical side we were O.K.... But I think for the first week at home I actually did all that nappy changing and that sort of stuff, most of the washing. Yes, that seemed to work pretty well and Rebecca was able to have plenty of naps which helped keep her strength. (Graham)

I would try and do as much as I could really... In those first 2 weeks it was just to really change her and when she'd get up in the night and not need feeding but just comforting, I'd get up and do that. But, yeah, just to do as much as I could really because I couldn't feed her at that stage. I mean for the first week or so I was, like, this is pretty easy because she's asleep all day, they don't do much and when they wake up, it's only because they want food and you wind them and then put them down and then you change them and that's it really. But, yeah, and obviously I'd try and do shopping and stuff around the house, that sort of stuff really . . . (Joe)

I actually took 4 weeks' full [paternity leave and holiday]. Just being at home was just really good . . . 4 weeks at home was just great, really, really nice. We kind of got into the swing of kind of how things were and how things would be and got a feeling for [the baby] being around. If I'd only taken the 2 weeks . . . it would have kind of felt quite short . . . and it tends to be either the baby or housework, kind of, I'm either doing one or the other. (Sean)

I thought also I wouldn't settle into it as quickly as I have. I thought I would be more, because I see babies as so delicate I thought I wouldn't necessarily know what to do with it. But it's kind of instinctive . . . Yeah, I think we take it pretty evenly, I mean until Susan starts expressing [milk] then I can't do the feeding but I do everything else. (Chris)

These very early descriptions of 'being there' involve the men in the physical tasks of caring – nappy changing and bathing – as well as more 'emotional' acts of 'comforting' and 'getting used to the noises'. Where babies are breastfed the men are excluded but as Chris says, 'I do everything else.' Domestic 'stuff' around the house and shopping are also tasks taken on by the men. In many ways this short period of time – largely made possible by paternity leave – enables the men (as well as the women) to begin to learn practices of caring and in many ways signals real potential for sharing of care to be realised: but the men's return to work changes everything.

Returning to work

The resumption of paid work is described in various ways by the new fathers. For them it signals 'going back to normalness', 'the best of both worlds', 'a relief' and 'a release'. Feelings of 'guilt' are also expressed as they resume work, which is described as 'less emotionally tiring' and less demanding than doing the 'mundane stuff' associated with caring for a baby. There is also a sense that responsibilities have now spread to encompass the home as well as the workplace ('I'm used to a lot of responsibility outside of here and being able to come home and not having that'). Joe notes that 'the nine to five part of my life is pretty much the same as it was before whereas Jane, her whole life has changed completely'. The men recognise the hard work entailed in caring for a new baby and some express concerns about how their wives/partners will cope alone. But in some cases returning to work provides a palpable sense of relief ('it's very nice to just jump in the van and . . . get back to work'). There is an inevitability woven across the men's narratives that they will return to work and their wives/partners will remain at home (through the initial months at least) caring for the child. Clearly the ways in which paternity and maternity leave are structured in the UK impose and assume a particular pattern of (almost exclusively maternal) early caring which is then (mostly) followed. Only one father speaks of wanting to stay at home and care full time for his daughter but that his wife will not let him. Another has reduced his working week by one day (but not his working hours) and another father speaks of eventually doing the same through 'compressing' his working hours. Another hopes to work part time once maternity leave has finished.

Following the men's return to work a series of things happen: they have less time to be involved; their wives/partners become more prac-tised in caring for the child; the periods (evenings and weekends for most) when they are involved in caring encourage task-based activities to be undertaken – for example, bathing, going for a walk; the men become less attuned to their babies' daily needs as they change quite quickly through the early weeks. In the following lengthy extracts their gradual shifts around day-to-day caring are revealed:

I managed to get about 3 weeks off in the end and it was quite nice for those 2 or 3 weeks, it feels like a special time in my head because I was around the whole time and at nights I would get up with [my wife] because you don't know what you are doing so we were doing it together and she was feeding him and then I would be, like, trying to burp him or change and then you go back to work and it is, like, you kind of have to sort of not withdraw from it, but I needed to get more sleep so Hannah dealt with the night a bit more and then whole days and then suddenly you become a bit more secondary . . . now a lot of that is . . . Hannah is kind of doing most of the care . . . Then when you go back [to work] suddenly the routine is continually changing so just when you think you have got it, he is changing because he is growing so quickly but I don't think I quite know all of the issues now . . . I get to see him a bit at the weekends but just lately I had deadlines as well so I was working sort of 7 days a week for a couple of weeks and quite quickly you can feel out of it. (Ben)

Maybe because I actually had, 5 weeks is quite a long time to be [off], it's not that we were sharing it equally, I wasn't breastfeeding by definition, but that was quite a long time to be doing all of that stuff, prior to going back to work. So now I'm very much aware that I'm not doing a lot of it actually . . . So it's hard work for her, much harder work for her than it is for me, just in terms of the time. (Richard)

I mean, I say that I'd love to have her all day and I would do, but after 3 or 4 weeks I don't know if I'd feel the same, I'd like to think I'd want to look after her all the time, but going to work is quite nice, you get that break and, like I say, it's great for me, I sort of see her in the morning and have a play with her and I come back and I play with her and it's great. Whereas obviously I can sort of have her for, say, 5 or 6 hours in an evening, or on a weekend or something like that, but outside of that at the present time that's the maximum I've got with her, so I would have no idea of what it's really like to sort of . . . (Joe)

They're with each other all the time, Sophie's much better at picking up on cues and knowing when [the baby] is needing food or tired or anything else. During the week I get home just before six, I do the bath, I do the change, you know, put the clothes on afterwards, I do the feed and then, for the ten thirty feed, she's put down at sort of seven-ish and then the ten thirty we now generally take in turns . . . There's a bit of a discussion. Normally, in fact, to be honest, normally Sophie does it because I am normally working and she kind of feels sympathetic to that. So during the week that's kind of . . . [at] weekends I find she's kind of thrust on me. You know, 'I've had her all week, she's all yours' so, yeah, definitely more hands-on at the weekend, feeding with her, playing with her, keeping her amused, changing her, organising. (William)

After the evening feed I'll try and tend to wind [the baby] just so that Maria has got that release for an hour or whatever it is. It's good, I mean I never see her much during the day obviously so I try and spend as much time with her as possible, yeah, definitely . . . just having the sort of time off, getting involved in the early years of her life really. Yeah, just being a whole part of the changing the nappies, the dressing and putting her into her buggy and taking her round the block a couple of times or whatever . . . little things like that, just making sure there's a plentiful supply, making sure we've got bucket loads of nappies ready, you know, yeah, bibs, you know, making sure they're all kind of washed and ready and ready for action. (Mike)

Paid work outside the home clearly shapes men's involvement in caring for their child(ren) in significant ways. Work requires the men to be able to function in appropriate and acceptable ways and so they may sleep in another room in order to be 'ready for work'. Men's involvement becomes 'fitted in' to particular parts of the day or week and becomes associated with specific activities, and all the while the women become more practised in recognising and meeting the child's needs. Men are more likely to describe their input once they return to work as providing 'assistance', 'support' and 'helping out' and to begin to talk more explicitly of responsibilities around caring in terms of 'providing' and 'protection'. As Gus says, 'the whole sort of provider thing has really sort of kicked in'.

It was noted in chapter 1 that there is a tendency in the Western world for the onset of 'parenthood' to 'crystallize a gendered division of labour' (Sanchez and Thomson, 1997: 747) and that seems to be the case here. But what seems qualitatively different is that the men still anticipate being involved in more hands-on activities but around the work commitments they have: the divisions in some respects have become more blurred. This is significantly different to the ways in which the men recall being fathered (see below) which, as other research has discussed, indicates generational shifts in expectations and daily practices of hands-on caring and involvement. The ways in which fathering and mothering and caring for children are organised and experienced has been debated across a range of academic disciplines for many years. Key questions concern whether the practices of caring for a baby are innate and instinctive and an essential aspect of being female or whether they arise from particular ways of organising societies and gendered responsibilities within them. So, in patriarchal and capitalist societies where paid work outside the home is highly valued men have traditionally been associated with this sphere, whilst raising children, which is much less valued, is something that women at home have been closely and 'naturally' associated with. Of course, in late modernity societies are more fluid and relationships and possibilities much less tethered in ways these depictions might imply: but they provide an important backdrop against which to consider here how the men talk about their fathering practices and fatherhood. Women as mothers have, then, been much more readily assumed to possess 'instincts', and so the appropriate emotional capacities to care, and men have not. But across the men's narratives of transition a language of paternal instincts, bonding and attachment are drawn upon as the men talk about becoming and being a 'father'.

A shifting sense of self: Being a 'father'

Becoming a father leads most of the men to talk of their priorities shifting. This predominately involves changed attitudes to work, which is described as less important by some, and more important by others, as a necessary means of being able to 'provide'. At the same time work and home are 'juggled' as family life is 'fitted in' around (mostly) unchanged patterns of working. Both are experienced as demanding more time than is available. Social lives are also curtailed. In the following extract Gareth, who is self-employed, talks about the changes he has experienced since becoming a father to twin sons, which have led him to feel 'obviously more protective':

Now I've got focus, I've got to provide for these guys so therefore I'm going to go out and provide for them. There's a definite undertone and it's not, like, a conscious day-to-day, hour-to-hour thing but there's definitely that going on all the time, I'm always thinking of ways to make money . . . almost the reason you work changes whereas, in some ways, therefore, work becomes more important because you think: I really need to make sure this is good and I can get a good next job and that it suits my family and everything else. So I think you're less working for yourself . . .

In many ways Gareth describes the 'catch 22' situation where work becomes more important in order to provide for his family, which in turn means spending less time with the family. Nick, too, talks of a changed attitude to work but where work now 'takes a back seat':

Work is a far lower priority and less of a preoccupation . . . you know, I used to do a lot of work at home, I'm not sure I've done any work at home in the last few weeks. I'm not on top of things at work like I used to be. I don't feel guilty about that. I used to beat myself up if I wasn't on top of everything because that meant doing stuff at home. So work takes more of a back seat.

But Gus talks about the added pressure he now feels as 'the provider':

I've thought more about money, to the point where I've got my bank statements out and broke down everything I've spent, and I've 'right, this leaves me with this much, but add the nappies' and now of course she's not working . . .

Clearly, the men's responses are also related to their type of employment and associated job security. But for all the men, changed priorities
are interwoven with a sense that as fathers they have new responsibilities which are tied to economic provision and emotional commitment.

Fathers in Western societies have traditionally been closely and, at
different historical times, exclusively associated with economic provision. Mothers, in contrast, provided the 'emotional' aspects of care.
But all the participants in this study positioned themselves – to a greater
or lesser extent – as being emotionally involved with their child(ren)
as well as economically responsible. This was expressed across their
narratives in a number of ways (as seen earlier in the chapter) and in
particular as they reflected on their early weeks of fathering. What is of
interest here are the ways in which the men draw upon a discourse of
'instincts' ('a strange sort of paternal instinct'), 'bonding' and 'attachment' – more usually associated with mothers – in seeking to articulate
and make visible their relationship with their child(ren). An emotional
and tender fathering relationship is claimed in ways that would be
unnecessary by mothers because it would be assumed. In the following extracts the men talk about 'instincts', 'a bond', 'attachment' and
how these are established through practice and a growing relationship
with their child(ren). Some also draw a distinction between their caring practices as a father and those of their wife/partner. Mike, whose
partner has been employed in a job involving children, reflects on this
and his own developing caring skills around his daughter:

But I think or I suspect that from a female point of view it's just, it may just
be a natural instinct so irrespective of what background work wise you've
had I think it's something that just comes naturally and I think even for
myself, like this morning when I left [the baby] started whimpering and
crying and she'd just woken up after another hour sort of sleep: oh, she's
been fed, oh, we haven't changed her nappy for a couple of hours, maybe
it's that. So we change her nappy and she seemed to calm down, it's just
trying to link what could it be, what haven't we done for a while . . . [so] at
the moment it's just kind of guessing and using your instinct and your kind
of 8 weeks of work experience so far that you've had and using that.

Frank talks of his own 'gut instinct' but this is also related to spending
time with the babies (twins) and so recognising what they need:

But, you know, at the end of the day more often than not, your gut instinct
is more right than anything else and I think because you spend time with

them, especially now you are starting to know that grizzle, well, we know what that is and you are starting to know what they're griping about.

Although he later makes a distinction between a mother's and a father's bond he explains this through the time a mother spends with the child:

As much as the instinct is there, it's definitely more a mother's bond than a father's, but I think it's more about because you spend time with them and you start to realise and understand them.

In the extract below Nick, too, reflects on the 'emotional impact' of being a new father:

The emotional impact is different from what I expected. I do as much as I can. At the weekends and in the holidays if Shelley gets up during the night with him, I get up during the night with him, even if it's just to sit down here for half an hour. I don't do the feeding, he's only breastfed so I can't do that . . . I always, we bath him together, he's always in the bath with me so that's been a special time. I change lots of nappies and if I'm not at work then I'll bring him downstairs and play with him in the morning and try and let Shelley have a half an hour on her . . . I'm not sure whether there's anything more that I could be doing, given that I'm out at work. There is no aspect that I don't get involved in apart from the breastfeeding . . . But there is something, there is something emotionally, I guess emotionally I don't feel I'm doing as much with him as I would like, but I couldn't justify that in practical terms . . . But it is more emotionally draining than I thought and at times I've found it less emotionally rewarding than I thought it was going to be. Actually when you get to the end of the day and he has screamed all day, I find it hard to think, well, you know, that's been a good day . . . I knew that was always a possibility, well, I know you can have good days and bad days and babies are going to cry a lot. But, yes, sometimes I've just thought it's not a very rewarding experience.

In this extract it is clear that, whilst Nick is significantly involved in the practical aspects of providing care (around work commitments) to his baby son, he does not find this early fathering relationship as 'emotionally rewarding' as he had anticipated. What is of interest here is, first, that he anticipated such an early, instinctive, emotional relationship and, second, that he is able to say that 'sometimes I've just thought it's not a very rewarding experience'. This is not because it is a bad thing to say, but because it marks out the gendered expectations of what fathers and mothers do and what it is possible for them to articulate in relation to their child (see chapter 6). It is not unusual for new parents to find aspects of the hard work of caring (doing the 'mundane stuff') to be in some respects repetitive and unrewarding, but it appears that it is more acceptable for a father to voice such feelings. It would be very differently construed if a new mother were to risk such honesty.

In the following extract William happily talks of having 'no idea at all' about looking after a baby – again, a very difficult thing for a new mother to admit – and, in contrast to Nick (and the other fathers), conveys a much more traditional view of the 'paternal role':

In terms of actually looking after a child . . . no idea at all. I felt very inadequate to be honest, you know. Sophie completely led that . . . but, you know, it's definitely a lot easier the older she's got because we've felt more confident, but in simple terms I think there is still a distinction, I feel, between the maternal role and the paternal role. I think mothers and fathers do provide different things. It's hard to list them but I think the mother is more emotionally attached . . . the fathers are more the breadwinning, sort of the looking after the family sort of role. But I think the influence and the interest a father has in the child has changed, definitely.

But even William acknowledges societal change with regard to the father's 'interest' in the child and that over time (interviewed at 12 weeks) things had become 'a lot easier' as his confidence has grown and relationships and routines become established. Across William's and the other participants' narratives, experiences emerge which illuminate how structural features (e.g., work) shape their fathering practices. They recognise 'paternal identity' as sharing some emotional traits with those assumed around maternal identities and also that caring becomes easier as it is practised over time. Apart from where babies are exclusively breastfed, the new fathers (mostly) position themselves as 'doing most things' but returning to work limits the frequency of their caring and reduces it to more task-based activities.

Significant shifts in men's hands-on and tender involvement are, then, discernible during these early postnatal interviews and are further highlighted when set beside the men's reflections of their own fathers' involvement in their childhoods. What the following extracts convey is how gendered possibilities and practices relate to shifting understandings of masculinities. In turn, these shifts have been facilitated by corresponding structural changes, most notably the introduction of statutory paternity leave in the UK. Whilst the following extracts are dependent on memory and *who* is telling the story it is clear that structural features and gendered practices are seen to shape how the participants' own fathers were involved in their care:

I mean, the way he's described it he did have a few days off work but I think he focused on doing nothing else and my mum looked after me and then he went back to work after a week or so. (Graham)

I mean, he probably wouldn't have had the flexibility that I've had with leave and stuff but, yeah, my dad being quite old fashioned ... I can't really imagine it. (Chris)

Yeah, I don't think he was hands-on, well, I know he wasn't hands-on. Historically that wasn't what fathers did in society at that point so I think very different. (Nick)

Yeah, I just want to be involved as much as I can and I'm sure my dad would have been as well if he could, but the way things have changed over time, it allows nowadays that you can now be involved, so I never missed an antenatal class or an appointment ... (Frank)

I think things are different. I know my dad said when I spoke to him about it that he did a lot of the bottle feeds at night and was quite involved and when I told my mum that she laughed ... he was working long hours so it was a much more old-fashioned set-up I think then, in that a bloke just worked and it was, like, just the woman's job to do that. (Ben)

Based on their recollections of their own fathers' lack of hands-on involvement in their young lives, both Joe and Stephen are concerned that their fathers will not be interested in their new grandchildren:

The one person I was a bit, not worried about, was my dad because when me and my brother were born, I can't ever remember him being very lovey dovey or anything like that, but he's brilliant. He has been really, really, really good actually, he's been great ... and he cuddles her and he was never like that with me or my brother ... (Joe)

[My dad] really annoyed me before [the baby] was born. He was, like, 'oh, I'm not interested in babies, they're just babies' and stuff like that and he's quite a big guy and apparently when I was young, when we were babies, there's three of us and he didn't want to pick us up because he felt a bit cumbersome, type thing, he might harm us, type thing. But as soon as he saw [the baby] that's it, he cracked completely [laughs], he wants to hold him, he doesn't mind looking after him so, yeah, he's over the moon, he loves the little chap and, yes, he's great, yeah, he's completely changed and

I'm not annoyed at him anymore [laughs]. I knew he'd change his mind, sort of thing. (Stephen)

Nick expresses similar concerns to Joe and Stephen, but acknowledges that his father's reactions might be hard to bear however he responds:

I think it's a difficult either way, a difficult situation because I think if he does lots of great things with [the baby] I think I will probably resent the fact that I don't remember him doing those things with me. But if he doesn't do them, I'll resent the fact that he's not doing them with him. (Nick)

Whilst generational shifts are clear here and indeed no surprise, yet again the ways in which the men talk about their relationships with their fathers emphasise the importance to them of male (fatherly) relationships even where they are not necessarily associated with emotional closeness.[4] What also emerges from the men's reflections is a clear sense of changing masculine identities and associated gendered behaviours – and articulations of these – especially in relation to practices of family life.

Across the early postnatal narratives the men demonstrate in various ways, and to various extents, that they have been 'hands-on' and feel emotionally involved and invested in their child(ren). Becoming a father has changed, in significant ways, aspects of their lives but being back at work also ensures that other aspects remain similar and may feel unchanged. The men talk in different ways about being a father and 'feeling like a father', some pointing (in surprise) to their own 'competence' in meeting many of their child(ren)'s needs whilst others are still puzzling over how the identity of father actually relates to them. Others emphasise the immediate bond/love/attachment that they felt for their child(ren) which they associate with being a father. Again, this range of experiences is not unusual and resonates with the findings in other studies (Williams, 2008; Plantin *et al.*, 2003) as well as with the earlier motherhood study. Richard talks in the following extract about how he feels now that he has become a father:

---

[4] This is not to prioritise the male-to-male (or father-to-father) relationship but to underline the importance that the participants placed on it across the study in relation to a range of different types of father/relationship. One of the participants whose father was absent for most of his childhood also said, 'I tell you, it's made me appreciate my mum more ... massively. I mean, she had three on her own and I just think, oh, my God ... the first time I saw her after the birth I was so emotional with her'.

So the feelings I have towards her aren't necessarily yet kind of fatherly ones, I don't think so. I think maybe I just haven't recognised them . . . I certainly kind of feel entirely different about myself and everything else because of this but I don't yet think there is anything explicitly fatherly going on, apart from the sense, the way in which our more practical relationship with the baby is and obviously . . . Ros is doing all the work and I'm kind of going to work and those sorts of things.

Here Richard acknowledges that he feels 'entirely' differently about himself 'and everything else' but that he's uncertain about what 'fatherly' feelings might actually feel like. Again, what is clear through the range of responses is that transition is a process in which (paternal) identities are not fixed and 'put on' but are gradually and reflexively identified with, through practices and growing relationships. Again, the difference between new fathers and new mothers is striking in that as soon as a woman has a child she is defined in relation to her child as a mother – an all-encompassing identity to which are attached societal expectations of behaviour. But becoming a father does not invoke the same societal responses and this has a range of consequences for men: they must actively seek to make clear/claim paternal identity and at the same time they are not expected or supposed to be (naturally) competent at caring. These competing visions of men, masculinities and fatherhood can be seen as both potentially limiting and liberating. But one consequence is that men as fathers (mostly) do have more choices available to them as women take up their (assumed) primary caring role. Graham alludes to different choices being available to him ('leave that to the mother') in the following extract:

So I wouldn't say I believe in a hard and fast way of fatherhood, of whether you do the hands-on stuff or you leave that to the mother but obviously it's very important to have plenty of contact and have a good relationship with the child, provide that kind of support in one way or another, whether it's supporting the mother in the baby care or providing it directly and providing plenty of interaction and stimulation and that sort of thing. I'm sure it's a very important role but I think it can vary.

In addition, acts of performing early fathering outside the home (in the public sphere) are also interpreted and responded to in different ways as a result of these competing societal visions of fatherhood and motherhood.

Performing fatherhood outside the home

Fathering practices and societal visions of fatherhood have, then, always been subject to change. One very noticeable change in more recent years has been men's much greater visibility in the public sphere, being out and about with their young babies/children pushing them in prams and pushchairs (strollers) and carrying them in baby slings. Such displays would in previous times have risked being seen as 'unmanly' as Mike recognises in the following extract:

maybe for a new father to be walking a child round in a pram or whatever round their neighbourhood would perhaps have been seen as unmanly or whatever...But, yeah, these days I'm showing baby off and taking her around in various different pushchairs or whatever and now that I'm a father I'm kind of noticing more fathers with their children as well...yeah, I think in terms of the kind of era thing I think, yeah, it's almost more acceptable now to be, you know, a man, a male showing your emotions or showing or telling people you take part in what was perceived to be a female role, cooking, cleaning, ironing, childcare for want of a better word, so, yeah, things have definitely come along which is good.

As well as acknowledging that he is 'noticing more fathers' now that he is one – something others also speak of in terms of 'joining a club' and there being 'kind of like this daddy bond' – Mike also talks about the greater acceptability of a man to show his emotions and to do things once 'perceived to be a female role'. He goes on to proudly describe taking his daughter out for a walk around the village where he lives:

and then when you get all the friends and family and villagers 'oh, let's have a look' and stuff like that and it just kind of makes you stand up straight and think, yeah, flip, ain't it...that's my daughter.

Others, too, describe early solo outings with their new babies:

I feel very proud when I go out round town with him. Partly because he always, whenever I put him in his carry he always falls asleep, which is really nice. I think I hold myself differently as I walk around town wearing him and I think people respond to you differently, you get a very different response in shops and stuff. People talk to you...there was a notable difference how people responded, in a really nice way. (Nick)

Yeah, I think I particularly enjoyed some of the very basic things with the baby, like I take him shopping to the supermarket and that also gives Susan a rest and he quite likes being in the top of the trolley. He does have a gaze around while he's awake but then pretty soon drops off to sleep... and, yeah, I take him for walks in the pushchair and that sort of thing... when I'm out with him and then obviously you get a lot of cooing over and that sort of thing, and I get chatting to people in the supermarket about him and that sort of stuff so that's nice... Yeah, I mean, I didn't find it difficult but I think Susan did. (Chris)

There are little things, like people are so much nicer to you, they are so much nicer to you in that if you have got a buggy, if you are waiting to cross the road, they will always stop... and, like, people are just looking at you and, like, smiling, people are just generally a lot nicer to you... if I'm on my own with [the baby] and people just start speaking to you and they are just generally nicer, it's like Christmas day! (Joe)

[I] took [the twins] out for a spin [in the pushchair] yesterday to cruise some girls... Well, they seem to get all the women stop and having a coo over them!

The fathers' sense of pride is once again palpable here. They clearly enjoy taking their babies out ('I hold myself differently') and the positive responses they receive. At the same time descriptions of 'cruising for girls' and taking the pushchair for a 'spin' imply particular masculine behaviours in which the pushchair is ascribed attributes usually associated with a sporty car. However, Chris notes that although he hasn't found taking the baby out in public difficult (in fact he has enjoyed it) he thinks that his wife has. This remark by Chris denotes the very different responses that men as new fathers and women as new mothers may experience and evoke in their early forays into the public sphere with their new babies (see chapter 6). In these extracts the men are responded to in highly positive ways as they engage in caring practices outside the home. The men's fathering displays are seen as novel and it seems that *almost* any performance by them would be positively received.

Interactions with others also help to shape how men experience these early weeks of first-time fathering and their selves as fathers and help to mark out the shifting parameters around contemporary configurations of fatherhood. One of the fathers (Graham) who has changed his working pattern (not his hours) to 4 days a week describes taking his baby to a postnatal group – where he is the only father:

I suppose I'm a very hands-on father, yeah. It's very interesting actually, it's very good for my self-esteem to go to this postnatal group on a Wednesday morning...I am the only father that goes to that and I'm afraid that some of the mums are not all that complimentary about their partners' parenting skills. There's one there, for example, whose partner had never changed a nappy [laughs]. So, yeah, I think I'm quite hands-on. (Graham)

The responses of the other mothers affirm, in positive ways, for Graham his 'hands-on' fathering and also confirm that not all men are so involved. Graham later remarks: 'it's nice to know that I can be a dad, I can do that stuff, that's good'. But he also acknowledges that juggling work and home life has been 'more difficult than I'd imagined'. Chris, too, expresses surprise that he has been more competent at caring for his baby son than he expected. He now wants to alter his pattern of work so that he and his wife can 'take it in turns' in caring for their son:

Susan and I would like to take it in turns with the looking after him...and it's, like, a lot of people's reactions, they are really surprised when I said that at that time and it's, like, 'well, why are you surprised?'...she gets paid a bit more than me and, well, from a selfish point of view I'd rather not send him at all [to a nursery] but I know there are lots of benefits to nursery but...I would sort of like, it would be nice to bring him up myself but...So we are going to send him the minimum of two, maybe two and a half, days.

The reaction to Chris wanting to reduce his (paid) working week in order to bring his son up 'himself' is a great deal of surprise. Yet aside from his desire to be involved in the daily caring of his baby, at an economic level this arrangement will also make sense as his wife 'gets paid a bit more'. But once again the ways in which deeply embedded gendered ideas of what fathers – and so mothers – are expected to do is apparent.

All the men are much more involved in doing hands-on, emotionally involved fathering across these early weeks than their own fathers are recalled to have been. But there are different levels and practices of involvement displayed across their narratives – from Graham, who has reduced his days of paid work, to William, who talks in much more traditional ways of separate roles for mothers and fathers. But even William says that he does 'a bit more than half at the weekend...I do all the bathing, changing and stuff. I think when I'm around the house I'm probably more hands-on than Sophie...but she does more in total'. What is not captured in the men's narratives is their real-time engagement in caring practices. But there is a tangible sense of emotional caring being undertaken through which loving relationships are being established and these are recognised by the men as having great importance. Corresponding to this, responsibilities are construed as (much) more than just economic, although economic provision remains significant ('I've got to do what I do best and bring the money in', Gareth). But it is also apparent that the mothers have (mostly) very quickly been positioned as the primary carer and that plans of 'sharing caring' where some sort of equality had been implied (see chapter 3) have not been realised. Chris, who has been able to take several weeks' leave, continues to talk in terms of equality and equity and it being 'fair' to 'swap over' the feeding through the night. But in other cases 'sharing' does not mean equality but is rather shorthand for involvement – but a more hands-on, practical involvement than in previous generations. As Dean says, 'it's pretty shared, I mean it's shared, although I would say 70/30 Ellie'. 'Sharing', a description which continues to be widely used, is a 'slippery concept' (O'Brien, 2005), and amongst the participants it is more about the allocation of tasks and activities – the 'stuff' that must be undertaken in meeting the needs of a dependent baby. Responsibilities are also associated with meeting a baby's needs but across the men's narratives these responsibilities are intricately woven with how selves as fathers and other (non-father) identities are maintained.

Conclusions

In this early postnatal period the men acknowledge that their paternal relationships are seen as different to those that their wives/partners might have to the child. They make sense of this through sometimes implicit assumed biological differences, but always alongside gendered dimensions of how lives are organised and lived. So whilst Richard alludes to 'womanly skills' and Ian claims that 'multitasking is not something that men can do', more generally the men recognise that because wives/partners stay at home they are the ones who become more adept at 'maternal practice' (Ruddick, 1989). And so, the men resume work and the women, quite literally, are left holding the baby – or two. Following the brief interlude of paternity leave, patterns of work create a situation in which fathering becomes fitted in around paid work. But work can also offer 'a release' and 'relief' and underscores the choices that are more available to men. However, expectations that men work and provide (during these early weeks and months) can also make it more difficult for men to stay at home and take on a primary caring role during this period. Fundamental – and recurring – questions of capacities to care, gender, practices of choice and agency, 'preferences' and power, and how these are navigated, negotiated and reconciled, are raised across the data.

In this chapter we have seen men draw upon a language of bonding and paternal instincts and convey a sense of more emotional, tender and caring masculinities, potentially signalling a significant shift that could interrupt the practices associated with 'fatherhood' (and 'motherhood'). But does this herald a move towards greater 'gender equality' and convergence; a shift towards less gendered behaviours which could signal 'undoing gender'; or a new iteration of patriarchal power and men's greater ability as fathers to articulate preferences and so choose the dimensions of their involvement across the spheres of home and work? These questions will be revisited in the next and subsequent chapters.

5 | A return to a new normal

Juggling fathering and work

No, I would go mad, I'm fairly sure I'd go mad, yeah, I couldn't be a stay-at-home dad.

(Gus)

The complex and contradictory landscape of contemporary fatherhood has been explored in the opening chapters in this book. It has become clear that for some men new imaginings and new possibilities have emerged as they become fathers: but how are these understood and accomplished in everyday life when set beside mothering practices and societal visions of motherhood? In this, and the following chapter, later episodes of the men's unfolding experiences of transition are explored as their child(ren)'s first birthday approaches. A longer view of their experiences is illuminated in a final section of this chapter, through data collected from some of the participants following their child(ren)'s second birthday. Once again a focus on the men's unfolding narratives reveals in different ways what 'being there', 'sharing care' and doing fathering involves and looks like as life returns to 'a new normal'. The themes outlined in earlier chapters are traced through as men reflect upon their earlier expectations, everyday fathering practices and sense of self. For the men, these revolve around paid work outside the home and doing ('fitting in') fathering in early mornings, evenings and weekends and in periods that are created through, for some, changing their working *patterns* rather than hours. The emotional highs and lows experienced as the men juggle and manage family, work and relationships are laid bare: but so too are the discourses and practices of gender which underpin and enable or preclude particular manifestations of caring masculinities and fatherhoods.

Throughout these later narratives the men again engage a vocabulary associated with a discourse of care giving and demonstrate their own growing expertise. They talk knowledgeably and confidently and in ways unthinkable only a year before of 'weaning', 'solids', 'semi-solids', 'ninth centile', 'teething' and 'potty training', documenting their child(ren)'s developmental progress. Over time they have become more practised and more confident in their fathering and, importantly, there is now a sense of having a more interactive relationship with a child who is much more responsive. As Gus says, 'now he's more of a person and also he notices me as his dad . . . he recognises me'. One of the most significant changes to have occurred during the interval between the interviews is the gradual establishment of a 'routine'. All the men refer to routines as a way to describe the details of their involvement and make visible (to me) their fathering practices. The routine also enables things to be managed, and gives a sense that life is being coped with ('a good routine and we have a manageable system'). In these later narratives, caring trajectories are less uncertain in terms of meeting their child(ren)'s needs, although how this is divided and/or shared is another matter. For the men the establishment of a routine has enabled them to feel more comfortable and competent in their fathering practices and their 'role' as father is clearer. At the same time changing feeding patterns, 'weaning' and 'introducing solids' also provide an opportunity for some of the fathers to talk of being *more* involved than in the early months. Focusing on these routines makes visible different fathering practices, the spaces in which these occur and so dimensions of these men's paternal identities. It also illuminates how paternal, maternal and parental responsibilities are assumed and where and how differences, similarities and 'convergence' in relation to these occur and are made sense of and explained (Doucet, 2006; O'Brien, 2005).

Around the routines, discourses of nature and instincts *and* time are linked together by the men in order to explain why their lives have become organised in the ways they have. Paid work outside the home continues to provide an important backdrop and economic security can become *more* important ('But then all of a sudden you think, oh, we need to be financially secure and I hadn't anticipated that sort of desiring security', Ben) (Dermott, 2003, 2008). Caring *routines*, then, convey a sense of tasks, control and managing within particular boundaries. What they do not conjure up or fully accommodate is what goes on around the routine: the all-encompassing thinking responsibility – 24/7 – that has long been associated with essentialist ideas about women and their maternal capacities. But assuming or accepting such constructions of the maternal, potentially or actually, sets limits around men's involvement in fathering and can also be drawn upon by men to explain and/or defend their level of involvement. What becomes apparent in relation to these debates are men's experiences of both exclusion ('wandering around the park on my own with the baby . . . sort of spotting other clusters of mothers together') and greater freedoms and choices ('I couldn't be a house husband, no way'). In this chapter men's capacities to care will be explored as they talk about both the hard work of raising a child ('I always knew that it's a 24/7 job but not realising it is literally 24 hours a day') and their sense of joy and achievement as their children move beyond the new baby stage to become more responsive and interactive.

During the intervening months since the birth all the wives/partners have either returned to work ('so that's been a big adjustment') or are about to do so. As a result, caring for the child(ren) has become organised across a wider support network including grandparents, childminders and nursery schools. The babies have grown and become 'much more interactive and mobile', 'characters' who it is possible to 'communicate with a lot more'. Fathering is described as being 'full of nice surprises' with 'joyful responsibilities', although 'going to work for a rest' can also offer an outlet. One participant is to become a father for a second time as his son approaches his first birthday and announces that this time round he is 'definitely more blasé about it'. But the intervening months have also been difficult ('it seems like a whole blur') and for some a sense of 'normality' still evades them ('it's just been such a rollercoaster this past year. I would like to settle down to some sense of vague normality'). In the early months two of the participants became more involved in caring for their young babies than they had planned as 'postnatal depression kicked in' for one of their wives and another was hospitalised following a diagnosis of 'postpartum psychosis'. Amongst the new fathers one has also been diagnosed with depression and signed off work whilst others talk of feeling under stress. Reflecting on the first 3 months of parenting twins, one father admits:

Sometimes you just wanted to crawl into a corner and just sit there and burst into tears, but that just wasn't an option, you have to keep going.

But for all the upheavals, stressful and joyous moments, the men talk in these later interviews in much calmer and more confident ways about their current, 'normalised' fathering practices and experiences.

Practising fathering

All the participants are now practised in hands-on caring as well as providing in economic ways for their children. Their caring fills the spaces either created around their changed work patterns, or evenings ('If I'm lucky I get back when he's going to have his bath so I take part in bath time') and weekends and has become a 'new normal' part of everyday life. Interestingly, in the extract below Nick explains how he tries to think differently about the time he *does* have available around a 40-hour working week to be involved with his young son:

I think with my son the relationship has developed because I've been involved as much as possible and I think I've been fairly consistent day or night, weekday, holiday. There are 40 hours of the week that I'm not here but there's however many hours that I am here and I'm trying to work more on that. I think it could be very easy to think, well, I'm not here from Monday to Friday so I'm not involved in those bits, well, actually I'm not here for a bit of Monday to Friday, the bulk of Monday to Friday I am actually here. I maybe asleep or whatever, but I am here. So I think just being around ...

The men describe typical (usually weekend) days when they take, sometimes exclusive, responsibility for their children. As in the earlier interviews this continues to involve nappy changing, feeding, bathing, taking out and is (mostly) task- and activity-based but, significantly, these now form part of a recognisable routine. As Richard explains:

It kind of just feels ordinary actually, so it's, like, just normal. I mean partly because it's sort of, I'm not sure this is how it feels, but quite a lot of it is just thinking of a series of tasks, tasks around her, when you are going to feed her and so on, but also in terms of what to do with her. So on the one hand it's normal and manageable because she is fairly well behaved, has a good routine and we have a manageable system.

The fathers have become much more practised at recognising and meeting their children's needs and continue to be significantly involved in sharing care. But they also recognise that their wives/partners have spent more time at home through maternity leave, which has enabled the mother–child relationship to develop in particular ways within routines, which in turn requires that the fathers be 'debriefed' when they take over. Across these accounts differences in caring styles are acknowledged as well as the roles they have become associated with ('I'm always the one to do the fun bit'), but the men's capacities to care are also clearly demonstrated. In the following extracts Joe, Ben and Frank describe their caring practices:

I mean, obviously Jane sort of knows [our daughter] better than I do because of the amount of time she spends with her. But in terms of, say, what you would do with feeding her, settling her, changing her, I mean I sort of do that as often, well, over weekends anyway and when I can and probably more than Jane. I'm sort of, like, a play figure for her really, I come back, get back from work and give her a bath and let her splash around and play with all her toys and . . . she loves all that sort of stuff . . . I always wanted to play, like, as active a role as I could. (Joe)

I have tried to do as much as I can and it's fairly even, she does more but I do, when I'm around I think I do a fairly equal share. She's not breastfeeding anymore so then most of the tasks are fairly even, although he goes to her more for comfort, I'm more for laughs. It's a real cliché sort of role but they've defined themselves already . . . So there is a set routine for him and either one of us or the other is here to do that. (Ben)

At the weekend now, Gill has got a Saturday job so every other Saturday she works in a small business, which means I have them for the day. So I'll get up and give them their morning bottle, I'll give them breakfast and then the whole day is with me. So I provide everything for them which is great . . . we've shared the workload and been quite thorough in debriefing on how Gill has got them into that routine. There wasn't any trepidation at all really, no, it was, I was looking forward to it. (Frank)

Chris and Graham are the only fathers who have at this stage reduced their working hours (rather than just patterns of work) in order to share caring for their young sons. Chris has responsibility for childcare on one and a half days a week, his wife one day and a nursery the remainder. He talks about their arrangement:

I think it's good for us that we both take turns and it's good for baby as well because we do things, you know, not necessarily do things in the same way. So I think I could do it more but I don't think at this stage I would want to do it full time.

Other fathers talk of having 'found a balance' (Gus) and things being 'pretty much split down the middle' and 'fifty-fifty' (Nick).

The practices of caring are described in a range of ways which are encompassed in Mike's description of it being 'part gut instinct and part . . . just the way the routine has developed'. But not all the men are able to make visible or narrate practices of shared caring. For example, Dylan draws upon his wife's 'strong instinct' and the 'absence of someone else telling you what to do' to explain his lack of caring involvement:

The first 9 or 10 months have been a complete shock and in the absence of someone else telling you what to do, it's difficult, you know, you don't really know how to treat [the baby] . . . I just, I find, I don't have the same strong instinct that she does actually, instinct wise, to go rushing to him if he's crying and to do these things. So I think a father, well, I'm not as responsible probably as I should be and I'm only just realising now how much care he needs. (Dylan)

Dylan here illuminates the ways in which men are more able to position their selves as fathers in ways that are not available to women as mothers. In contrast to most of the other fathers in the study, Dylan clearly draws upon an essentialising discourse of women's 'strong instinct' in order to explain his lack of involvement. But James, too, draws upon this discourse, describing his wife as 'intuitively' knowing what to do whilst his responsibilities are more 'about money':

No, I think it's tough for both of us but [my wife] seemed to click, she knew what she wanted and intuitively it was, you know . . . if you do this then she stops crying and I thought, oh, Christ, I'm going have to start writing this stuff down 'cos I can't remember any of it, it was just so difficult . . . Yeah, it's just so deep embedded, I mean it's just a basic instinct really. I mean the mother nurturing the baby, I guess, and the father having to [laughs] kill wild animals and bringing back the food . . . so I mean the responsibility is just, I mean, yeah, I'm more responsible about money and how we're spending it. (James)

But most of the fathers draw upon a range of discourses and talk about nature ('Well, with me it comes naturally') and *their* paternal instincts ('I do think I have quite a strong paternal instinct'), together with processes of learning ('it just comes like anything really, with practice'). The amount of time each parent spends with the baby – as dictated by structural features of paid work and paternity leave – is invoked to explain how relationships are developing and how caring is organised and practised. As Mike says:

Maria's instincts were more switched on or more focused . . . I mean, I was off for a small part of paternity leave and then went back to work and I think, yeah, Maria had obviously built up perhaps a stronger bond with [our] daughter because I wasn't there all the time, because of work. (Mike)

The implication here is not that Mike lacks 'instincts' but rather that work means he has had fewer opportunities for them to become as 'switched on' or 'focused'. However, even though the men all return to work they are also more involved in fathering than in previous generations: these caring practices take them into physical spaces which have traditionally been more closely associated with mothers.

As the men go about the daily (or more commonly, weekend) practices of caring outside the home they are at times confronted by arrangements which illuminate the gendered organisation of public spaces: something that had not been 'visible' to them before. These (sometimes) physical arrangements subtly reinforce gendered, and so societal, visions of masculinities and associated behaviours which do not correspond with men as fathers. In the following extract Nick describes taking his young son swimming:

One of the interesting things I'd never even thought about before we had [the baby] was where changing rooms are in public and I was quite surprised at how many places have a changing room in the women's loo or something and there isn't one in the blokes or there isn't a separate one. I had never even given it a thought before and then suddenly I'm out somewhere and 'bloody hell' there isn't anywhere to change the baby unless you're a mum. (Nick)

Mike also describes getting 'strange looks' and feeling 'apprehensive' and out of place in a similar setting:

I mean, ages ago we were in town and had to change [the baby] and the pair of us went in and I was a bit apprehensive and I got some strange looks off a couple of ladies in there. I mean, they weren't feeding or anything like that but it was just a look to say 'well, why are you in here?' sort of thing. I can imagine it would feel quite strange if I were to take [the baby] in on her own and there maybe some other mums in there or something. But at the end of the day I'm the father and I've got to change her, I've got to take dual responsibility, I can't sort of pass her to a passing female and say 'will you just change my baby for me?' (Mike)

Richard, too, recognises how mothers and fathers populate public spaces in different ways:

I had her on a Friday and I remember wandering around the park on my own with the baby, sort of spotting other men on their own with their babies and then of course clusters of women . . . but all the men are on their own, almost certainly doing what I'm doing which is our one day a week with the baby, which is not necessarily a problem and it's fine. But then you realise, and this again is probably a cliché, but the men don't have those little groups to support them in a certain sense, they actually probably don't need it, but if we were doing it every day, we probably would . . . it's just actually having something to do, that's the challenge of the one day a week [childcare] I have is, like, 'what are we going to do today?' (Richard)

Ben also describes taking his young son to the park and to a music group:

When I go to the park, there is, like, the odd dad occasionally, I am the token dad quite often. I went once to the music group which was hysterical . . . I took him to this music group and Hannah assured me there would be a couple of dads. So I get there and there's not and I'm, like, the only bloke with a big circle of ladies clapping and singing songs which I didn't know . . . So there's a real, you see this massive network of stuff going on for women with their babies everywhere and there's not, like, a blokes' music group. (Ben)

These extracts richly illuminate a number of interlinked issues emanating from historical patterns of caring and constructions of powerful masculinities (Doucet, 2006). For example, because women are assumed to be the ones who change nappies, men are therefore seen to be out of place in a baby-changing room (representing a 'risk' in some indeterminate way?); because men take responsibility for providing childcare alone much less often than women they have not developed (or do not feel the need for?) support groups of other fathers; support also implies weakness which is not a characteristic associated with hegemonic masculinities; men can be comforted by assurances that in their forays into this new world they will not be the only dad there, although quite often that turns out to be the case. In contrast, and again drawing attention to the gendered dimensions of social spaces and behaviours, Joe describes spending a day with his young daughter:

I had baby the whole day and I really loved it. It was on a Saturday as well so I had her the whole day and I was really looking forward to it and we went over to my dad's house and then we just went for a drink to, like, a family pub sort of thing and took baby and she quite liked it and I was, like, laughing and saying [to the baby], 'it's more fun with dad'; like, I have her and take her to a pub! Like, with Jane she has coffee mornings.

Joe reflects with humour on the contrasting places that he and his wife individually (and perhaps more comfortably) frequent with the baby. Across these extracts the men's experiences confirm a disjuncture between individual practice and more general societal visions of gendered fathering and mothering practices. Some areas remain more obdurately associated with mothers ('coffee mornings') and attendance at the health clinic with the baby is another 'feminine' space where, as Chris observes, 'if there is a father it's usually accompanied by mum as well'. But some small changes are discernible as men begin to seek out other fathers. For example, Dylan says:

I've found another dad who is doing the same thing on the same day so we get together . . . you know, by the time we've sorted ourselves out it's about 11 o'clock and we might go swimming or something like that.

Across the men's narratives it becomes clear that much of their caring is undertaken outside the home ('we went to the park all morning', 'I like taking him for walks, it's good, just to stroll about', 'I do lots of the outside walking'). This seems to be linked to activity-based caring, which fits into the routines that have been established around the children *and* the times or days when the men take greater responsibility for providing care. It also links to what other research has argued is a practice of delineating paternal spaces in which caring takes place, as distinct from those associated with maternal spaces of the home (Doucet, 2006). Fathering, then, is described in emotional language as feelings of 'love', 'bonding' and 'attachment' but also as a set of practices and tasks which include activities outside the home. The men do not seem to have available to them a storyline of *just being* a father, but rather must use the restricted times and spaces they have available, to actively *do* and make visible their fathering. Paradoxically, it is these limited times and spaces that are a consequence of men's work patterns outside the home which have shaped fathering in particular, activity-based, ways.

The introduction of 2 weeks' paternity leave in April 2003 in the UK signalled recognition at government level that men's caring (and not just economic) involvement in fathering should be encouraged/facilitated. More involved fathering has been championed as a good thing. But take-up of paternity leave has been lower than hoped and criticisms have been levelled at the scheme and levels of pay offered to those who make use of it (James, 2008). As noted earlier, all the men in the study were in paid employment and all expected to – and indeed took – time off from work following the birth of their first child(ren) but not all made use of the 2 weeks' paternity leave (see chapter 4). Irrespective of the scheme's inadequate financial provision, a reason cited by some of the participants for not taking up their entitlement concerned the 'derisory' length of only 2 weeks' leave. In very powerful ways the periods of time allocated in the UK to paternity leave and maternity leave have consequences for societal ideas of what men and women do: how caring and work inside and outside the home and responsibilities to our children are envisaged and organised.

In the following extract Mike reflects on contemporary arrangements which he feels 'are a long way off equality' for fathers:

I think there is more common acceptance, or I would like to think there is, that fathers have got equal sort of roles... but I think we are a long way off equality-wise with things like paternity, for example; I mean, I had 2 weeks and it's something like £90.00 or 10 per cent of your wage, whichever is the less, and I should imagine nine times out of ten it's going to be the ninety quid or whatever it was... it's a nice offer, a great gesture, but that is all it is... I think you just want to spend as much time as you can at home during the first few weeks so I think we are going to be a long way off those kind of rights or equality and all that. I think the government has extended maternity leave for mums and stuff, it's a shame they can't do something in tandem...

Gus, too, reflects on maternity leave enabling his partner to stay at home, but because she is the main breadwinner this means that he has to work longer hours:

The only thing that's difficult is when Anna is off work because those 6 months, everything still has to be paid for, but Anna is not earning... and she's the main breadwinner, so...

Although Joe's wife is not the main breadwinner – they both earn 'similar money' – he, too, recognises the practical restrictions that the period of paternity leave places on his involvement in more childcare:

> I mean, for us really, I mean, I joke with Jane, for us, our financial situation, it wouldn't have made any difference at all because Jane and I are on very similar money so it would have made no financial difference whatsoever. I suppose the only sort of barriers would be that it wouldn't have been practical because I just get my 2 weeks' parental leave, I don't know what my work would do, I mean they are quite good, they might have said 'you can have a few months and come back later' . . . But, like I say, I don't think there is any financial duty on the male, on the husband, to go out and work, I think if the situation fits then, yeah, it's something the family decides and in terms of parenting, no, I think it should be fifty/fifty, equal.

But notwithstanding the barriers presented by only 2 weeks of paternity leave, Joe had earlier said that there was 'no way' his wife would have let him be the one to stay at home although he expressed an interest in doing this.

The arrangements, then, which structure men's and women's engagement in caring for a young child reinforce particular essentialist assumptions and ideals. But whilst current paternity and maternity leave arrangements in the UK have been described as discriminatory because they promote inequality between the sexes (Browne, 2007), they also emanate from within a patriarchal system of gender inequity which has consequences for both men's and women's lives. For example, whilst on the one hand women can exercise 'maternal gate-keeping' and, drawing upon an essentialist discourse, lay claim to an intuitive and natural relationship to the baby/child, men can prioritise work outside the home and, without having to explain their actions, can remove themselves from much of the minutiae of daily caring for a baby/child. However, as noted in chapter 1 research has shown that some women can have ambivalent feelings around mothering and do not find full-time caring for a young child 'intuitive' or fulfilling. They may also find that caring must be fitted around paid work outside the home (as has been the case historically for many women living in disadvantaged circumstances who may not have a choice) and they do not recognise 'maternal gate-keeping' as a practice but may seek to encourage the reverse! At the same time research also suggests that caring masculinities are more recognisable and accepted in contemporary visions of men's lives and that more men want to be able to participate more fully in the emotional and caring dimensions of raising a child. But clearly, appreciating men's and women's lives as more fluid and complex does not lead to a straightforward 'trade-off'. The arguments around these issues – about men's involvement in caring and new forms of patriarchy and power – were visited earlier (chapter 2) and will be explicitly contemplated in later chapters. But now, bearing in mind a question posed in chapter 2 of how, for men, 'family responsibilities affect their working lives', we turn to focus on the ways in which men narrate their selves as fathers and workers (Ranson, 2001).

Selves, the world of work and family life

For all the men 'it is hard to remember what it was like pre-baby' (Ben) and some wonder at what they filled the time with before becoming a father. In the following extract James reflects on the preceding year:

> I cannot remember my life before daughter, you know, it used to revolve around things like the football calendar! Now I've not a clue who is playing Wednesday, you have no time for anything like that, no time for hobbies or anything like that, it's just, it's just full time really, it's just work and home and daughter really and that's about it really. It's not a bad thing, it's a good thing, but it is just totally, totally different... it's a full-time job and I try to get home as early as possible, say 6/7 o'clock and suddenly the baby is handed over and it's 2 or 3 hours before she goes to bed, so Alexa [wife] gets some rest because it's just so draining every day.

Here James conveys a sense of a very full, time-pressured and demanding life in ways that capture the relentlessness of work and home demands, sentiments which are largely shared by the other fathers. Trying to 'be there' and engage in more involved, hands-on fathering whilst 'keeping things together' leads several of the fathers to talk about raised levels of stress and, in one case, a diagnosis of depression leading to being signed off work. The pressure for men (and women) to accommodate work demands and family responsibilities 'doesn't give much leeway' (Chris), as caring is fitted in around paid work. Weekends can involve further 'juggling' as some men take responsibility for their children as their wives/partners fit their paid work into this available time. Family life and relaxed time spent altogether can become squeezed out with the constant demands of fitting everything else in. Dylan, who is self-employed, reflects on how he has 'reconciled' his job and family life:

I've always lived for my job and so on, but now I'm beginning to realise it's not all about that, I want some time with my son . . . but I wouldn't give myself many marks out of the ten at the moment, I have to say, as a father and I wish I, one can always do better and I wish I could do better. As I say, it's only going to come through giving up other commitments, the work commitments or finding some superhuman energy from somewhere, but that doesn't come.

Dylan uses a recognisable phrase, 'living for my job', and talks with regret that he has not been as involved in fathering as he had anticipated and the difficulties of achieving this. He then reflects further on his experiences of becoming a father:

Yeah, all sorts of issues have come up that I never dreamed, you know, the male pride thing, that is very important now, more so than ever . . . that my existence is justified . . . that I sort of still feel the need to prove myself perhaps in my job more than anything else and perhaps it's not valid or recognised to prove yourself as a father.

Paradoxically, 'the male pride thing' seems to be more important now there is a child to provide for, which is reinforced by a sense for Dylan that he needs to 'prove' himself through his paid work because proving himself (just) through fathering 'perhaps it's not valid or recognised'. Given its long associations with women's 'natural' capacities, caring for a child is not a valued undertaking in developed societies and can be almost invisible unless 'problems' arise. This is made clear in the way in which Dylan talks about how he needs to prove himself through his job and so, implicitly, demonstrate success in recognisably masculine-associated and measurable ways. Fathering, then, is not enough or does not bring with it the values which are attributed to success in the world of paid work.

But what is also striking across some of the men's accounts is that when they have not been as involved in a hands-on way as they had anticipated, this is expressed in terms of regret or sadness but never guilt ('I don't beat myself up about it'). An example of this can be seen in the following extract where Gus talks about a period of working exceptionally long hours:

I am pretty much doing exactly what I thought I'd be doing really. I mean, the last couple of months have been busy at work and there's weeks where I work sort of 75 hours and so, you know, I just don't... Like I said earlier, there were 3 days where I just didn't see him, I sort of went into his room and I'd see him asleep but I never saw him awake. But there's nothing we can do about that and I don't, you know, I don't beat myself up about it, it just, it has to be done sometimes.

What is interesting here is how it would be perceived if a new mother were to provide the same description of (excessive) working. All sorts of questions would be asked about who was caring for the baby. Indeed, in contrast to the women in the motherhood study who rationalised and felt obliged to provide lengthy explanations about their decisions to even return to (part-time) work, these men are not so compelled (see chapter 6). The moral and gendered terrain which inflects so many dimensions of mothering and motherhood clearly does not operate in the same way for men as fathers around family life and paid-work practices.

The importance of paid work and having a recognisable (and valued) worker identity outside the home runs through many of the men's narratives. Even where initial (antenatal) plans had envisaged significant amounts of sharing caring, the time actually spent in being responsible for caring can become eroded as men's lives as fathers unfold. Whilst the men continue to meet work commitments – or increase their work hours in order to compensate for wives/partners being on maternity leave and new costs associated with a baby/young child – the women become more practised at parenting through their greater time spent with the children. As Sean acknowledges:

Because Ella is with [our baby] more she is happier with Ella and Ella knows more of the things that make her smile; she's become far more of a dab hand at everything than I have. So generally the expertise lies with Emma.

Several of the men have wives/partners who they acknowledge can either earn more than them or who can earn an equivalent income. But in spite of this, for the most part it is the men who take the primary worker role in situations where more than just economic considerations are clearly being accommodated. Breastfeeding is of course one consideration, but so too are the apparent choices which circumscribe men's lives as fathers in different ways to women's lives as mothers.

As Gareth's twin sons approach their first birthday he, like the other fathers, reflects on his early experiences of fathering and compares it to paid work:

Oh no, looking after them is far harder for me personally despite all my stresses and grief at work, I would, I don't want to sound too harsh and uncaring or unfatherly but I would rather, given the choice, if it was just the choice of the two, looking after kids all day or go to work, I would much rather go into work, by far. It makes you feel bad saying it I guess, in a way, because it's your children and stuff but if it was that or that, then I definitely would rather go to work. I couldn't be a house husband, no way.

It can be assumed that having twins involves more work than a single child and this must also be the case for Gareth's wife. In this extract Gareth recognises that the ways in which he compares looking after his children and going to work could sound 'harsh' or 'unfatherly' but he goes on to emphasise the importance to him of his 'breadwinner' identity:

I like working too much. I love going to work so, I mean, for me obviously I love them but I love going to work more than I do sitting here all day looking after them . . . I definitely see myself as a breadwinner . . . But, yeah, I definitely see myself more in the kind of, in terms of them, silent, strong person in the background that . . . I don't know whether it's a traditional thing but that's just the way I feel about it, whether that's right or wrong I don't know.

What is significant here is that a breadwinner discourse remains available to Gareth and the other fathers. They do not need to justify working outside the home because traditionally this has been prioritised in relation to men's lives and correspondingly valued. It is the men who do not provide financially for their children who have been, and still are, criticised. But what the longitudinal approach taken in this study allows us to do is look back to the ways in which Gareth had envisaged work and caring being practised when he was interviewed during the antenatal period. In the first interview I had asked Gareth 'and will your wife return to work?' and he had replied:

Yeah, definitely. It's not just a random . . . she spent, I mean, she did a postgrad diploma and then a Masters so this isn't a job she wants to walk away from. I mean, she's been seven years studying for it. She's sort of 25 [years old] and 10 years ahead of all of her peers with regard to age and the same level of position, so, yeah, it's not something she is going to walk away from lightly.

But in practice it is also not something that she is going to be able to continue with easily because Gareth 'love[s] going to work' more than staying at home and, for a whole range of reasons, he is not positioned as the parent with primary responsibility to care: so he has a choice. He is also able to articulate a preference which does not require further justification. This is not to say that Gareth is uncaring or a bad father but just that he can express and act on a choice which does not seem to be available to his wife. In the end, for most of the wives/partners paid work is fitted into evenings and weekends when the fathers can provide childcare around their own working commitments. This ends up being the case for Pam, as Gareth explains:

I'm very busy at work which is good. Pam is back at work but that has had a knock-on effect for me personally because I spend all day with the boys on Sunday and Tuesday night, I have them from Tuesday afternoon until Wednesday morning and then all day Sunday, which is cool because I get to spend time with them. But it's also quite hard.

One of the arguments which has been put forward to explain aspects of gendered inequalities in relation to caring arrangements has centred on some men having more choices and greater freedoms available to them. In some ways this is indeed the case (see chapter 6) but in other ways it is, of course, too simplistic an explanation. So, whilst Gareth can appeal to a recognisable discourse which (traditionally) associates hegemonic masculinity with breadwinning and through which personal success is measured, such constructions also restrict other possibilities/opportunities. For example, Joe is not the one to stay at home through the early months caring for his daughter even though he expressed a desire to do so and Richard's experiences of caring for his daughter are solitary when set beside the 'clusters of mothers together' that he sees: power, then, can be seen to operate in different and sometimes diffuse ways but also in *both directions*, albeit unevenly.

However, it was also noted earlier (chapter 2) that men now have the 'discursive resources' available to them with which 'to make claims upon their employers' (Hobson and Morgan, 2002: 14). And a strand of discourse premised on ideas of 'family-friendly' and 'flexible working' policies and 'work–life balance' is alluded to, or explicitly invoked, in the men's narratives to explain their fathering and work practices. In contrast to the durable discourse associated with being a breadwinner, notions of flexible work and work–life balance are still relatively new in the UK context and have not (yet) become so deeply ingrained. The men talk in various ways about reconciling work and home life. Gareth talks of this involving 'a juggling act the whole time' whilst Ian feels that by rearranging his working week 'there isn't any conflict between work and home'. Ian is also the only father to take '2 weeks' unpaid parental leave' during the first year, which 'wouldn't have been an option' had the couple not unexpectedly been left some money. In the following extract Ian talks about his wife preparing to return to work:

She's hoping to go back part time although that is not quite settled yet. Interestingly, we haven't talked about me going part time and Polly going back full time ... I think it could have been a consideration but I'm in a very small company and I'm very lucky that they are as flexible as they are. I couldn't do the job I'm doing part time.

Ian is grateful that his employers are 'as flexible as they are'. Expectations that employers should be flexible in order to accommodate changes in the family lives are not assumed or taken for granted. Similarly, Ian's job is not one that he feels could be done part time and there has been no discussion that he might change his work to part time: he commented earlier that his responsibility is to 'keep bringing money into the house'. In contrast, Richard combines working from home with travelling occasionally to his geographically distant office and his wife is the one who commutes to her workplace. This flexible arrangement is facilitated by Richard's flexible employment in a university, which in turn enables him to both work from home and be necessarily involved in a 'lot more caring':

I might well be doing a lot more of certain caring sorts of things than others, but not because I'm a wonderful new man sort of thing, it's just that's the division of things ... she's doing the commuting. But just in terms of practical everyday kind of looking after, I actually do quite a lot of that.

For the two of the fathers, Chris and Graham, who have reduced their working hours, experiences of combining caring and work are mixed. For Chris it 'is just about sort of manageable', but for Graham it 'has not proven all that successful'. Fitting everything in and lack of time are clear issues in most of the men's accounts, alongside other concerns such as being seen as a committed worker by colleagues and employers. Some fathers talk of their geographical proximity to their workplace in order to explain how they are managing work and home life. Joe, Nick, Gus and Stephen all live in very close proximity to their workplace, as does Mike:

I'm really fortunate, I work 10 minutes away from where I live, so I needn't leave until, like, ten to nine and I get home so early as well and if I'm needed I can just, you know, be back in 10 minutes. So it's an ideal situation.

Nick also appreciates the time he saves in not having to commute ('I don't waste 2 hours a day travelling as lots of people do'). But for others, work and home demands are felt to be precariously (un)balanced. James, who confides that he has felt under such pressure trying to balance work and home life that he'd contemplated going to see a doctor, is sceptical about the extent of the family friendliness of the company he works for and its motivations:

I went back to work and it really hit home and that I'm not going to be able to do this job and have a family and you think, well, I've just got to work harder at both ends, but you know literally there are only 24 hours . . . things had to change from a work–life perspective . . . we had a bust up and a few people walked out of the office so Human Resources got involved and set ground rules . . . as I say, they said they were family friendly as a company . . . but most employers don't do a great deal for their staff because it's all about money.

But Frank has a very different experience of company policy and family friendliness:

I did get sent home a couple of times because I was so knackered and told to go home and get some sleep because I was being totally unproductive at work and I was quite zombified and I think I sat down and had my quarterly review with my line manager and I said, 'I don't know what happened in the last 3 months, you'll have to fill in the gaps because I haven't got a clue.' It was literally, I was on autopilot for about 3 months so I didn't know anything.

In this extract Frank conveys the complete exhaustion that can be experienced as new parenting unfolds: being on 'autopilot' and 'totally unproductive at work'. Fortunately for him, his employer appears to be understanding but clearly this is not the case in all employment areas. Interestingly, one of the fathers, Nick, has actually worked in an HR capacity as part of his wider job and ruefully notes that this role has always been about 'supporting mothers back to work on a part-time basis' but that he has never come across 'a father who wants to go part time. No father has ever asked for it, it has never come up'. Employer practices around 'family-friendly' initiatives are, then, patchy and subject to the forces of economic conditions. But they are also highly significant if notions of a work–life balance are to be more than just rhetoric, and if parents are to be able to work flexibly in ways that can accommodate individual family needs and shared caring.

Returning, then, to the question posed earlier, 'family responsibilities' affect these new fathers' working lives in various and individual ways: prompting some of the men to change working patterns in order to take on caring responsibilities, whilst for others magnifying the importance to them of their worker and provider identity. But even where the latter is the case it is also clear that these men are still involved in significantly more hands-on caring for their young children (often concentrated into evenings and weekends) than in earlier generations. But their practices of fathering still do not equate to the all-encompassing responsibilities and *thinking* that *primary* caring involves and this will be returned to in the following chapter.

Selves as fathers

Shifts in contemporary European societies were traced earlier in chapter 1. As a consequence of these shifts it was acknowledged that different and more fluid ways of thinking about selves, gender and life trajectories had become possible (chapter 2), including new understandings of masculinities and men as fathers. All the men in this study felt that they were involved in fathering practices in ways that were different to earlier generations. For some this involved an immediate and instinctive 'bond' with their child and corresponding sense of being a father, for others the relationship with their child was established more gradually through the early months. In the earlier motherhood study it was found that most of the women felt initially compelled to talk of their mothering feeling 'instinctive' and 'natural' (which some later retracted; see Miller, 2007). But men becoming fathers are not necessarily expected to experience or express an instinctive 'bond'; however, many did. As Chris and Stephen explain:

Yeah, I was quite surprised that it was so instinctive but, yeah, because I thought it would take longer because although I really wanted to be a father and I've always wanted to be a father, you don't know how easy, not easy, but how easy you are going to settle into it, so, yeah, I was surprised. (Chris)

Yes, I personally think it came naturally for me [being a father] because it was the right time in my life and I felt as if it was the right time to have a child for me, so that's why it's not been such a big impact. But saying that, it's still quite a lot of hard work you have to put into that and it's not something, I don't think you can teach that to somebody. It's something they'd have to pick up . . . I've got quite a strong bond with [my son]. (Stephen)

Interestingly, the 'right time' in a life to have a baby and always wanting 'to be a father' are used to rationalise the connection they have 'instinctively' and naturally felt. But Stephen also alludes to picking up fathering through practice, over time. Gus, too, uses the passage of time and his child's growing responsiveness to describe his increasing sense of feeling 'like a dad':

I definitely feel like more of a dad now, you know, with him being older . . . because he's more, before he was just this, you know, this thing, but now he's more of a person and also he notices me as his dad, you know, he recognises me, he looks out for me in the same way that he looks out for his mum . . . but, yeah, until he takes on a personality and starts doing stuff and also I think shows you love and shows you affection . . . so now I really feel like a dad, you know, and so it's, I wouldn't say the weight of responsibility, that was always there but, yeah, I feel more like a dad now, definitely.

Changes in how the men now see their selves as fathers are, with the passage of time, more distinct, as paternal relationships of 'love' and 'affection' have developed. Joe talks of how he has changed, although not in a 'day in, day out' way, and his surprise at this:

I do see myself as a lot older and a lot, at the back of my mind, sort of more responsible. I went to Italy on a stag do, like, 3 weeks ago and always at the back of my mind now I sort of know that I've got responsibilities . . . I mean I have changed, I really have changed and you sort of think if something happened to me, what would happen so, yeah, I am a lot more responsible in the back of my mind. I don't think I've changed sort of day in, day out but, yeah, at the back of my mind I'm older and a sort of sense of duty . . . responsibility and feeling older, I maybe didn't expect that. I mean, obviously she is my number one priority really now in the world and that's going to continue really all the way through her life. I don't think that's ever going to change at all so, yeah.

Gareth, too, talks of an 'incremental shift' as he muses on his feelings about being a father:

I do and I don't [feel like a father]. I do when I'm, like, obviously days like today when I've got them, of course, absolutely in the physical sense, yeah. But I don't think I feel any different in that sense, nothing so profound as that you know, it wasn't a huge shift, it's kind of, yeah, it's been incremental really . . . it's just another feeling of sort of love really I guess.

In the following extract Dylan, too, contemplates his feelings about being a father and whether he has a sense of himself as a father:

It's just beginning, it's taken a long time . . . It's a gradual thing and you don't want to totally change either because that's what I'm feeling, I'm losing myself.

Dylan implies a sense of fear around 'losing himself' which is inter-esting because it signals both change but also a sense of Dylan having agency and an ability to obstruct the process of change in ways not available to women when they become mothers (T. Miller, 2009). The identity of 'mother' is all consuming and is applied to women once they have a child in such a way that other dimensions of their identities can be overridden, whilst the identity 'father' enables other possibilities. This means that men may work hard to demonstrate this aspect of their identity and render it more visible, or they could reject or deny it: clearly, again, gendered choices operate in different ways here. Across the men's narratives a sense of being more mature, having responsibil-ities ('in a really good way you know it's not a bad thing') and 'fun', together with new pressures and demands, characterise how the men talk about being a father. Some lament the loss of a sense of a self outside that of parenting ('I think it's possibly other things have been squeezed out between the parenting and the work') and others have felt uncomfortable at their unexpected frustrations encountered in the hard work of caring for a baby/young child ('when he's upset and crying my tolerance of that, or ability to cope with that, is pretty slim . . . that has surprised me') and frustrations sometimes spilling over into work ('I suppose towards the end of a working week I'm getting a bit tired and so I get a bit snappy, which I don't like myself for'). Becoming a father, then, signals personal change and offers a new perspective (and reflexive position) from which to understand a gendered and changing self.

All the men have a sense of having more responsibilities now they are fathers. Although Stephen actively assists in caring for his young son around his work, and his partner also works full time, he still describes his responsibilities in recognisably traditional ways:

I feel as if I've got, definitely more responsibility now . . . I think the responsibilities [in this generation] are the same, I don't think they will ever change. You have a child and you have to provide for the child, provide for Claire and so on and so forth. So I don't think the responsibilities have changed at all.

But most of the other fathers acknowledge that their involvement in hands-on, more emotional caring for their children is qualitatively different from just economic provision. The earlier chapters followed the men's narratives as they anticipated and subsequently practised fathering. In the extract below Gareth – who earlier spoke of his love of work – contemplates the meaning of the changes around caring and parenting:

But I think it's fantastic that the men are becoming more and the guys that I speak to that are new fathers that are around my age are so much more involved than my perception of what it used to be like. On a Sunday morning when I have [my twin sons], it's funny because there's two guys in the village who have got children and I meet one of them at the park . . . I talk sport with one of them, I don't talk any baby stuff really. I mean, I'll keep them updated, I'll say, oh, you know 'how are they doing?', I'll say 'oh, the top teeth are coming through', you know, and then we'll go 'did you see the game of football?' . . . We do very briefly speak about child related . . . I don't think the conversations necessarily become feminised, I think the behaviour is going that way.

Here Gareth wonderfully captures both a sense of change *and* continuity. Men as fathers are more visibly engaged in practices that at one time would have been almost exclusively regarded as 'feminine', but some things remain unchanged with more recognisably 'masculine' topics of conversation being engaged in by the fathers. For Gareth, then, men's 'behaviour' as fathers is becoming more 'feminised' (emotionally caring and hands-on?).

Other fathers, too, describe experiences since becoming a father which suggest in different ways a sense of shifting gendered possibilities. In the following extract Richard talks of his response to tragic news stories:

I have sat down and watched television a couple of times and...sort of news stories and suddenly realise you are welling up and all that sort of thing...you suddenly become much more aware or much more thoughtful about the nature of loss and all that sort of thing...it's not that I never thought of those things before, but you suddenly have some sense of the depth of them or you discover where your heart is and that sort of thing.

Describing 'welling up' at sad news stories and discovering 'where your heart is' does not conjure up images of strong, unemotional, masculine behaviours (although it is interesting that Richard again uses 'welling up' and not 'crying': see chapter 4) and again helps to illuminate more fluid concepts of gender. Ben also thinks that things have changed in the ways in which men can talk about being a father. In the following two extracts he relates his recent experiences of going to a stag night and then a trip to the pub, both activities associated with more 'masculine' forms of leisure activity:

I found myself there [at the stag night], you are with a bunch of eighteen blokes and within 10 minutes I'm showing them pictures of my boy on my phone...Yes, I'm sure that's all changed a lot lately because they were kind of a really regular group of lads and, you know, they were asking me 'when was he born?' and then other ones that had obviously been through that knew roughly what stage you were at now...so I had quite in-depth conversations with some of them about it.

...but I do remember going for a drink with two really close friends of ours in the local pub, probably since I've seen you; like, my first Friday night out in the pub just with a couple of mates and we sat and talked about our babies and then went home. That's like the cliché of what you know you are not supposed to do. But you couldn't help it because you just have to spill out all this stuff – you know, what's your baby done?, oh, mine is doing this, oh, right I remember that, up four times a night and trying to go back to work. So, yeah, you have a lot of shared experiences and I think it's maybe changed in that it's all okay, I don't think there's...or maybe that's just my circle, that they are not people who are too macho and proud to get out a picture of their child or something. But I'm sure that's changed massively, I'm sure it has.

Clearly Ben is aware of the range of behaviours more readily associated
with being at a stag night or in a pub and 'the cliché of what you know
you are not supposed to do', but he also recognises that things have
'changed massively' and now 'it's all okay'. For Ben, then, it is not
just that some behaviours have changed – become more 'feminised' –
as Gareth suggests above, but amongst his friends the topics of conversation have as well. Joe, too, says he 'thinks dads take on a much more
hands-on approach' now, but he is also aware that support groups for
fathers may not exist (yet) in the way they do for mothers:

I mean, Jane goes to lots of groups with baby, loads and loads, every day
she's got something that she does and I'm not sure whether there's like a
similar support network for fathers.

In talking about a changing sense of self and their practices of fathering the men help to illuminate a range of issues that are pertinent
in current academic and more popular and policy debates around
fathering, mothering, parenting and caring. Their transition is made
sense of by drawing upon a range of discourses and situating their
experiences within these. The discourses available to these men can
be seen to encompass masculinist constructions of durable, 'worker-
breadwinner'-related strands, to less embedded, and relatively novel,
family-friendly notions, alongside ideals of the involved father who is
emotionally and physically engaged in caring for his child(ren). These
strands represent a wider 'repertoire of possible story lines' when compared to those available to women as mothers (Miller, 2005: 160).
But notwithstanding this, the men's narratives do reflect noteworthy
change – the possible 'costs' of which will be considered in subsequent
chapters.
   Looking back on the first year, what has become clearer is the impact
of becoming a father on how the participants see themselves, and their
relationships with others. Many of the men, including Ben below,
speak of 'becoming a family' and doing 'family things':

But I think that we've been very happy and that's been a, not a change,
but it's been really lovely being a family and I do think of us now, rather
than being sort of just me and Hannah I do think of us as a family which
is kind of a big change in your identity . . . But, yeah, my identity definitely
feels changed.

The sense in Ben's account is of having, in part, a collective identity as a family rather than just being an individual. Ben describes further the changing relationship:

you change as a couple as well because you now have a relationship that includes this little boy which has become, I think at first it's quite hard because the permanence of it hasn't sunk in and now I think you realise that that is it forever now, hopefully anyway ... our relationship, mine and Hannah's is, I think it's different to what I expected, but it's really nice being parents together.

Joe also talks positively of having 'loved every minute' of being a father but also acknowledges that it has been 'harder than he expected' and at times relationships have felt under 'stress':

I've loved every minute of it, I wouldn't change anything for the world. In some ways it's sort of been maybe harder than I expected in that, there were a couple of months where it was quite hard for the baby to settle and I probably never really appreciated how hard that was really, and it can put a stress on your relationship, not your marriage, but your relationship with your wife because obviously you are sort of tense and maybe looking for excuses ... and I never probably appreciated before that your life sort of fits around baby, well, ours does anyway, it fits around her routine.

Frank feels that through sharing and supporting each other 'when one person is having a bad day ... it just strengthens your partnership' and in a similar vein Stephen, too, talks about the importance of being 'committed to your partner'. But for Dylan, the competing demands he has felt as he has become a father have led to difficulties in his relationship with his wife:

I never expected a child to be so much, to need so much attention or work or time and that's taken time away from Lisa and I and our sort of relationship as well. We have got to be, I think any new parent would probably tell you that and that's been tough as well just holding our own relationship together has been tough at times and there's been pressures that I never would have expected and awful times really, horrible rows and things.

Gareth also talks of things at times being 'difficult':

Yes, it's very difficult ... you know, as much as we try to talk and stuff, it does get, yeah, we do have our moments where we don't agree and she feels like she's doing everything and I feel like I'm doing everything and, you know, it's very difficult ... but I kind of guess we are okay, I guess, I mean we're still here.

Nick, too, has experienced unforeseen personal difficulties which have unfolded following a traumatic birth and the subsequent illnesses his wife and son have suffered. He felt able to (and that he should) 'hold everything together' (be strong) during this period but there have been consequences for his own health:

But I think the first 6 months were incredibly difficult ... it must have been, it was after Shelley was making huge, huge improvements in her own health, that I had health problems and I was diagnosed with depression which I think is a direct result of the last 6 months ... you know, the emotional strain of the last 6 months. So the health problems have sort of gone between us ... I am pretty sure a lot of that was the impact of the first 4 or 5 months, having to hold everything together for everyone and then, I guess, having held everything together and then my son's health improved and then Shelley's health improved so I took my foot off the gas a bit.

Clearly transition of any sort implies a period of change, and becoming and being a father has brought about significant life-long changes for these men. As Joe said earlier about his young daughter, 'she is my number one priority really now in the world and that's going to continue really all the way through her life'. These changes appear more significant than in previous generations because of the societal and individual expectations that fathers will be more involved in emotional and physical aspects of what were previously, more exclusively, constructed as feminine practices, relationships and domains. By the time the children approach their first year, practices have become well established into routines and relationships have become more interactive and embedded. The men have, over time, worked out their 'niche in the family' but this period of transition has, as the extracts reveal, encompassed significant lows and highs, emotionally and physically.

Looking back at the first year James reflects on his personal journey:

It has certainly got easier, probably easier isn't the word to use, but it's got less hard I think. I think that last time we met was just unbelievably difficult, that period, it was just awful, and coming out of that nice period and going into this sort of back to work, trying to become normal, but there isn't such a thing as normal when there is this, well, it was still a little stranger [the baby] around at that stage, to be fair ... it's not until really that the relationship probably started building from that point onwards really, kind of 6 weeks because you're still coming home and it's still a crying machine that's, you've not really got a, it was difficult for me … I still didn't have a relationship with her. But it was after that point when she was sort of connecting on different things, like when you come home and you make her smile like that and starting to build a bit of an understanding and a bit more of a relationship and it got slowly, slowly easier until you find your sort of little niche in the family …

Towards the end of the first year James has found his 'niche' as a father 'in the family'. But how do the men's experiences continue to unfold and what do fathering practices and involvement look like a year further on at around the time of their child(ren)'s second birthday?

Fathering at two years

Nine of the original seventeen participants were interviewed at around the time of their child(ren)'s second birthday. These interviews had not been included in the original research design, which had replicated the earlier motherhood study, but it was decided to follow up on a group of the men in order to capture a later episode of their unfolding experiences. As these interviews are undertaken several of the men and their families have moved house and/or become fathers for a second time, are on the point of becoming parents again or speak of second pregnancies being planned. One couple has married. In the interviews 'routines' are again referred to ('we've always instilled a routine') but as a taken-for-granted aspect of everyday family life, which is acknowledged to be 'hard work', 'tiring', 'all encompassing', 'constant' but also 'fun, fraught at times, but fun'. The men continue to participate in care-related activities and tasks ('we share out most of the practical tasks, given that my wife is part time at work and I'm full time'). But this mostly continues to be concentrated into evenings and weekends. The fathers comment on their children's rapid development, including their greater capacity now to communicate what they want, which according to Frank means caring has 'become easier even though it is still relentless'. Paid work also continues to be an important theme and there is talk of progressing on the 'career ladder' and 'career progression', changing jobs (in one case, due to redundancy) or working differently in order to try to achieve 'more flexibility' and a work–life

balance. An understanding boss might be vital in men achieving a sense
of a work–life balance:

And work are very good – if anything happens or if I'm running a bit late
I'll just phone up and my boss is absolutely fine. (Mike)

But my boss is quite understanding, he has got three of his own. (Frank)

But the competing demands of home and work have also left several
of the men in 'a state of tiredness all the time' (Nick) although they
are now much more practised at reconciling these demands. James
describes the demands of a job, a growing daughter and a relationship with his wife as being a 'triangle that's difficult to square'. He is
about to start a new job as a result of the work pressures he has felt,
which have led him to seek medical help (something he had discussed
tentatively in the earlier interview):

When I went to see the doctor and described a typical week to him, he was,
like, 'well, no wonder you're not very well, what do you expect?'

In the following extract James excitedly describes his new job:

But, yeah, there will be lots of travel in it as well, even though I would never
admit to Alexa, I do miss the getting away and seeing different places. You
know the first two projects are two places I've never been.

The opportunity to get away will, James anticipates, give him some
release from what he has elsewhere described as the pressures of
'squeezing in the rest of life around work and all the chores I've got to
do to keep ticking things over'.

Graham, too, has changed his job (within an organisation) in a bid
to find a better work–home balance. He had altered his working hours
and pattern of work (to 4 days a week) following the birth of his
first child and now has another young baby. Here he defines 'relative
success':

and when it works well I feel like I'm doing an okay job at work and I'm
getting done what I need to do at home in the way of childcare and so on
and the less good scenario, which I suppose still happens and happened a lot
when I was doing the previous job, is where I don't get the work finished but
I have to go home anyway and then not very happy necessarily with the care
I'm providing at home either if I'm just trying to get by and putting [our son]
in front of the video or something, it's not necessarily the best approach.

Men's involvement in caring continues to be activity and task based in and outside the home and 'typical days' are described by all the men. William reflects on his involvement over the previous two years and comments that he 'can't think of anything that Sophie does that I don't do, if that makes sense'.[1] He then describes a typical day:

So a typical working day would involve me being up and out the house before daughter wakes up . . . I'll get home, it's a little bit variable, but typically between about six and maybe half six-ish and we'll have a little sort of play together, the two of us, outside if it's warm enough and not raining or otherwise just inside. Probably not for too long because we try to keep her, the theory is that she has a bath around half six but we recognise increasingly that that slips, and it slips often in response to the fact that I'm home a bit late more than anything else. So I still do the bath 95 per cent of the time, I'll do the bath, wash her hair, dry her hair and so on and so on and then give her, her milk, read her a story . . . So actual time together during the day is definitely limited actually, during the working week, maybe an hour a day or something like that, which I don't think . . . I don't consider it long enough . . . weekends is kind of like my time with her.

What becomes clear through this extract – and other fathers' descriptions of their typical days with their children is just how much paid work features and how little time is left, or available, for hands-on caring. As William describes his typical day it gradually dawns on him that in reality he only spends 'an hour a day or something', which he doesn't consider to be 'long enough'. William also acknowledges that he probably works more than he needs to:

I think I probably work too, well, Sophie would say . . . definitely, and I still with work, do more than I need to do . . . still work later than I have to do . . . But looking towards the future . . . I do it because it's part of developing and kind of climbing up the career ladder and everything else, so there's kind of a bigger plan to it, but it is still frustrating, yeah.

Earlier, in chapter 4, it was noted that William saw himself – or at least drew significantly upon – a traditional discourse of breadwinner and provider; and this hasn't changed. But what is interesting is that alongside his 'bigger plan' and career aspirations he still does take *some* responsibility for bath and bedtime activities with his daughter and is

---

[1] William had not been available for a second postnatal interview because his job had required him to spend some time abroad.

(and expects to be) more involved at weekends. He also sees no difference in what he and his wife can do for/with their 2-year-old daughter
(although his wife might feel differently). So even though William in
many ways treads a very traditional pathway through fathering (and
appears to have choices available to him that his wife, who would like
him to work less, does not) even he is more engaged – and expects to
be – than in previous generations. Two years after the birth, paid-work
practices for the men, and so, correspondingly, the time they have at
home, appear to have become more embedded and normalised. Costs
associated with a growing family increase, house and/or job moves
become more pressing and what once seemed like new possibilities in
how lives and caring are organised – and explicit plans for sharing
(see chapter 3) – may become obscured as daily life is got through
('survived'). This is not to say that the men all revert to traditional,
patriarchal ways of fathering and doing family life but rather to point
out what becomes a 'domino effect' over time as transition unfolds.

Aspects of the practices which lead to the domino effect run through
the earlier empirical chapters. But the effect was richly illuminated in
a 2-year interview with Ian. Ian had changed his place of work from a
company office to a home-based one as a result of his firm relocating.
Like other fathers who had tried this, he spoke of the difficulties of
achieving any work-related activities alongside caring for his son, and
so his office (a room upstairs) and working hours were clearly marked
out. As his wife had also returned to work (part time) his son went
to a local childminder for part of the week. This, as Ian explains,
had been arranged by his wife (Polly) as she was the one doing the
'balancing':

I think Polly led it and obviously it was Polly who was actually balancing
the days that the childminder could look after our son against the days she
was going to work. So that was more up to her.

Even though Ian is significantly involved in many aspects of caring for
his son, he says that this is not as much as he would like it to be:

I think I'm just sort of a little bit less involved than I sort of would like to
be, in that Polly does have more time with [our son] because she only works
two and a half days a week, so obviously she is looking after [our son] the
rest of that time. So she is generally a bit quicker at doing anything, but in
particular tasks to do with him, if I were to do it, it might take longer.

Ian here, like other fathers (see chapter 6), recognises that by doing tasks more frequently his wife has become quicker – and probably more accomplished through more practice – at doing them. Ian continues:

Because she is more practised at doing it and is less likely to tolerate [the baby] messing about, because if you do something more, you know, you don't want to bother wasting time. I'm trying to get sort of, I do keep a broad spectrum of various things, like I took [our son] to the doctors the other day. I've heard that dads ought to take their children to doctors, the fact that men aren't seen to be involved in going to doctors is one of the reasons apparently that men are less inclined to go to doctors in later life.

I then ask Ian if there is any aspect of caring for his son that he does not do and he asks his wife who has been sitting in the next room. She replies 'packing his bags for Brenda' (the childminder). The following extracts are taken from the interview as it then unfolded with Polly and Ian in discussion:

POLLY: Yeah, I tried to get Ian to [pack the bag], I decided, when I was ill at the beginning of the year I said, 'right, you do a Monday' and I had a list. But my list was all scribbled on and then Monday maybe he'd be out and so we haven't kept that up. But we ought to do that again. But I suppose the only thing I can think of [that he doesn't do] is choosing what [our son] wears. It's partly again because I have a system and he has, if he wears disposable nappies, he wears smaller trousers than if he's in bigger, bulky washable ones. So I know which trousers to put on and I'm saving that for this occasion and Ian doesn't know. So he might get his head bitten off if he chose the wrong thing!

IAN: Yes, so I think that looks interesting to put on and then it's invariably the wrong thing.

POLLY: Or I say, 'why have you changed to that?'

IAN: So...

POLLY: You don't have confidence in doing that, do you?

IAN: No.

POLLY: I also, I tend to be responsible for the washing as well so I'm aware of what [our son] needs and what he's wearing and what fits him and, again, because I'm responsible, I tend to be responsible for the change bag as well, I pack that... Yes, and I buy them as well.

IAN: Yes, and if I get involved it does sometimes make it more difficult because Polly then has to throw what I've done... [laughs].

POLLY: Poor Ian!

IAN: Disputes about how many washable nappy outers have been used.

POLLY: Were there any clean ones?
IAN: They can be reused on a short-term basis and whether they get reused
    or whether new ones get got out.
POLLY: You see, I have systems.

This exchange (which will be instantly recognisable to many parents) beautifully illustrates how practices and behaviours are taken on and become part of the gendered, accepted and 'dailyness' of routines of caring. The very early weeks of fathering (and parenting) which unfolded in chapter 4 involve both parents together learning how to care for their new babies but this cannot continue in the same way once paternity leave and/or saved holiday is used up and the fathers resume paid work. From that time practices of caring by men can mostly only be performed in periods around working and so are task and activity based: both because of time and in order to fit within a routine of care that can make possible both coping and (some) sharing. Since the men resume work outside the home the mothers spend significantly more time with the babies and so not only do they become more practised at recognising and responding to their children's needs but more adept at doing so too. So, in the exchange above, it becomes clear that Ian doesn't pack the bag for the childminder because, according to Polly, he doesn't choose what his son wears because she 'has a system'. Polly's system also includes an acquired knowledge about which clothes are more appropriate for the child to wear (depending on nappy size – this is not rocket science) and she might be cross if Ian were to choose the wrong item of clothing. Because Ian knows that he might not choose the item of clothing that would fit with Polly's system he avoids this task and so becomes unpractised and lacking in confidence. Because Polly also does the washing she knows not just what fits her son but also what is clean and so she takes responsibility for getting the changing bag ready for the childminder. But not only does Polly do the washing but she is also the one who buys the child's clothes. Although Polly talks of having written a list at the outset (to help Ian pack the bag for the childminder) it becomes clear very quickly that it is probably just simpler and quicker to do the task herself and so she becomes more competent and practised. Similarly, 'debriefing' – a practice referred to by most of the fathers when they might take over caring responsibilities at a weekend – is also time consuming and probably here feels unnecessary in relation to getting a changing bag ready

for the childminder. The *domino effect* of one small, apparently incon-
sequential act (in the wider scheme of things) – packing the bag for
the childminder – has, then, much greater implications for a chain of
responsibilities which becomes assumed and reinforced *and gendered*.

Taking responsibility for caring for children in short episodes
inclines men to never (quite) become as competent as their wives/
partners, to never quite develop the 24/7 thinking that mothers (as
primary carers) become so much more practised and adept at (see
chapter 6). All the men in the study speak of the unexpected hard
(and undervalued) work of caring, including William in the following
extract:

Oh, the first few times I had care of [my daughter] was just shattering. I'm
sure everyone says that! But, you know, just handing her back, the relief and
then I'd go and lie down for a while!

Ben, too, acknowledges this:

I know how hard work it is to do it all day, just to have the responsibility
of looking after him all day and entertaining him and getting from one meal
to the other and on your own it's really hard work.

But their lack of constant practice is also a factor here (which is not to
imply that mothers do not also find caring for a child hard work), as is
the recognition of the hard work of doing it 'on your own' and filling
the day. As well as coming to appreciate just how much is involved in
caring emotionally and physically for a child there is also a troubling
realisation for the men of just how undervalued (and invisible) raising
a child is in our society. This sentiment is captured by Graham:

I suppose in terms, it's not an exceptional thing, so you can be exceptional
in another line of life, another part of life and unique, but in parenting,
although you are unique in your own family and you know you've got a
unique child and so on, so you should feel it is, but in a way it's more difficult
to feel that this is something that is really important and good, and I should
feel good about having done this.

The ubiquity and everydayness of parenting is captured here by
Graham but also an implication that, whilst women have become used
to their parenting work being assumed, undervalued and invisible, this
(being novel) is more difficult for men to accept. Graham clearly is
caught between acknowledging the importance of parenting and his

own difficulty of accepting this as a valuable, 'exceptional' thing, having been raised in a society where paid work is a much more highly prized and valued expression of masculinities.

Conclusion

The data from these later interviews indicate the ways in which men as fathers are able to slip back into the familiar territory and patterns of the workplace, not always completely willingly but certainly with societal approval. They are at the same time able to draw upon recognisable discourse of the (modified) breadwinner, but this is alongside recognition of change in what they do and how they can articulate their practices of caring using language more often associated with femininity. But men have available to them different discursive resources when compared to women (Vuori, 2009). These resources operate in relation to caring and paid work in ways which enable these men to exercise agency within a greater range of possible gendered storylines. But there can be limitations too – for example, when men may be seen as potentially disruptive to (historically) maternal spaces. But this group of men do want to be more involved in caring for their children, although they recognise and/or experience stress in trying to reconcile the competing demands of paid work and family life. There is greater fluidity, then, articulated in relation to gendered practices and patterns of caring but also evidence of a domino effect which reinforces particular styles of paternal and maternal involvement. Any notion of 'gender convergence' is at best partial, occurring in pockets of time around paid work. These discussions, then, of caring, responsibilities and a domino effect return us to fundamental debates about biological and/or gendered differences between men and women and their capacities to care. These are considered in the following chapter, which brings together data from both the fatherhood and motherhood studies.

6 | *Gendering practices*

Motherhood and fatherhood expectations and experiences

So I think I've clearly got a female gene in me or something along those lines . . . I think it should be equal roles and responsibilities for the fathers if possible.

(Mike)

So, who is left holding the baby – and why? In this chapter the themes which have arisen across the earlier empirical chapters will be explored further through a juxtaposition of data from the two companion studies on transition to fatherhood and motherhood. Conceptual and theoretical considerations specifically in relation to practices of gender are revisited and reflected upon as the chronological unfolding of transition to fatherhood and motherhood is compared. The data from the two studies will show how men and women make sense of their transitions in different, similar and complex ways which simplistic, categorical explanations, traditional discourses and dualist language does not, and cannot, sufficiently capture. The longitudinal approach taken in both studies has enabled the capturing of shifting experiences and their framing within and between an array of discourses in which temporal, intricate shifts in selfhood and agency are revealed. Threads of discourses which are premised on assumptions around biology and nature, preferences and choice, and social contexts and obligations (Dermott, 2008) feature in the narratives produced as participants make visible their engagement in, and between, care and paid work. Practices of agency, self-surveillance, re-editing of individual narratives and what can be risked voicing – and when – all illuminate the differently configured, gendered and morally underpinned contexts in which fathering and mothering experiences are framed and unfold.

   In the previous chapter questions around the ways in which paternal and maternal responsibilities and identities are assumed and the implications of this were contemplated. Chains of responsibilities were

outlined as a consequence of a domino effect of actions and men's
resulting 'exclusion' from particular activities, often as a consequence
of workplace demands. In the first part of this chapter this focus is
continued as the men describe and make sense of their caring practices. As noted in earlier chapters, the recognition and advent of the
'involved father', in discourse if not wholly in practice, has prompted
new considerations about what such a shift might signal (see chapter 2;
Plantin *et al.*, 2003; Vuori, 2009). For example, does it represent real
social progress or something more sinister connected with new forms
and uses of patriarchal power and what does it mean for understandings of gender and debates around essentialism? (Hearn *et al.*, 2006;
Gatrell, 2007; Plantin *et al.*, 2003). The context of late modernity is
also significant as caring arrangements have become more complex
in this contemporary setting. Changing work patterns across the life-
course (for women and men), alongside changing demographics, family
relationships and different ways of living, can mean that caring support from other family members is not readily or regularly available.
Added to this, 'modern society demands a high degree of achievement'
and this has filtered into ideas around child-centred, 'hyper' parenting
(Bjornberg, 1998: 202; Ghazi, 2001). These have extended the parameters and expectations of 'good', quality caring and parenting to include
doing a range of additional, 'added-value' activities (e.g., Ben taking
his 10-month-old son to the music group) which previously did not
exist. Caring for a new baby and growing child is, then, (unexpectedly) hard work ('it is literally 24 hours a day') as contemporary life
is experienced as being even busier. It is also more time pressured and
economically precarious as 'the capacity of the family to live on a
single wage' has, for many, been eroded (Featherstone, 2009). Family
life and paid work are 'squeezed in', 'juggled' and often 'balanced' in
unsatisfactory and complicated ways (Rossi, 2006). These features of
contemporary life, then, form a backdrop to the 'micro-politics' and
everyday practices that fathers and mothers can engage in. By focusing
on the ways in which these arrangements are narrated by the participants in the fatherhood study, a sense of their agency together with
their 'choices' is made visible: so too is the *potential* of constructions of
masculine power. In the extracts below, the men grapple with descriptions of caring, which at times invoke and fall back upon traditional,
biologically informed dichotomies of 'mothers' as emotional and sensitive and 'fathers' as logical and physically strong. But there are also

more nuanced and intricate descriptions of their fathering practices which further illuminate and confound this contested landscape.

New fathers explaining caring responsibilities

Within the descriptions emanating from the later postnatal interviews the parameters of the new fathers' agency is implicit (a theme returned to later in the chapter) and narrated through a range of strands of discourse. In her work on intimate fathering, Dermott (2008) draws attention to the different ways in which her participants explain the similarities and differences between mothers and fathers. This involves the men appealing to three main groups of ideas: biology, personal preferences and choice, and social forces and gendered obligations (Dermott, 2008). In the transition to fatherhood study the men also draw upon these culturally recognisable discourses: not in clear, categorical ways but rather in complex narratives which weave together different threads of each of these discourses. This again illuminates the men's greater freedom when compared to mothers to narrate their transition experiences. Most of the fathers say that they do not think there is a difference between what mothers and fathers can do in relation to caring for the child except breastfeeding ('in terms of actually caring for our daughter I don't think there would be any reason why Jane or I would do that better really', Joe). But some then proceed to draw upon differences in order to explain their own fathering involvement. Others also talk in more generic terms about 'parenting' rather than thinking of responsibilities as specifically being paternal or maternal ('it's the responsibility of the parent really, I can't see how it would be different . . . I don't think it's different from fathers to mothers', James). But conceptualising caring responsibilities as shared, the same and so effectively 'genderless' is one thing; describing actual daily practices reveals something more complex (Deutsch, 2007; Townsend, 2002; Plantin *et al.*, 2003).

In the following extract Nick talks of sharing care for his young son and being able to 'take it in turns' because he has not been at work following a diagnosis of depression. But he also sees differences:

I think there are times that Shelley finds it easier to pacify him. I don't think she does have a better or deeper instinct of what the problem is. I think she may verbalise it more than I do but I think half of it is guesswork: it might be this, it might be that, it might not be. I don't think she has a greater understanding for, you know, a greater instinct of what the problem is. I think it is easier for her at times to pacify him but then he's also been at home for the last 9 months with her and so he will have a different level of bonding with her. But there are also times when he's clearly fed up of being at home with her for the day and it has been a very hard day and as soon as I walk in the door, he'll come to me and be pacified immediately. So it sort of works both ways.

Nick feels that both he and his wife have 'instincts' but that his wife may be more sensitive to his son's needs because she has been at home (on maternity leave) and so 'a different level of bonding' has had the opportunity to develop over that time. But he still feels that this 'works both ways'. He goes on to describe a 'normal day':

I think a normal day, at the moment, because I'm not at work at the moment, we sort of take it in turns in getting up in the morning... What's apparent is I like to be more active with him, I like to have sort of more structured things to do. I would much rather go out for a walk this afternoon than just sit and play for 90 minutes on the floor. I'd much rather go and play in the park and have a structure. I'm still very involved in his meal times and predominantly I bath him and Shelley feeds him in the evening and puts him to bed... Yeah, [it's] probably as I expected, I thought everything would be pretty much split down the middle. I think there are aspects that I don't take on as much as Shelley. Shelley seems to do far more cooking and preparing his meals for the freezer, not when he's just about to eat, than I do, but I think that's not about the care of [our son], I think that's how we run our house.

What is interesting here is the way in which sharing, and things being 'split down the middle', does not mean equally sharing the same things, or (at least) the way in which they are practised. Nick prefers there being 'a structure' to his caring and so goes to the park rather than staying at home. But this may also be associated with expressions of masculinity which Doucet (2006) notes in her research. Amongst her sample of stay-at-home fathers in Canada she found that 'caregiving such as promoting their children's physical and outdoor activities, independence, risk taking, and the fun and playful aspects of care' were linked to men's strategies to delineate paternal caring from maternal caring: fathering in outside spaces achieved this (Doucet, 2006: 196). There is also a division of labour (and so responsibility) in relation to cooking and preparing and freezing food for their son which could imply more of a 24/7 thinking responsibility being assumed by his wife, but is described by Nick as a consequence of 'how we run our house'. But feeding and food have been traditionally associated with mothers (possibly stemming from associations with breastfeeding) and there is a clear cultural and gendered association between women and food purchasing and preparation. Other fathers, too, identify food preparation *and planning* the children's meals as an area where they do not have the same responsibility and/or expertise as their wives/partners. In contrast, Chris says that he and his wife share food preparation for their son: 'Yeah, we make all our own food ... we tend to cook it up and then freeze it and then have it in containers.' But Chris and Graham, too (who are also the only two fathers to have changed the number of days they work in order to care), are exceptions amongst this group and in the following extracts, Ian, Gus and Richard reflect on their exclusion from this particular aspect of care:

I do quite a lot of the cooking normally for Polly and me but I don't do that much for [our young son] actually because Polly normally has a mental map of what she's got frozen and what she needs to do. (Ian)

Because one of the roles that Anna, one of the things that she does regularly is she gets his food ready for the next day. So goes into the freezer, gets out, you know, a cube of whatever, puts it all into pots and then sets up the three sterilised bottles that she needs for the next day, it's something she does every night. I should probably do it but I never do ... I think, you know, it's always said to me that blokes can switch off a little bit more. I'm sure scientists have done tests on our brains which says, you know, blokes can just sort of switch off, whereas women when they go to bed, a million things can be going around their head and you know it's ... (Gus)

It's that men can't do it because men can't do practical things. Actually it is easy to feed the baby but knowing what to feed her tomorrow is difficult. (Richard)

What is interesting here are the men's explanations for how these practices have become managed on a daily basis. These imply both a biological inability linked to brain function – 'blokes can just sort of switch off' and 'men can't do practical things' – and recognition at the same time that these practices are constructed and have become set up and practised in a particular way that could be interrupted: 'I should probably do it but I never do.' Through these practices the mothers have developed what Ian calls a 'mental map' which leads to a domino effect and chain of responsibilities (see chapter 5). Richard, who works from home part of the week and whose wife commutes to her job, continues to describe how caring for their child is practised:

I do different things. I mean Ros sort of sits around, well, doesn't sit around, on her days she kind of does lots of cooking and stuff and sticks things in the freezer and has baby sitting around watching her whereas my model is we have to go out.

Like Nick and the other fathers, Richard's 'model' of caring involves going out (Doucet, 2006). His apparent inability to *just do* caring alongside other activities in the manner that he sees his wife do is echoed in other fathers' accounts. Dylan explains this difference in models of caring through his wife being 'more experienced':

I think the difference . . . because Lisa is more experienced now in childcare than I am and she will have gone shopping and made phone calls and done blah, blah, blah and I'll just be focusing on [the] baby . . .

In many ways, running through these extracts are examples of men's ability to continue to position their selves as novice and secondary, not necessarily in calculating and obstructive ways but in ways that have evolved through deeply embedded, gendered practices of care. Dermott (2008) points to a lack of time being an important factor in 'determining parent–child relationships' (86).

For the men in this study their involvement has occurred in the periods around mostly full-time working lives whilst their wives/partners have become *more* experienced through full-time caring during maternity leave. The division of caring practices around their children can, then, come to assume (quite quickly following the end of paternity leave) gendered patterns of emotional and more physical interaction as a consequence of how time is allotted by each parent to caring. The novice and secondary aspect of fathering is conjured up in the following extract as Richard says, 'you tell me what to do and I'll do it':

It's the division of labour that we have, it isn't straightforward in a kind of hard work task labour [way] . . . , I do quite a lot of things like, I do lots of the outside walking . . . and lots of the changing. The thing that Ros clearly does take responsibility for, partly because she's taken responsibility for and I've allowed her to, is the sort of intellectual labour of worrying about where [our baby] is yet, what she's supposed to be doing now she's 10 months old. As I say, we didn't sit down and have that agreement, I never said 'bugger that, I'm not doing it', but it's just that that is how it's worked out. But it was, like, you tell me what to do and I'll do it, I'll manage to do it.

In this extract interestingly Richard alludes to how responsibility – and more specifically the 24/7 all-encompassing responsibility that has so long been associated with mothers – operates. In their family, Ros has that responsibility – 'the sort of intellectual labour of worrying' about their child's development, etc. – because 'that is how it's worked out' and Richard has 'allowed her to'. This arrangement appears to have been arrived at through practice rather than Richard consciously opting out of certain activities and he is happy to be 'told what to do': but this way of doing fathering is only available to Richard (and accepted by wider society) *because* his wife is doing the 'intellectual labour of worrying'. Graham, too, recognises that caring for a child is more than a set of activities – 'it's just such a big job that takes up so much time *and thinking*'. Practice is also emphasised in Frank's descriptions of a father:

He's there to feed, to change, to bath, to love, to cuddle, to comfort, I think that is what a father is there for, to provide everything and anything that your family needs, not just the baby. So it's being the support, yeah, I think that's everything a father should be. I don't think it's different to the mother's responsibilities, but it's more of a, I think the way it's delivered it's more of a, there is a feminine way of doing it and a masculine way of doing it and I think being a father is more of a masculine way which I personally thrive on . . . So, yeah, it's the same cuddle but it's a different cuddle, maybe it's more soft whereas mine is probably a bit more strong and sort of rough. So it's the same sort of things, but delivered in a different way but I think that benefits children, that family unit.

Frank here begins to tease apart what he sees as 'feminine' and 'masculine' ways of delivering caring – 'the same sort of things, but delivered in a different way' – and emphasises his physical strength in contrast to his wife. But regardless of how they are delivered, in 'masculine' or 'feminine' ways, Frank still describes practices of caring – cuddling and comforting – that have traditionally been associated with feminine traits rather than hegemonic masculinity. These descriptions, which resonate with others threaded through the men's narratives, both confirm significant changes in the aspects of caring in which (some) men are now involved *and* also the need to think across a range of masculine positions and expressions. Mike, too, suggests he may have been born with a 'female gene' as an explanation for his involvement (around his full-time job) in all aspects of caring for his daughter *and* domestic chores in the house: things he clearly recognises as being traditionally associated with being female. Frank also implies that although there may be differences between men and women this does not mean that men cannot become more practised through the 'hands-on experience' of doing caring. In the following extract he describes getting up to his twin sons at night:

Maybe men don't find it instinctive, so they have to get hands-on experience and I think some of them shy away from that responsibility, that step that they need to take ... I don't know whether it's me because I'm quite straightforward thinking, practical, hands-on, I will always think about the situation, how best to do it and then reflect and then say, 'did I do right, did I do wrong, what would I do next time' and then having a strategy in place for the next time it happened ... but I think in between mothers and fathers I think it's your own, devoting the time and understanding to the children and I think that's what we do as well as we can with the time we've got ...

So what 'negotiations' and/or 'freedoms' are apparent in these accounts of dividing responsibilities in a setting infused with a legacy of inequality? A recurrent concern for feminists has been to explore how power has played out in constructions and assumptions around caring and practices of patriarchy (see chapters 1 and 2). A facet of these concerns arises from men's greater ability to exercise choices and operationalise 'preferences' in their lives which have been denied to women. In the following extracts a greater freedom to choose is implicit in the ways in which caring and work have been organised. In the first extract William reflects on how caring for his young daughter is shared, drawing upon recognisable feminine attributes:

So there are lots of shared things and I think still the emotional thing is more maternal perhaps, like the sensitivity and the reaction to [our daughter] and what needs to happen in the immediate term is probably more Sophie's forte really, whereas mine is a bit more the protective provider really ... [but], yeah, I think to a large extent it's practical actually I must admit. I mean, I think, I'm sure I could have looked after [our daughter] and Sophie could have been at work and, you know, we could have filled those roles and it would have worked. My honest opinion is that although that switch would have worked, it would have been less effective and I think it would have been less effective because there's some kind of basic instinct that makes us better at one role than another. So that's my, I think it could have worked, but I think it works better the way it is, yeah.

What is illuminated here is how choices, and what others have called 'preferences', can work for men in this arena (Dermott, 2008; Hakim, 2002). Although William does not explicitly state making a choice of working outside the home rather than being the primary carer for his daughter at home, he has recognisable and accepted discourses to draw upon which enable him to justify his preference to be the 'protective provider'. He is also able to invoke ideas of the maternal as more emotional and sensitive and refers to 'basic instinct', but at the same time acknowledges that their roles could have been switched, but thinks this 'would have been less effective'. Perhaps not surprisingly (given the hard work of caring that he alluded to earlier, in chapter 5) he thinks that the caring arrangement 'works better the way it is'. Gareth, too, invokes the strength (and the associations) of the term 'maternal' in the following extract:

Yeah, you know, when you say 'she's maternal', I kind of think that's more applicable to women rather than saying 'he's paternal'. I just still think maternal is a much stronger word than paternal in terms of emotional commitment to the children, I don't know. I think women find it a lot easier, it's more innate to women naturally . . . But, as I say, definitely I think there is more of an emotional attachment for women and they're just . . . as I say, on a purely practical basis, Pam is just so much more natural at it whereas I have to be more logical and think about what I'm doing, whereas Pam just does it.

In many ways, of course, Gareth is right in that the term 'maternal' *is* much more readily associated with children and caring than 'paternal'. This means that Gareth can appeal to ideas of women's 'natural' capacities to care in order to justify his working and caring practices and preferences (see chapter 5). But whilst it is possible (and acceptable) for Gareth to talk of Pam being 'so much more natural' at caring this is not a sentiment that could be easily switched in order for Pam to invoke 'paternal instinct' and justify her wish to continue her career (see chapter 5). Gareth sees Pam as practised and caring in ways which seem natural and effortless, whereas he has to 'think about what he's doing'. And this apparent difference sits at the core of the debates and explanations around the division of labour and care for our children: Pam, according to Gareth, 'just does it'.

The men in this study have all demonstrated levels of involvement and a capacity to 'be there' in emotionally caring and invested ways that have not been visible in their own fathers' generations. But does this represent progress – a relaxing of constructions of masculinities and associated conventions – or men moving into and exerting choices and power associated with a particular hegemonic model of masculinity: a consequence of which is to subvert women's agency in this arena? Certainly these men are able to draw upon a wider range of discourses than women as mothers. A language of 'bonding' and 'instincts', which has previously been much more closely associated with mothers, is threaded throughout the men's narratives. But is this evidence of them appropriating and claiming an essentialist relationship to their baby/young child and so potentially diluting in some way the mother–child relationship, or a consequence of their closer involvement in the birth and early weeks and the greater availability of a 'caring masculinities' discourse? Paradoxically a continuing strand of much feminist scholarship has been to challenge essentialist claims made about women, not to lay claim to and protect essentialism. In the extracts above the complexity of these debates is laid out, as pathways through caring are described. It is also clear that it is acceptable for those fathers who wish to prioritise paid work and career progression over caring for children to do so, even though they may not be the higher earner within the couple (as was the case for Joe and Gus). Men's emphasis on paid work is unquestioned and taken for granted, but the flip side of this is that it can be difficult for men who want to – or have to – take on the primary caring responsibility, as other research has shown (Doucet, 2006: 186). The extracts also reveal that the fathers may continue to demonstrate a lack of expertise (because of a lack of time and practice or a 'mental map', or differences in brain functioning) and can move more easily – and less guiltily – in and out of paid work and the home when compared to mothers.

Bringing the data together: transition to first-time fatherhood and motherhood

The comparative focus taken in the remainder of the chapter will range across experiences of selves, practices of agency, caring and paid work. By juxtaposing data extracts from the two studies the ways in which 'gender differences are articulated and justified' will be further explored (Dermott, 2008). The data are organised around the three interview points which both studies share: antenatally (7–8 months into the pregnancy), early postnatally (6–8 weeks following the birth) and later postnatally (9–10 months following the birth), and the first difference relates to who features in the narratives.[1,2] In significant ways, the men's narratives are largely constructed in relation to their wives or partners, but although husbands and partners figure in the women's narratives they do so in much less pronounced, more peripheral and 'fleeting' ways (Dermott, 2008). This disparity corresponds with differences in constructions of 'maternal identity' and 'paternal identity' noted in earlier work on fathering. So that 'whereas mothers seem to construct their maternal identity independent of their relationship with the child's father, fathers' constructions of paternal identity are more grounded in – or mediated by – their relationship with the child's mother' (Pleck and Levine, 2002). 'The figure of the father', then, is in significant ways 'constructed through women' but against a powerful and complex backdrop of gendered moral rationalities (Vuori, 2009; Duncan and Edwards, 1999).

Anticipating fatherhood and motherhood

In the antenatal interviews both the men and the women in the two studies seek to present their selves as preparing 'appropriately'. But the physical embodiment of pregnancy for women and the corresponding lack of this for men, and so the potential sense of detachment, provoke different societal expectations and individual behaviours. The men's novice status is accepted and expected during the antenatal period but there are implicit assumptions that women (who in the motherhood study had not been pregnant before) will have some instinctive sense of what is involved. But many of the women spoke of feeling 'confused' during the early antenatal period as others expected them to know what to do. In the following extract Philippa recalls a visit to the

---

[1] A further (fourth) interview was undertaken in the fatherhood study at around 2 years following the birth (see chapter 5).

[2] As noted earlier (chapter 4) the interview timings with the men were extended to accommodate their working schedules.

antenatal clinic and conveys a sense of irritation at being expected to 'automatically know' as she steps into this new setting:

... they kind of assumed things, like you knew you had to take a urine sample with you and stuff and there was a bit of kind of... and I didn't on the first occasion and they said, 'oh, I can tell it's your first baby', and I thought no one ever told me. I don't know, there were just little things that I just found irritating, this kind of assumption that it was... you were kind of stepping into something and you'd automatically know where to go and who to see...

But whilst both men *and* women may feel they need to learn or be told what to do through the antenatal period, societal ideas around maternal destiny presumes that women will possess innate maternal knowledge (Letherby, 1994; Romito, 1997). Women becoming mothers (may) also share these ideas, and strands of essentialist discourse are woven through the narratives of the women in the motherhood study – especially when they talk about the birth and being able to care for a new baby. But some of the men also, at times, draw upon essentialist discourse as they envisage 'bonding' and experiencing instinctive feelings once their baby is born. However, in contrast to how the women are perceived, societal assumptions about what men do during the antenatal period are much less clearly defined (Marsiglio *et al.*, 2000) and may be experienced as such. Here Joe talks of feeling uncertain about 'what most dads [to be] do':

But I don't know what most dads do, whether sort of most dads as soon as they find out [they are to become a father], sort of change their life straightaway. It hasn't really been like that, to be honest, I don't know if that's normal or not?

For women the imperative that they demonstrate their appropriate preparation for motherhood (through attendance at clinics, scans, changing dietary and exercise habits) is morally underpinned. They risk being labelled a 'bad mother', even before they give birth, if they are not seen to conform in appropriate ways: already they are seen as mothers. Men's novice status in this domain enables them to demonstrate their appropriate preparation in very different ways. This is manifested through, for example, curtailing social activities associated with being a 'regular guy' ('I won't be drinking as much... I'm just a regular guy but we all drink too much apparently', Gareth), the physical preparation of the house and/or baby's room, reading books (mediated by their wife/partner) and being generally supportive. But for men becoming fathers this is a much less morally inflected and 'policed' arena: but then they are not the ones physically carrying a baby.

The embodiment of pregnancy clearly involves physical and emotional changes which men cannot personally experience. It is not surprising, then, that the women talk much more about struggles with trying to retain their sense of self through pregnancy, as their altering body signals change to everyone else. In the following extract Peggy reflects upon this:

I think you have to fight more to keep your individuality . . . You know, you have to fight to be the person that you . . . rather than everybody's preconception of what a mother ought to be, or what a pregnant woman ought to be, or what you ought to be doing.

The struggle to retain a sense of their individual identity is necessitated because others 'read' and conflate bodily changes in pregnancy with instinctive maternal identity into which an individual, non-mother, identity is subsumed. In contrast, impending paternal identity can only be overtly 'read' and associated with men through, and when they are with, their pregnant wife/partner. Although some of the men spoke of experiencing emotional changes (e.g., feelings of maturity) since finding out they were to become a father, struggles over a changing sense of identity were not a feature of the men's antenatal narratives: but trying to feel a sense of 'connection', a 'way in' sometimes was. In contrast to Peggy (above), James talks here about his changing sense of connection through the pregnancy:

I think, yes, the first few hours it was complete and utter shock and then it was just in the denial bit and then just pushed to one side and really, to be honest with you, it didn't affect me until probably about a couple of months ago when sort of things started to get larger [laughs] and I could feel things moving around. 'My God, it's moving' and then, yes, then you sort of feel a bit more connected with it I think. But there is a sort of detachment feeling in the early phase . . . well, nothing has changed really . . .

In this extract James talks frankly ('a sort of detachment feeling') as he describes his unfolding and tenuous sense of feeling 'connected' as the pregnancy can be 'pushed to one side'.[3] It is the actual birth of the child that heralds for these men their first physical possibility of connection, 'attachment' and 'bonding'.

Caring for the baby once it is born is a feature of the antenatal narratives across the two studies. The women talk tentatively of their concerns about being able to 'cope' – but these concerns are mostly alleviated by drawing upon assumptions (and hopes) that instincts will 'come naturally' to them once the baby is born. The men also draw comfort from their partner's assumed natural mothering instincts. So whilst Ian talks about his concerns that 'on the practical side there are all the things you worry about that you might not be able to do very well', Helen says 'but I think maybe when the baby comes I'll... it will be very natural to me'. Indeed all the participants are pinning their hopes on nature and instincts: their own or their wives'/partners' or both. But whilst the men and women can equally express concerns about coping and practically caring, their narratives emanate from deeply gendered assumptions about women as mothers and primary carers. The potential risk, then, of not coping is much greater for the women, which perhaps goes some way to explaining why the women's anxieties about coping are narrated through recognisable and reassuring maternal discourses of nature and instincts. For example, in the following extract Sheila talks powerfully of being 'terrified' but ends by stressing 'instinct':

Terrified... the responsibility, doing things right, just looking after a whole human being... but then again it's... well, everybody else can do it and I'd rather just do it by instinct.

Sheila, Helen and Ian, like almost all the participants in the two studies, recognise and express concerns about 'doing things right' in relation to caring for their as yet unborn children. Their concerns show that they are attuned to societal ideas about 'right' and 'wrong' and 'good' and 'bad' ways of caring for a child and being a mother and a father (Garcia Coll *et al.*, 1998).

A comparison of the antenatal data from the two studies also illuminates the very different positions in which women becoming mothers

---

[3] Two of the women in the motherhood study also spoke of a desire to metaphorically push the pregnancy to 'one side' as they voiced their dislike of the physical, embodied changes they had experienced whilst pregnant.

and men becoming fathers are placed and from which they can narrate transitions. It demonstrates the ways in which gender as 'a central organising strategy' shapes the reproductive terrain and assumed behaviours across it (Lupton and Barclay, 1997: 12). The location of childbearing and motherhood at the interface of the cultural, social, moral and biological has critical implications for both what can be said – and what not – by the women as they anticipate motherhood. But for the men, constructions of paternal identity and fatherhood are not situated so emphatically within these overlapping spheres. Their biological associations do not carry with them embodied, physical change, the moral domain is not policed as vigorously and the social and cultural dimensions are more fluid and less prescriptive than those around motherhood. But births herald the possibility of new forms of engagement.

The early postnatal period

The most significant difference between the men and women in the two studies at the time of the early postnatal interviews (6–10 weeks following the birth) is that the new fathers have resumed their employment outside the home and the new mothers remain at home caring.[4] But as the men inhabit the familiar worlds of work and, the newly unfamiliar home-with-baby, 'priorities' for them are said to have changed. Work outside the home can be more economically important but also less significant in their lives as the men become involved in caring fathering practices and fitting into establishing routines ('his wellbeing is more important than money'). In contrast the (previously employed) women's horizons have receded, as early mothering is largely restricted to the perceived safety of the home. This follows early mothering forays into public places where mothering acts have been felt by the women to have been judged 'incompetent' by others. The narratives produced in these interviews reveal differences in practices of agency and self-monitoring in relation to performances of mothering and fathering and what can and cannot be voiced about early experiences. In the

---

[4] Another practical difference was that because the women were at home as the primary carer it was reasonably straightforward to arrange the early postnatal interviews with them but because the men had resumed work it proved much harder to arrange interviews with them and so the interview timetable slipped a little (see p. 85).

interviews with the new mothers most of the women began by stating that they were *now* coping, but also that it would have been a different matter had they been interviewed much earlier ('I would say probably only the last week that I've actually got on top of it', Helen).[5] Indeed it is very hard to narrate what are felt to be profoundly difficult and unexpected experiences as they are actually being lived through; they require the passage of time in order for 'some reflexive grasp' to be possible (Frank, 1995: 98; Miller, 2007).

In the following extracts Diane and then Nick reflect upon the early weeks and their experiences of mothering and fathering:

I just didn't really understand what was wrong with me. I didn't understand what [my baby] wanted. I'm thinking as a mother I should know is she hungry, wet, bored, what is it? . . . You think other people will look at you and think you don't know your baby, there's something wrong with you . . . It didn't come naturally. (Diane)

But it is more emotionally draining than I thought and at times I've found it less emotionally rewarding than I thought it was going to be. Actually when you get to the end of the day and he has screamed all day, I find it hard to think, well, you know, that's been a good day . . . but, yes, sometimes I've just thought it's not a very rewarding experience. (Nick)

It is almost unthinkable that a new mother could use the language that Nick does to describe some of his early fathering experiences: 'less emotionally rewarding than I thought it was going to be'. This is not because they might not have shared these very thoughts but because the risks for a mother of voicing such sentiments would be perceived as too great (Lupton, 1999). Diane in the extract above also talks of her early baffling mothering experiences and says that 'it didn't come naturally' – a sentiment voiced retrospectively by most of the other mothers – but there is a distinct difference between these two extracts. It is not just that Nick is able to talk more freely about negative aspects of caring (without fear of moral sanction), it is also where they appear to locate the responsibility and the root cause of these experiences.

---

[5] Ironically in the final interviews in the motherhood study and/or the end-of-study questionnaire several of the participants then revealed that they had been pretending to cope during these early postnatal interviews. The pressure to provide a recognisable and apparently coherent account of their early mothering experiences had led them to construct narratives of new motherhood, in particular 'coping', and so recognisably, 'good mother' ways.

Nick points to a screaming baby and a long day filled with screaming which (understandably) does not feel 'emotionally rewarding' or a measure of a 'good day'. In contrast Diane's narrative is all about *her* failure to know what her baby wanted and so her assumptions that something must be wrong with her. Nick is not asking the same questions of himself about *his* inability to stop his child screaming all day and so what could be wrong with him. Implicit once again in these extracts are the gendered assumptions which permeate ideas around nature and nurture at societal and individual levels: Diane felt that she should 'naturally' know how to care for her new baby, she felt she was lacking in some maternal way because it took practice (rather than feeling instinctive) to be able to recognise and meet her baby's needs, but Nick is not expected to instinctively know. Indeed, perhaps Nick's description is evidence of a lack of a biological instinct to care in emotionally engaged ways as some have argued. But if this is so, it does not account for all the hands-on and emotionally invested caring that he actually does for his young son (see chapter 5), nor does it account for Diane's apparent lack of innate maternal instincts which only become more attuned with practice and over time.

The surveillance of maternal behaviours by others is something that Diane also alludes to in the earlier extract when she says 'you think other people will look at you', the implication being that she feared her mothering would be found wanting. A concern that their early mothering performances were subject to scrutiny and negative appraisal was shared across the new mothers' narratives but interestingly was completely absent in those of the new fathers. However, these different concerns were not just an irrational fear expressed by the women but were borne out in practice as the new mothers and fathers went out and about in the public sphere (see, e.g., chapter 4). Below, Gus and then Gillian describe early excursions out with their babies:

... because I'm sure every father that you've interviewed has said it, but my baby is incredibly cute and so you will be walking around town and people will stop and go, 'ah' ... it's generally old ladies that do it but, you know, they'll start chatting, 'oh, he's gorgeous', you know. And I was paying at one of those pay yourself things in [the shop] and the pram was parked behind me and I'm scanning things in and I could just hear these two old voices in the background, these two old grannies going, 'oh, he's lovely, is he yours?', 'oh, he is lovely' and they were all sort of ... that's really nice. It's always great when people tell you that your baby is gorgeous, isn't it?

I know I'm a mother but I don't quite feel like a mother yet...I went to [the shop] once and she screamed the whole way round, then I did feel like a mother because all these old ladies were there and they were going... 'that baby shouldn't be out', 'it's too hot for that baby to be out'. I could hear them rabbiting on behind me. So then I did feel very much like a mother...a dreadful mother.

Societal expectations of men's responsibilities as new fathers are much less clear than those associated with mothers. In many Western societies they continue to embrace economic provision but are much more ambiguous in relation to expectations of men's hands-on involvement as fathers (O'Brien and Shemilt, 2003; Marsiglio *et al.*, 2000). And so even though the parameters around caring arrangements for babies and young children are gradually shifting, almost any public display of early fathering practice is both highly visible and metaphorically applauded. Mothering, in contrast, is mostly *in*visible and taken for granted unless it is seen to be inappropriately performed ('it's too hot for that baby to be out'), when it may be subject to disapproval and critical comment. It is little surprise that most of the women in the motherhood study stayed at home during the early weeks following the birth in order to become more practised at recognising and responding to their babies' needs. Practices of agency as mothers and fathers are, then, engaged with and experienced against a socially and culturally configured backdrop that *assumes* particular behaviours of mothers and applauds these very same behaviours when practised by new fathers. These men, then, are also subject to a 'social gaze' but it is differently oriented. Other research findings, however, suggest that when men take on long-term, *full-time* caring and so step into the role assumed of mothers, societal disapproval, suspicion and 'scrutiny' may also result (Doucet, 2006: 185). Clearly, then, 'gendered judgements on what' mothers and fathers '*ought* to be doing' inflect how paid work and caring are perceived according to who it is that is combining the two, a mother or a father (180).

Later postnatal interviews: paid work and caring

The ways in which discourses of hegemonic masculinities and work can be drawn upon to narrate the contours of men's involvement in and outside of fathering was explored earlier (see chapters 4 and 5).

But as well as paid work being an important dimension of men's identities, increasingly it is a significant feature in women's lives too.[6] Yet
what becomes clear through comparing the data from the two studies
is that women feel compelled to apologise for, and justify, decisions
not to stay at home and take on full-time mothering ('I didn't feel it
was enough for me') but to combine it with paid work. The women's
returns to work are described in narratives which convey a sense of
'guilt', whilst the men talk more freely about 'career progression' and
the importance of work (and being a breadwinner) to their identity
and their new family. But this is not to suggest that paid work and
careers were not important to the new mothers – they often were – but
societal visions about what mothers should do shaped what could be
said. This in turn is further underpinned by what Hochschild (1989)
has called the 'economy of gratitude' which relates to how domestic labour and caring activities are divided and negotiated (Coltrane,
1996). Even though recent research points to changes in men's involvement in caring and women's increased activities in the workplace,
some aspects remain obdurate and seemingly impervious to change
(Dermott, 2008; Doucet, 2006; Featherstone, 2009; O'Brien *et al.*,
2007).

In the motherhood study all but three of the participants had
returned to paid work by the time of the final interview (at 9–10 months
following the birth) and all describe their decisions in tentative but also
challenging ways. In the following extract Rebecca, a school teacher,
recognises that her own ambitions do not marry with societal expectations:

I felt as though if I had a job I was doing something, whereas if I didn't, if
I was just at home with baby, 'oh, you're just a mother and a housewife'.
And I know that's the wrong thing to think but you still can't help thinking
it.

It became clear to both the new mothers and new fathers that caring for a baby was hard but largely undervalued and 'unexceptional'
work – aspects of which could be enjoyable and rewarding – but which

---

[6] It is also important to acknowledge that paid work is not always a choice for
mothers but an economic necessity. This can be the case for 'less privileged
women (for instance, immigrant women, women of colour) who have
historically been important economic actors both inside and outside the home'
(Segura, 1994).

was evaluated differently to 'real' work outside the home. Abigail, too, talks of her need to be a 'professional person' again:

I do like being a professional person and myself...I really felt by the end of my maternity leave that I was treading water and the whole world was getting on with their lives and mine was on hold...Even if I was achieving something with him, I didn't feel it was enough for me. That might sound selfish, I don't know?...I felt so trapped by the end of my maternity leave, I felt so isolated.

Implicit within Abigail's narrative is her recognition that her self and identity as a professional person had become lost amongst her mothering, 'subsumed into this kind of fluffy thing' as Philippa (another mother) describes it. Other women, too, spoke of needing to regain a sense of their pre-baby self in ways that the new fathers did not. The men's sense of self is not in danger of becoming swamped by their fathering practices or their paternal identity, but remains closely connected to paid work in taken-for-granted ways. As Gareth said with feeling (chapter 5):

I love going to work so, I mean, for me obviously I love them but I love going to work more than I do sitting here all day looking after them...I definitely see myself as a breadwinner.

But the caring–work equation is not so straightforward for the mothers to voice and in the following extract Philippa grapples to find what she thinks will be an acceptable way to express her decision to return to work:

...I don't know that I'd find [full-time mothering] stimulating enough...well, not stimulating enough but...I don't know really whether I would be good at it...I need to do both anyway, I think.

Decisions and practices of combining paid work and caring are articulated and rationalised in narratives that clearly reinforce gendered expectations of what mothers and fathers (can) do.

Practices of narrative construction

Reflexive practices of making sense and narrating a significant period of personal transition are themselves also gendered and differently engaged with, and this became clear through the longitudinal focus taken in the studies (Jamieson, 1998). In the late postnatal interviews many of the new mothers revealed that they had concealed difficult experiences of early mothering in the earlier postnatal interviews. But this is not a practice that the men engaged in and/or reveal (Seidler, 2007). The reasons for this appear twofold: first, the men did not feel compelled to *conceal* difficult early fathering/caring experiences in the ways that the women did and, second, because practices of reflexivity and narration hinge on a coherent sense of self and identity, which for the women is challenged and disrupted as they become mothers in ways that for men at this stage of their fathering journey, it is not (Miller, 2005; Frank, 1995).[7] A significant finding, then, to emerge in the motherhood study was that as early unexpected mothering experiences were gradually managed and the women's confidence in their mothering skills grew, they produced narratives which countered the accounts they had previously given. The opportunity to reflect on their transition experiences led many of the women to withdraw, rework and renarrate earlier accounts, to produce 'counter narratives' as they came to feel able to challenge aspects of the myths of motherhood and strands of associated discourse (Miller, 2007). In her final interview Helen reflects on her earlier interview (6–8 weeks following the birth) at which she presented a very upbeat account of coping with becoming a mother and now reveals how she was actually feeling:

> . . . I think in every way, that my life just turned upside down . . . I don't think there is anything that anybody can do to actually prepare you for the change it's going to have in your life . . . I know now and I can express myself as to how I was sort of really feeling . . . I know a couple of the questions you asked me, sort of, first I was bordering on bursting into tears, you know, but I mean I obviously contained myself but, you know, I wouldn't let this other side, sort of . . . Because I don't think I . . . you know, I didn't express it to anybody. You know, not my health visitor, not . . . Stephen, you know; my sister and my mum, you know, have been great sources of support but they have been so capable [as mothers].

---

[7] Across the narratives feelings of 'frustration', 'anger' and 'exhaustion' were at times voiced in powerfully emotive ways that suggest men feel less compelled to 'police' their selves in the narratives they construct: for example, 'It's only because I'm . . . you know . . . a sane, rational person and able to think "this is just a baby, it's not his fault" . . . but, there's a little part of me that's going, "Oh, my God, I just want to punch the wall, or something, you know, I just want you to stop, why are you crying, stop crying, please stop for the love of God, stop crying."'

But the opportunity to revise and renarrate earlier accounts – and so produce 'counter narratives' which challenge more dominant strands of discourse – is not practised in the same way across the men's narratives of transition (Miller, 2007). This may be a result of the men choosing not to reveal or rework in an interview difficult or unexpected experiences, which might be interpreted as weakness or failure. It could also be that they did not feel the same pressure as the women to conceal experiences (which might potentially be interpreted for the women, at least, as 'unnatural') as their journeys unfolded. Alternatively, their sense of their self has remained largely intact and unchallenged by becoming a father because their paternal identities and developing fathering practices have not been subject to the same societal assumptions – or scrutiny – as those which frame motherhood. In fact, all the men's narratives follow a more straightforward, teleological and less problematic trajectory in which expectations may or may not match experiences but are accommodated in lives and identities which for significant parts of days and weeks have continued to follow recognisable pre-baby patterns. And whilst many of the fathers and mothers talk of their transition to fatherhood and motherhood in positive and life-affirming ways ('I feel over the moon', Stephen), paternal identity still leaves spaces for feeling both 'detachment' and 'independent', as one of the fathers says in an interview when his child is 2 years old:

I guess if I'm really honest . . . There's still that element of detachment. I still feel that she's a really great thing to have around the house. That sounds terrible, doesn't it? It's wonderful to have her and I definitely feel like her father but I also still feel a little bit independent.

Narrating maternal and paternal identities

The evidence accumulated across a rapidly growing literature recognises that new possibilities exist for reconfiguring practices of caring and paid work (Hobson, 2002; Browne, 2007; Doucet, 2006; O'Brien, 2005; O'Brien *et al.*, 2007; Hearn *et al.*, 2006). But as this and other research has shown, there is not a 'free market of parenthood' as equality discourses might imply, but rather a complex mesh of moral and gendered responsibilities and rationalities, love, frustration and hard work that women and men must negotiate as mothers and fathers

(Dermott, 2008: 90; Duncan and Edwards, 1999). The empirical data in earlier chapters have illuminated the negotiations and reconciliations that men engage in as they anticipate and then narrate early fathering experiences in contemporary contexts where 'the inherent instability of gender norms' offers new possibilities (McNay, 2000: 2; Hearn *et al.*, 2006). In the final section of this chapter we turn to consider how far new possibilities as reconfigurations of mothering and fathering are evident across the participants' narratives through their appeals to changing masculinities and/or femininities. Immediately, taking this focus shows how successfully women's lives have been conflated with all things maternal through particular constructions of femininity and ideals of womanhood. This is in contrast to the men who grapple with and engage ideas of both masculinities and femininities to describe and locate their own fathering involvement.

The women in the motherhood study do not explicitly refer to constructions of femininities in relation to their pregnant bodies and early mothering: there is no need. It is only when they try to make sense of experiences which are unanticipated – usually associated with not instinctively feeling that they know how to do mothering – that they begin to question assumptions of feminine traits. But even these are initially internalised, as Diane says in an earlier extract 'what is wrong with *me*'. Not surprisingly the men's narratives provide much richer accounts of how and where ideas of masculinities and femininities can be drawn upon and, sometimes claimed, in describing and making visible their paternal identities and practices once the baby is born.

Fathers engage in fathering practices in spaces and ways which can emphasise and mark out both the 'masculine qualities of their caregiving' (Doucet, 2006: 196) and at the same time their selves as 'regular guys'. Across the men's narratives it is possible to see the ways in which ideas of masculinity are invoked as explanations of styles of care giving ('there is a feminine way of doing it and a masculine way of doing it', Frank), measures of their involvement ('I feel that I am probably doing more than quite a lot of men', Ian), and affirmation of their self as a 'real man' and a father ('My brother said to me . . . "you are like a real man, you are married and you are a dad"', Joe). At times this involves recognising that the caring practices they are engaged in might be (and in earlier times would have been) seen as 'feminine', and some behaviours as 'cissy' (Frank). But whilst Mike talks comfortably of having 'a female gene in me or something along those lines',

Gareth draws a distinction – 'I don't think the conversations necessarily become feminised, I think the behaviour is going that way.' Gareth goes on to confirm that the fathers he meets talk about sports events and other activities much more closely associated with masculine identities (e.g., placing a bet on a sports event; see chapter 5). But Frank confirms that he and his male friends do exchange fathering stories – 'Oh, absolutely' – but adds, they 'probably wouldn't admit to it but, yes, it does go on'. Earlier (see chapter 5) Ben also recognises and monitors his new paternal identity in societal contexts which he experiences as changing in terms of expected norms of heteronormative masculine behaviours. So at a stag do he finds himself sharing information about his baby son with 'a really regular group of lads' (some of whom are also fathers) and at the pub he and his friends are not 'too macho and proud to get out a picture of their [children]'. But Ben also monitors the boundaries of his changing self and so talks in an antenatal interview about reading a 'useful' book on active birth, but adds that he 'did keep it quiet amongst my male friends'.

Conclusion

All the men are caught up in managing in subtle and more explicit ways their individual selves, developing paternal identities and practices of what they gauge to be acceptable masculinities during this early period of first-time fatherhood. This involves them both 'distancing' themselves 'from the feminine' (Doucet, 2006: 196) but also at times *claiming* feminine attributes. For the new mothers, maternal identity (mostly) does not have to be claimed or justified, but explaining decisions to take up paid work alongside mothering do. Here the women draw upon strands of discourse which at one time would have been more closely associated with masculinities – for example, individualism and economic provision. As Abigail says, 'I like being at work for myself. I like the money and for us to be comfortably off again.' Paradoxically, then, many of the new mothers also seek to distance themselves from ultra-feminine and essentialist ways of being. But a legacy of long-practised caring arrangements can also be invoked, as when one of the mothers, Sheila, talks of not returning to work and 'wanting to be there' for her twin sons in what she acknowledges as being 'the old-fashioned style'. There is evidence, then, across both the motherhood and fatherhood studies of men and women interweaving strands of discourses associated with masculinities and femininities as they narrate their transitions: and marking out their differences. Through these practices, and even at this relatively early stage of their fathering and mothering 'careers', the men can be seen to be recon-figuring aspects of fathering and masculinities and the women – more tenuously, because it is riskier – challenging aspects of the myths they have encountered in constructions of motherhood (Doucet, 2006: 210; Ribbens, 1998). This takes us, then, to consideration of what men's increased involvement in caring practices actually means in relation to both understanding and constructions of gender (Deutsch, 2007; Risman, 2009). These questions are now revisited in the following, concluding chapter.

7 | Conclusions and reflections

I see that to be a good father I need to be able to do as many of the bits as my wife can.

(Nick)

It is not a man–woman divide anymore, it's a partnership, team work . . . I think it has changed a lot, a hell of a lot.

(Frank)

Like the breadwinning and all that stuff, that's all old hat now, but in a way I'm still trying to do it.

(Dylan)

[Work and family life], it's a triangle that's difficult to square.

(James)

This concluding chapter draws together the theoretical debates raised by the empirical data in relation to divisions of labour around practices of caring and gendered constructions of responsibilities. The intention in this book has been to provide a more precise focus on a group of men's individual and collective practices and their emerging paternal identities in contrast to broader brush-stroke approaches (Hearn *et al.*, 2006). This focus has revealed a greater degree of commitment to, and daily practices of, emotionally engaged, hands-on caring by fathers, but in circumstances which can confound the best of intentions, and reinforce *or* enable more recognisably traditional patterns of care. The participants' fathering responsibilities are claimed, denied, narrated and unfold in tender and loving and sometimes difficult and challenging ways. Their experiences are similar and varied (just like those of new mothers) and significantly the men's practices of caring can sometimes overlap with what new mothers do, in what is a new and foreign terrain for both men and women. But these practices, although they can closely resemble mothering, always begin from a secondary position in which a 24/7 caring and thinking responsibility (described earlier by one new father as 'the sort of intellectual labour of worrying') is never exclusively or primarily taken on, practised and, through practice, 'naturalised'. Even though the data capture a small window of possibility which is created immediately following the birth, as men take paternity/holiday leave and new caring practices around the baby are worked out and managed *together*, this period is soon over. Very quickly, intentions of (sometimes equally) sharing care – expressed in the antenatal interviews – are implicitly revised, or explicitly reframed, and early shared practices become routines of caring involvement which are fitted in around paid work. Soon gendered pathways of caring emerge and are followed. These patterns of caring become established as routines, across the early months, and so a *domino effect* is produced as connected links in a chain of responsibilities unfold (see chapter 5). It also becomes clear through the longitudinal and, latterly, comparative focus taken that the men's practices of agency as new fathers are configured and evaluated in ways that are different to new mothers (Miller, 2005, 2007). This returns us, then, to the questions posed in the opening chapters of this book and to consideration of how the findings can further illuminate debates around fatherhoods, gender and divisions of labour around caring for young children. Men's practices of agency as new fathers provide an overarching motif as these areas are now considered.

In a 1980s review of fatherhood and social change in the USA the observation was made that men can be 'technically present but functionally absent in the home and family life' (LaRossa, 1988: 451–2). This observation clearly invokes men's practices of agency as fathers, which are now claimed to be both significantly different *and* recognisable within this description. As LaRossa *et al.* (2000) have noted, 'researchers agree that change has occurred but disagree on the magnitude of change' (377). And clearly there is both cultural and individual variability. In a more recent UK study it was acknowledged that 'fathers are aware of the existence of ideal types of fatherhood that inform them what they *should* do but what they *actually* do is the result of circumstances that, in many ways, they do not choose' (Williams, 2008: 490, emphasis in the original). This implies that ideals and depictions of 'good fatherhood' can be readily conjured up and articulated through associated discourses – as we have seen in the empirical chapters in this book – but that practices of agency as fathers are shaped by the circumstances in which lives are lived. But in what ways do circumstances shape men's practices of agency as fathers? How are these different and/or similar to women's agency as mothers and how do choices and so-called preferences operate (Dermott, 2008; Hakim, 2002; Crompton, 2007)? What is implicit within the quotes above is the matter of men's privilege and power. But to talk of power in the abstract is of course simplistic and unhelpful. So, whilst some research has concluded over many years that men have a greater power to choose the parameters of their involvement in family life (Lamb *et al.*, 1987; Townsend, 2002; Hearn *et al.*, 2006; Gatrell, 2007), others have claimed more recently that involvement in fatherhood is more a consequence of contexts that are not of men's choosing (Featherstone, 2003; Williams, 2008). Masculine practices of agency, and so power, underpin these apparently competing positions on fathering involvement and in effect both these positions are tenable: that men do have more power than women in many areas that shape family lives and caring practices, and that these have emerged from and become embedded, and so durable, within contexts (and discourses) which for contemporary fathers may not be of their choosing and which can effectively block *and* facilitate particular choices for men as fathers (Marsiglio and Pleck, 2005; McNay, 2000). This was illustrated across the men's accounts collected longitudinally in this study. Whilst their intentions to share care – in ways that some envisaged as equal – were often elaborated in the first interviews, by the last interviews this had either been found to be too difficult to achieve in everyday practice and/or actively avoided.

Modified carers?

The study findings – that these men's practices of caring are more likely to take place outside the home and in pockets of available time around paid work – resonate with other research (Doucet, 2006). But within these parameters their care giving is practised in ways which are emotionally and physically more engaged and involved than facets of fathering identified in earlier research (Lamb *et al.*, 1987; LaRossa, 1988; Townsend, 2002). In many ways their practices coincide and overlap with the three demands – 'preservation', 'growth' and 'social acceptability' – which form part of 'maternal practice' as conceptualised by Sara Ruddick in the 1980s. But although the men are emotionally engaged and hands-on in their care giving, and many of their practices are the same as those that mothers do, they are (mostly) not doing 'mothering' (Doucet, 2006); although this is not to say that they care less, emotionally. Key differences emanate from the very different starting places from which journeys into fatherhood and motherhood begin, one embodied as the pregnancy is physically carried and one more detached and seeking ways in. These differences are reinforced through the gendered, societal and individual expectations that operate and inform possibilities around agency and discursive practices, which are further shaped and reproduced through the structural features of paid work and policies of paternity, maternity and parental leave. The difference in fathering and mothering that the men acknowledge either explicitly or implicitly (see chapters 5 and 6) relates to their wives'/partners' ability to do the sort of 24/7 thinking, and so managing, in ways that the men mostly feel they are not able to replicate, although in many aspects men can feel they are doing the same practices as their wives/partners but delivered in a more masculine way. This, then, returns us to questions of biological determinism, the significance of mother–child relationships and the interchangeability of mothers and fathers (Dermott, 2008; Holloway, 2009; G. Miller, 2009).

The generational changes reflected in the findings of this and other studies demonstrate that behaviours and responsibilities around caring are of course fluid and varied (Williams, 2008; Brannen and Nilsen, 2006; Miller and Mann, 2008; Brannen *et al.*, 2004; Hrdy, 1999). These attributes support arguments that caring relationships and practices – and so how we think about fatherhood (and motherhood) – arise in, and result from, particular circumstances. But how and whether biological determinism is accommodated within a constructionist mode of understanding of reproductive lives and caring relationships sits at the heart of much debate, which necessarily returns us to considerations of paternal and maternal subjectivities, individualisation and gendered practices of agency. At the outset, this book began from 'an optimistic belief that men can do the sort of caring for a child that we associate more usually with women as mothers' (p. 8). And yet as we have seen through the empirical chapters, most of the men have themselves come to note an important aspect in which they see and feel a difference: the thinking and so planning, everyday and longer-view managing of caring that their wives/partners quite quickly become competent and, from their perspective, 'expert' at, as they (the new fathers) resume paid work. But does this perceived maternal competency point to a greater biological imperative and innate emotional capacity for women to do caring? Or does this arise as a consequence of the legacy of gendered practices and concomitant constructions of caring responsibilities and possibilities in particular family and work settings? Additionally, this point of difference could also signify, or result from, a 'unique' mother–child relationship which is different to a father–child relationship (Holloway, 2009). In reporting the findings of a recent study on transition to motherhood, it was noted (using Winnicott's phrase from the 1950s) that 'the experience of becoming mothers turned [the] women, without exception, into "ordinary devoted mothers"' (Holloway, 2009). And this is exactly how I would describe the men in this study too – 'ordinary devoted fathers' who, like the new mothers in Holloway's study, 'wanted the best for their babies and did whatever they could to provide it' (Holloway, 2009). It is clear, however, that these men as fathers do not exactly replicate what mothers do but they clearly have a capacity to care in very similar (and at times indistinguishable) ways: but they are not 'interchangeable' in the sense that complete replication would imply (Dermott, 2008; Doucet, 2006; Holloway, 2009). In many ways the term 'parenting' implies interchangeability and so is problematic for all that is hidden and 'erased' – for example, maternal history – when this blanket term is used (Townsend, 2002; Baraitser and Spigal, 2009; Gillies, 2007). Indeed some of the fathers did emphasise 'teamwork' and 'parenting' rather than distinguishing between individual mothering and fathering practices and responsibilities. But there is a danger that 'parenting' is/continues to be an expedient category under which gendered differences are erased and legacies of 'women's disproportionate responsibility for childcare' are forgotten and through which women are lost and new claims by men can be made (Ruddick, 1997: 206; Townsend, 2002; Baraitser and Spigal, 2009; Roberts, 2008; Vuori, 2009). It should, then, be invoked with caution and care, which is not to suggest excluding men but recognising what fathers and mothers do, and can do, both individually and in combination.

Recent scholarship on men's involvement in fatherhood has led to a range of observations about what involvement looks (or does not look) like and what any changes may signify (Dermott, 2008; Hobson, 2002; Plantin *et al.*, 2003; Johansson and Klinth, 2007). If involvement in practical terms is 'fitted in' to the periods of time left around paid work (even where working patterns are changed) this invites and promotes a more activity-based type of engagement. 'Going out' with the baby denotes particular masculine styles of caring and the new fathers' forays into public spaces in this study were positively acknowledged by others, unless their presence appeared to be potentially disruptive in a space historically associated with mothers – for example, baby-changing rooms (see chapter 5). But this activity-based or quality-time-together style of caring often 'continues to burden mothers with [the other] child related chores' in ways that once again emphasise men's greater power to undertake particular styles of involvement (Gatrell, 2007: 368). Clearly the circumstances in which expressions of involvement are manifested are complex and confounding. Research increasingly points to the use of the term 'modified breadwinner' as a useful way to think about changes in practices and (some) men's involvement in family lives (O'Brien and Shemilt, 2003; O'Brien, 2005). However, the practices of new fathering captured in the longitudinal and more intricate findings here suggest that the term 'modified carer' be added to the lexicon of caring as a flip side of 'modified breadwinner' in order to illuminate and linguistically reframe more contemporary caring arrangements and men's involvement in these. Indeed the term 'modified carer' may capture both what men and women do as lives around caring and working are further reconfigured – reconciled – and subject to greater fluidity alongside other societal changes. For example, care-giving practices in some families involves 'an intricate relationship between parents and not simply a division of labour' (Doucet, 2006: 244). But at the same time, does men's continued capacity to express preferences and choose, at some level, their involvement in care giving simply reflect very slowly changing patriarchal arrangements or something more troubling? Indeed, is more physically and emotionally 'involved' fathering 'just a new, more subtle expression of traditional "hegemonic masculinity"'? (Plantin *et al.*, 2003: 5). It is to consideration of change and (re)conceptualisations of gender that we now turn.

Undoing gender or doing gender differently?

Does approximation in caring practices between men and women signal 'genderless' behaviours and/or evidence of 'undoing gender' as
posed earlier in this book? (Deutsch, 2007; Risman, 2009). If doing
gender means to 'act in such a way that mutual understandings of what
is normatively correct or even "true" from a gender perspective are sustained' how far do the changes documented in the empirical chapters
in this book indicate doing more than this, and so undoing gender
(Bjornberg, 2004: 36)? The legacies both of gendered caring arrangements (including 'maternal gate-keeping') and men's privileged ability
to choose the contours of their involvement (more so than women),
render this a very tricky ground on which to make claims of undoing gender. Thoughts and/or hopes that 'genderless' behaviours can
be discerned underestimate the complexities of the enterprise. Rather,
the data in this study have shown the ways in which new, early father
involvement is 'a socially constructed performance' set within a complex of *changing* expectations and norms of behaviour which encompass (new) claims of biological determinism (men's paternal instincts)
and which are relationally managed and played out in everyday performances: they are not 'genderless' but at best provide indicators of
gender being done differently (Marsiglio and Pleck, 2005: 263; Hearn
et al., 2006). This is because practices of care giving are experienced
within a landscape premised on inherited and culturally recognisable
ideals of masculinities and femininities, which are and have been powerfully shaped by and through expressions of unequal power, privilege
and patriarchy.

But whilst this is an important historical backdrop to summon,
the categories of masculinities and femininities, and indeed patriarchy, have all been subject to revisions and more precise elaborations which acknowledge diversity and fluidity (Connell, 2005; Seidler,
2006; Hearn *et al.*, 2006; Kimmel *et al.*, 2005). For example, 'we can
no longer speak with the same assurance about the ways men and masculinities are positioned within patriarchal cultures' (Seidler, 2006:
4), or indeed invoke the 'gloss masculinities' (Hearn *et al.*, 2006).
Similarly, the *legacy*, and so durability, of particular displays of
patriarchal power in relation to the divisions of labour around production and reproduction also cannot easily be ignored or erased.
Importantly, then, understandings of masculinities and femininities,

and so expectations and assumptions around gendered behaviours, need to take account of the contexts in which individual lives are lived and from which more 'collective practices' have emerged (Hearn *et al.*, 2006). Taking such a stance in this research has enabled the practices of a group of men negotiating maternal and paternal spheres and identities as they are anticipated, and newly encountered, to be followed. The empirical data have shown that these men's individual experiences often overlap with, and increasingly conform to, recognisably collective practices of doing involved fathering conjured up in normative and more caring masculinities discourses (Plantin *et al.*, 2003). But the men's narratives also reveal their capacity to refuse aspects of changing norms and deploy 'tactics of avoidance . . . and passivity' (Bjornberg, 2004: 48). So, do the findings from this research demonstrate processes of 'undoing gender' (Risman, 2009)? And what are the implications of changed fatherhoods for our understandings of masculinities, binary categories and dualist language in this context (Smith, 2009; Messerschmidt, 2009; Deutsch, 2007)?

In a recent article, Risman has suggested that 'perhaps a criterion for identifying undoing gender might be when the essentialism of binary distinctions between people based on sex category is challenged' (2009: 83). But is this enough to suggest actually 'undoing gender' or is it more an indication of gender being done differently? Men's greater involvement in the domestic sphere in terms of housework and childcare has been found to change 'their ideas on masculinity and fatherhood' (Plantin *et al.*, 2003). This is not to suggest that fathers want to take over or become mothers but rather that caring behaviours once associated with women can also be practised in sensitive and tender ways by men and there can be benefits in such arrangements (Doucet, 2006; Marsiglio and Pleck, 2005; Plantin, 2007). But does a reconfiguring of understandings of masculinities and femininities around caring involvement and practices constitute a challenge to the 'essentialism of binary categories' as suggested by Risman, and so 'undoing gender'? Doucet reported that in her Canadian study of stay-at-home fathers the men sought to 'distinguish themselves as men, as heterosexual males, and as fathers' (2006: 196). Similarly, attributes that could be seen as effeminate and/or weak were also narrated in careful and cautious ways by the men in their narratives in this study. Their often sensitive and loving accounts of new fathering experiences were located in ways that emphasised change, but also appealed to recognisable strands of essentialist masculine discourse emphasising strength and control and their power to choose particular pathways through work and caring (see chapters 5 and 6; Johansson and Klinth, 2007). But although change is clearly discernible amongst this small group of men living in the UK, discourses of 'the involved father' are not (yet) 'hegemonic' here as they have been claimed to be in Sweden, where 'it is not possible for fathers . . . to talk another discourse, at least not publicly' (Plantin *et al.*, 2003: 23). Even in the Swedish context this level of change in men's behaviours around their involvement in family life does not appear to constitute 'undoing gender' at an essentialist level (Risman, 2009). Whilst it clearly signifies *reconfigurations* of practices, and so shifts in what are, at a societal and individual level, understood and accepted expressions of masculinities and femininities, the legacies of inequalities around production and reproduction – 'cash and care' – still cannot be ignored or conveniently erased (Hobson and Morgan, 2002). In the UK changes in policies which could, over time, facilitate the process in which practices of hands-on, involved fatherhood become more recognisably normative are much more recent and tentative.

There seems, then, to be no way of escaping gender. Even where men talk of being involved in fathering in equally shared ways, practices of care are differentiated by them in ways that are delivered as either 'masculine' or 'feminine' ('there is a feminine way of doing it and a masculine way of doing it').[1] Gendered differences are also invoked through the dualist language of femininities and masculinities in order to demonstrate men's greater involvement and so change ('I don't think the conversations necessarily become feminised, I think the behaviour is going that way'). At the same time it is also acknowledged that men may 'find it much harder to own their feminine qualities' (Featherstone, 2009: 244). This is not a surprise when emotions and emotional displays have been 'interpreted as "feminine" and so as a threat to male

---

[1] It is interesting that in an end-of-study questionnaire one participant responded to the question 'Are you the main carer for your child?' by stating 'Jointly shared with partner', even though he worked full time and had not changed his working hours or days and his partner worked part time. He clearly felt a sense of jointly shared responsibility which was not something that equated to *actual* time spent with the baby. This again demonstrates the complexities around individual understandings, semantics and notions of being able to 'measure' all emotional as well as physical involvement in caring.

identities' which normatively are premised on selves that are rational, autonomous and controlled (Seidler, 2006: 25). Binary categories, for example, motherhood and fatherhood and associated dualist language, then, remain important both historically and pragmatically as facets of gender which can be reconfigured, claimed and monitored, but which are also deeply embedded. Certainly the findings from this study suggest that amongst the participants, gender is being done differently *and* at times in recognisably traditional ways as evidenced through appeals to being a 'breadwinner' and the men's assumptions about maternal competence. But when gender is being done differently it can at least challenge the *oppositional* dimensions of binary categories – as well as dichotomous understandings of gender – and continue the vigilance around the unequal power structures on which these have been erected. But what about when gender is not being done differently?

In considering how men's choices as fathers are framed within expert discourses in Finland, it has been noted that in relation to sharing in parenting 'the normative pressure for men to change is not strong' (Vuori, 2009: 12). Whilst the 'normative pressure' in Finland will, almost certainly, be much stronger than in the UK (as in Sweden, as noted earlier), this observation is helpful in returning us to the earlier questions about men's power to choose their involvement in fathering. Normative pressures, alongside government policies, workplace practices, unequal pay levels and obdurate strands of breadwinner discourse all continue to make possible choices that are not equally available to women as mothers and so can impede opportunities for gender to be done differently. In these circumstances men have continued to have more choices available to them ('I would much rather go into work, by far') and their articulations of 'preferences' continue to be normatively acceptable – and accepted – in wider society. Vuori (2009) suggests that within the shared parenting discourse, questions about men's involvement have turned into 'what do men want?', clearly invoking men's ability to choose (12). But even allowing for the impervious qualities of normative understandings about what men (can) do it is overly simplistic to reduce the debates just to men's power and choices, which are increasingly shifting, subjective and varied, subject to greater public and policy scrutiny and felt by some men to be 'unequal' and so discriminatory. But economic considerations and social identities outside the home (e.g., as worker and/or professional) do clearly continue to be significant and remain weighted

towards men's preferences: which can be articulated in ways that are
not so available or accepted when expressed by women who are mothers. What is underscored once again is the *value* that societies place on
paid work and production and men's role within it, in contrast to the
important caring work and practices associated with raising a child
and a next generation.

Current employment practices in many European contexts also
impede the possibilities of gender being done differently. Even though
fathers in the UK are increasingly configured in government policies as
'resources both financially and emotionally', paternity leave as currently constituted does not facilitate prolonged engagement and is
not available to all men becoming fathers (Featherstone, 2003: 247;
O'Brien, 2005; Browne, 2007; Crompton, 2007). Combining paid
work and care giving has largely been – and continues to be – a problem for working mothers to reconcile. Yet the importance of paid work
to self-identity (rather than being just an economic activity) for *both*
mothers and fathers has recently been reported in a European quality
of life survey (Torres *et al.*, 2007). This study focused upon 'time use,
work-life options and preferences over the life course' and reported
on trends in gender convergence. It noted that even though societal
attitudes to work had changed there continued to be a majority expectation that women (and not men) should reduce their working hours in
order to accommodate childcare responsibilities (Torres *et al.*, 2007).
Men have, then, provided, and continue to be taken as, the normative
reference point for paid work, employment policies and practices, even
though women are increasingly significant economic players in this
sphere. Thus, enabling gender to be done differently, and so 'shaping
fathers' propensity to take family leave', will only be achieved through
gradual cultural, and so normative, shifts (O'Brien *et al.*, 2007: 379).
Crucially these will also require supportive policy frameworks together
with financial incentives, which will be revisited later in this chapter
(O'Brien, 2005; O'Brien *et al.*, 2007; Johansson and Klinth, 2007).

Discourses, narratives and (emotional) modernist male subjects

Explorations of gender make clear its more fluid dimensions in contemporary contexts and the men's narratives in this study attest to the
reflexive possibilities that have ensued (Featherstone, 2009; Williams,

2008). The men's embodied, emotionally rich and varied accounts of their transitions to fatherhood are woven from strands of recognisable discourses which suggest refashioned masculinities and new possibilities. The resulting narratives are 'intersubjectively' and relationally experienced and normatively and morally informed (Doucet, 2006). Their accounts have been emotional, tender, sometimes troubling and challenging but always compelling and apparently heartfelt. So it has been interesting to note that in the rapidly growing body of literature on the topic of men, masculinities and fatherhood a recurring question has been the extent to which men's accounts of fathering marry with *actual* practice and, by implication, how 'trustworthy' these accounts are. There can of course be methodological problems in studies which seek to measure men's involvement in fathering and terms such as 'involvement' and 'shared parenting' are indeed 'slippery' and difficult concepts (Dermott, 2008; O'Brien, 2005; Marsiglio *et al.*, 2000; Marsiglio and Pleck, 2005). But a broader concern seems to be a 'discrepancy between what men say and what they do' (Johansson and Klinth, 2007: 2), about their ability to '"talk" the discourse coherently whatever their actual behaviour' (Plantin *et al.*, 2003: 19) in societal settings where change is more about imagery than practice (McMahon, 1999). This brings us, then, to consideration not just of practices of these men's agency as fathers but of their practices of reflexivity and the ways in which these are circumscribed through transition to first-time fatherhood.

Documenting processes of reflexivity and narrative construction as individuals make sense of transitional life events has been a primary focus in my academic work. A conclusion from the earlier motherhood book was that women in the study felt compelled to present their shifting selves as they became mothers in culturally recognisable and, importantly, socially normative, and so acceptable, ways. This led the women to produce accounts during their second interviews (at 6–8 weeks following the birth) which conveyed that they were now coping and mostly enjoying new motherhood. These coping narratives were then revised in the final interviews and/or countered in the end-of-study questionnaire when the women felt more able (less fearful of negative responses?) to disclose how they had really felt at the time of the interview ('I now realise I was not being 100 per cent honest with my answers... I was feeling quite disorientated and out of control', Helen, end-of-study questionnaire). Interestingly, then, when the accounts produced by the men are set beside those of the women it is apparent that they have not felt compelled to revise their accounts and have been able to 'tell it like it is' as their experiences of transition have unfolded. Even when their intentions and/or practices have shifted between interviews, and involvement is not as involved or equally shared as they had initially envisaged, they do not feel that it is necessary to produce an alternative version of their experiences of their involvement. Unlike the women, they do not appear fearful of a negative response. The normative pressures, then, felt by the women as new mothers as to how they thought they should feel – and so the storylines they should follow – are not so prescriptive for men as they become new fathers. This is because the modern discourse on fatherhood in the UK is not so well embedded or coherent and continues to emphasise economic *as well as* emotional involvement and thus other possibilities (Plantin *et al.*, 2003; O'Brien, 2005). What we see, then, is on the one hand these men's practices of 'reflexivity and the corresponding opening up of masculinity (into masculinities)' (Williams, 2008: 498) and on the other hand normative discourses, which continue to circumscribe expectations and behaviours in a range of possible ways, that are not so available to women as new mothers.

One facet of these societal expectations and individual behaviours relates to men's expressions of emotions. Across the empirical chapters the men grapple at times with experiences that have invoked emotions but for which they do not have a ready 'masculine' vocabulary. As noted earlier, the male subject is normatively positioned as rational, autonomous and in control of himself. In contrast, anything which is emotional can be seen as being out of control and so weakness: attributes more closely associated with femininities and women's lives. But transition-to-fatherhood journeys *are* emotional and in order to describe them the men display an emotionality which they can only elaborate and articulate by drawing upon a vocabulary which they recognise as invoking femininity. Interestingly, in relation to this, considerations of embodied and internalised experiences of gender have noted the dominance of the 'masculine perspective' in all areas of the social world except for 'parenthood and reproduction, where it was the feminine perspective which dominated' (Uhlmann and Uhlmann, 2005: 101). This in turn falls back upon and reinforces binary categories and dualist language: but what are the alternatives? Although it has been argued throughout this book that this group of men have greater access and freedoms to a wider range of discourses, and so possibilities, around their practices of fathering, these continue to largely conform to ideas of heteronormative masculinities, rationality and control. For men to talk in other ways might 'compromise their heterosexual male identities', implying that as men they were 'somehow lacking' (Seidler, 2006: 25).

We return, then, to the question posed earlier about what men *say* and what they actually *do*. The men have recounted their experiences through transition in ways which illuminate a range of displays of masculinities, in narratives which convey unproblematic chronology and trustworthiness.[2] When the empirical data are compared to those from the companion motherhood study it becomes clear that the men's narratives are not revised in subsequent interviews (or in the end-of-study questionnaire); nor are revelations made about previously difficult experiences that could not be voiced as they were experienced, as found in the motherhood study. These men are not subject (in the same way as the women were) to powerful 'myths' about fatherhood, or to the same moral scrutiny. Their telling of any difficult experiences is less problematic and, sometimes, unexpected and difficult personal experiences are candidly voiced. There is some irony, then, that it was the women in the motherhood study who, for a whole range of explicable, rational (in our society) and gendered reasons, felt compelled to say one thing, but actually felt and experienced another, not the men. This brings me, then, to considerations of constructions of masculinities and their reproduction within the social and gendered encounter that unfolds in the process of doing qualitative longitudinal research.

Qualitative longitudinal research

The interview is a social interaction in which data emerge as a co-production (Birch and Miller, 2000). In-depth interviewing and, in particular, qualitative longitudinal research focusing on significant life transitions invite reflexivity: participants are prompted to look back, across and forward to events and experiences in a life. Indeed such a research approach emanates from a position which assumes a 'modernist subject' who, in the interview encounter, is more likely to

---

[2] 'Trustworthiness' as understood in relation to 'selves as both recognisable, coherent *and* tenuous' (see Miller, 2005: chapter 7).

enact 'performances of self in which radical difference is suppressed' (Alldred and Gillies, 2002: 147; Miller, 2005). The modernist subject is, then, understood to be a storyteller engaged in a 'project of the self', who can reflexively give an account of a life – a self-narrative – in ways that are coherent and culturally recognisable (Frank, 1995; Giddens, 1991; Holstein and Gubrium, 2000). But notwithstanding important critiques of some of these implicit assumptions, and the difficulties posed by periods or events of 'upheaval and uncertainty', the men in the transition-to-fatherhood study (who were also self-selected) conform in many ways to notions of a modernist subject.[3] They also largely conform to those social actors conjured up in normative ideas of the 'good father' who is involved, present *and* employed. In fascinating and changing ways aspects of gendered dynamics also shaped the data collection process. The study was conducted by a woman who is also a mother and so was (often) positioned (as a result of these attributes) as having an 'innate expertise' on aspects of the research topic (e.g., being asked for advice or confirmation of actions). But in the interviews the male participants were both novice (in relation to fathering and fatherhood) *and* practised, and expert at having available to them a range of hegemonic discourses (e.g., around work and masculinities) which provided them with more (recognisable and accepted) possibilities in their narrations and practices of agency as they became parents. It is important, then, to take account of these gendered dynamics and the ways in which 'men's potential interests in presenting a "masculine self" might' also be played out (Marsiglio and Pleck, 2005: 263; Deutsch, 2007).

The men in this study mostly appeared comfortable to talk about 'the unfamiliar terrain of the personal and the emotional', although one commented in the end-of-study questionnaire that he was 'glad I didn't ask about sex' (Seidler, 2006: 32). In contrast, the following exchange took place in a first (antenatal) interview with a participant and is included here to demonstrate the interactional and gendered

---

[3] University ethics approval for the research made it a condition of the approval that participants must opt into the research. Although the study was subsequently widely advertised, this had the effect of producing a white, employed and older sample than had originally been intended in the research proposal. But getting any men to join a longitudinal study as they anticipated fatherhood felt like a small victory!

dimensions of the interview encounter. This exchange happens as the participant reflects on his wife's pregnancy:

PARTICIPANT: The pregnancy itself ... I suppose it has limited us, what we have been able to do sort of socially, you know, that side of things and dare I say it has actually affected our sex life as well. I didn't know what to expect really. Is that the side of things that you are interested in?

TINA: Absolutely everything.

PARTICIPANT: I have been quite put off, actually, by the pregnancy.

TINA: That is not unusual.

PARTICIPANT: And that is actually something I haven't really spoken to anyone much about because amongst mates you probably don't ... but I have spoken to [my wife] quite a lot about it. I think early on that was fine but I have just been put off by this child and I think it is really strange for me.

Several things are interesting here. First, it is clear that the participant recognises that talking openly with a woman he has just met (first interview) about the act of sexual intercourse may be transgressing normative displays of behaviour in an interview and/or a masculine self ('dare I say'). He proceeds to check out that the study is interested in 'that side of things' and I encouragingly confirm that it is, although in fact this is the first time – and one of very few occasions – that sex is discussed by the men in the study. I then reassure him that his disclosure that he has been 'quite put off' sex 'by the pregnancy' is 'not unusual'. I recall this from some of the literature I have read, but the reassuring words are spoken before I have remembered this and I am clearly trying to reassure, give permission and create a space for him to say more, which he does. In acknowledging that he hasn't 'really spoken to anyone much about' this (apart from his wife), he underlines that this is not a topic for discussion amongst his 'mates' where going off sex would generally be seen to run counter to heteronormative constructions of what real men do and corresponding displays of macho behaviour. In this exchange we both (but I more directly) tread carefully around an emotionally difficult subject whilst tacitly being sensitive to, and trying to maintain (and so reinforce), shared notions of masculine behaviours – and so I reassure him that his experience is 'not unusual'. It became clear in many of the interviews that men are limited in the opportunities they have available to them to talk freely in ways that could be seen as more emotionally attuned and so

more closely associated with feminine ways of being. It is little surprise
(although I was initially surprised) that almost all the interviews lasted
longer than those in the motherhood study. In the following extract
Joe talks about how the interviews have made him feel, invoking the
limited opportunities he (and other men) can have to talk in such ways:

So I didn't really know what to expect when we had our first interview, but
for me they are really, really good, to speak to a stranger about and none
of your friends are ever going to ask you a question, like, about fatherhood,
or anything and I've never sort of thought about that before. So for me it
makes me think really about sort of questions that you never really thought
of and it's been really helpful for me, yeah. I've really enjoyed them.

But of course talking about emotional things can also be difficult
if you are unpractised, as the following exchange, which took place
towards the end of a first (antenatal) interview, illustrates (emphasis
added):

TINA: Ok, so looking back over the time since you've found out you were to
   become a father what is the most significant change that's taken place
   in your life?
PARTICIPANT: Do you mean that from a sort of practical point of view or
   an emotional?
TINA: It can be any of those or all of those.
PARTICIPANT: So the most significant change is, ok, *I don't know how to
   put it,* I think kind of, good question, can't I have a different one? The
   most significant change probably for me has been, and this may not
   sort of sum it up properly, but, like, an awareness. We talked about this
   growing up sort of thing and the fact that I've kind of been preparing
   myself and maybe sort of subconsciously but I think I've gone from
   being someone who was entirely carefree to someone who perhaps is
   more aware of some of my obligations but that hasn't translated itself
   into actually being responsible yet but I've just been preparing myself
   for that. *Does that make sense?*
TINA: Yeah, that makes absolute sense.
PARTICIPANT: So I don't think things like painting a room are particularly
   change because we would have painted that room anyway for other
   reasons so I think it's a mental thing but I've kind of just prepared.
TINA: That's really interesting. So it is like sort of a mental or emotional
   preparation?
PARTICIPANT: I think so, yeah.

TINA: That's great and so the last thing is, is there anything else that you'd like to add?

PARTICIPANT: That's an easy one. No, I don't think so. No, it's very interesting to get involved in this and to hear your comments of other fathers as well. I'd be very interested to read whatever...

This exchange is once again interesting for all the things it illuminates about articulations of masculinities and emotional selves as well as the research process. First of all, clarification is sought about whether my (lengthy) question is about 'a sort of practical point of view or an emotional' one and I am unhelpful in narrowing it down and leave it wide open for the participant to decide ('It can be any of those or all of those'). The participant can then be seen to grapple with *how to* narrate complex and changing ideas and his individual emotions ('I don't know how to put it'), which he comes to describe as 'an awareness' and a 'mental thing'. When I try to clarify and confirm what he has said – 'so, a mental or emotional preparation?' – he doesn't quite concur and I do not push him further as his discomfort and difficulty with talking about his changing emotions has been palpable. We move onto safer ground and like other men in the study this participant confirms his interest in being 'involved in this', the study, and hearing from me about 'other fathers as well'. This relates to the observation made earlier that the men in this study, unlike the women in the motherhood study, do not reveal difficult experiences *retrospectively* but rather as they are lived. Related to this – as seen above – is the point that some men do not appear to have the language to articulate personal, emotional change and/or are not used to doing so, and so are not practised at or comfortable doing so.

The interview as a catalyst for reflexivity is clear in the above extracts, but so too are the subjects which do not feature ordinarily in men's casual conversations with their male friends. The interview process was described by a number of the men as 'cathartic' and 'enjoyable', again alluding to the opportunity to reflect on unfolding transformative experiences in ways which would not normally be available to them – or men more generally. As another father said:

It has been an enjoyable thing to do. This is sort of time, sitting down and talking for an hour, it's fabulous! I don't really get time to do that.

But there was also some uncertainty about what was 'required' in this novel territory as well as an implicit understanding that they could not be seen as 'expert' in this arena. As one participant said, 'how much detail do you want me to go into?', adding later, 'sorry, I'm not very good with words'.[4] This uncertain setting (especially the first interview) and the uncertain and first-time journeys on which the men were embarked led some to seek confirmation of how their unfolding experiences might fit with other participants, and so how 'normal' they were. Such confirmation was difficult for them to acquire in other everyday masculine talk and encounters. At times they openly made decisions about what to talk about ('and one night a lot happened, I'm not going to say what, but a lot happened and we had to take [my partner] into a psychiatric hospital'). Others implied that the interview would prompt them to reflect beyond the interview encounter ('later something may come up and I'll think, "oh, I should have said that"'), and tiredness as a consequence of the interview topic (a new baby) was also apparent at times – 'Sorry if I've been a bit drippy, I'm a bit tired.' On occasions wives/partners were also around (in another room but clearly within earshot) whilst the interviews were conducted. At times they would interject, correcting details around timings of the birth, for example, but their presence did not appear to inhibit the men in how they narrated their experiences.[5] On occasion their presence was useful in enabling me to better understand how the caring relationships they described actually worked out in practice (e.g., see chapter 5, p. 141), again illuminating the intricacies of what is said and what is done.

Taking a longitudinal approach in the research importantly facilitated a much more nuanced picture of the temporal ordering of these men's experiences of early fathering and fatherhood to be discerned (Doucet, 2006: 243). It also enabled a comfortable and familiar research relationship to become established and between interviews

---

[4] This participant was the only man to say this, but in the motherhood study almost exactly the same words were used by another participant. It is of interest because it makes us consider again our understandings of modernist, reflexive subjects (see Miller, 2005: 158).

[5] But the presence of a wife/partner did sometimes make me feel uncomfortable. This was because I was aware that I was taking up their 'family time' as interviews were fitted into weekends or evenings when the men had been at work and the women had usually been at home all day with their new baby and sometimes (and not surprisingly) seemed exhausted.

emails were exchanged and photographs (sometimes) sent following the birth (Miller and Boulton, 2007). Had the research adopted a singular, 'snapshot' interview approach then the observations and conclusions would have been quite different. Following analysis of the interview data collected in the first interviews it could have been assumed that the 'involved father' or 'new man' as more normatively associated with men in the Nordic countries had, amongst these participants at least, arrived in the UK, as intentions of sharing care (sometimes equally), being fully involved and even organising paid work differently were envisaged and narrated (Johansson and Klinth, 2007). In the second interviews the men acknowledge the hard work and enduring dimensions of caring for a new baby but are involved in sharing most aspects of the caring as the couple *learn together* how to meet their baby's needs, but this is a short-lived period. By the final interviews (at 9–10 months and then at 2 years) much more recognisably, traditionally gendered behaviours are practised as responsibilities for specific activities of caring are fitted in by the men around paid work (even where wives/partners may also have returned to work). And what this underscores is just how deeply structural features, and cultural practices and expressions of masculinities and femininities, continue to shape how possibilities are imagined and practised (or not). This is not to be defeatist but rather to suggest that changing practices around *who cares* is both absolutely possible (as imagined in the first interviews and illuminated in the second) and also slow and impeded (currently) by unequal policies of maternal and paternal leave entitlements and inverted values around paid work and the work of raising a child. The longitudinal dimension of the research has, then, been crucial in revealing change and continuity and constraints and possibilities across the domains of fatherhoods and motherhoods.

Practices, policies and future directions

It was noted earlier that men have been taken as the normative reference point – the 'standard worker' – with regard to employment and the workplace (Crompton, 2007: 240). It can be useful, then, to invert questions that are asked in relation to men, work and family life in order to reveal their underlying gendered assumptions. For example, Johansson and Klinth have pondered 'what factors could have a negative impact on men's readiness to stay home with their children?' but this is not a question (often, if ever) asked of women who are mothers (2007: 5). Contrastingly, working men who are fathers could be asked a question much more often asked of women who are working mothers, about how 'family responsibilities affect their working lives' (Ranson, 2001: 4). There is a need, then, to reframe even how we conceptualise and imagine ways of doing family lives and paid work. Even though more women combine paid work and caring for children than ever before, some by choice and some because they do not have a choice, the breadwinner discourse is still much more readily available to, and associated with, men. And so, amongst the minority of fathers within this study who actively avoided taking on caring in the ways they had envisaged, the breadwinner discourse provided a useful device to be drawn upon in framing their narratives in which the familiar role of economic provider was prioritised and invoked. This small handful of fathers could be seen to use their more powerful position to prioritise work and so rationalise the more limited extent of their hands-on caring involvement. But the breadwinner legacy, even in its modified form, can also obstruct men's involvement, which is reinforced by current policies of paternal and parental leave (O'Brien, 2005; O'Brien *et al.*, 2007; Browne, 2007). These policies and associated understandings frame family lives and caring responsibilities in clearly gendered and, according to Mike (in chapter 5), 'unequal' and so discriminatory ways for fathers, as *maternal* care is prioritised.

But as has become clear, addressing and reconciling matters of gender and equality and/or convergence or 'symmetry' in relation to caring and paid work is not just a matter of getting the right legislation in place: although that of course helps (Doucet, 2006: 233). Indeed political, legislative and policy change are all critical tools in countering men's more privileged position which has emerged historically 'through the normative constraints put upon women' (Bjornberg, 2004: 50). But if change is to occur then policies must be normatively recognised and entitlements economically sufficient and comprehensive enough to be taken up. For example, evidence from a recent cross-national study showed that if fathers are to take up parental leave it should be 'an individual entitlement, paid at a high rate of compensation, and be flexible, making possible shorter and longer blocks of leave either full or part time' (Featherstone, 2009: 134; O'Brien *et al.*, 2007). But even then 'seemingly progressive pieces of legislation' can contain 'counter-productive clauses which render them highly ineffective as agents of equality' (Browne, 2007: 254). And at the same time, policies designed to promote men's greater involvement in the domestic sphere *may* encourage 'change at the interactional level', but can never 'ensure it' (Deutsch, 2007: 119). At this level a number of other factors – for example, employment status, social class and other aspects of personal biographies – will also be at play. However, notwithstanding this there have been some successes – even if these register at a normative and discourse level rather than a collectively practised one – of men's shifting responsibilities around involved caring for their children, as evidenced across Scandinavian countries (Plantin *et al.*, 2003; Hearn and Pringle, 2006; Johansson and Klinth, 2007). These examples offer some hope for the future, as does (in theory at least) the promise of a 'system of flexible parental leave' made by the new coalition government in the UK. Responses to the need to reconcile work and family lives have, then, been varied across the European stage involving (some) change to social policies and family and employment laws (Rossi, 2006). But the need to (re)conceptualise caring (the right to give and to receive care) as a core dimension of 'democratic agency' and to challenge the 'hegemony of the work ethic' remains fundamental in any discussions on reconciling work and family life (Sevenhuijsen, 2000: 20). For many fathers and mothers, necessarily combining paid work and caring, in ways demanded by fluctuating labour markets and economies, can be not only a difficult and stressful balance to try to achieve, but the two spheres can feel 'utterly incompatible' (Rossi, 2006: 239). This, then, remains a challenging and contested terrain.

Conclusions

All the men, just like the women in the motherhood study, share a profound sense of having achieved something 'amazing' as they have become fathers for the first time (Miller, 2005: 138). Encouragingly this small group of men, like many others, are fathering a new generation of children for whom normative practices of caring will be experienced as emotionally and more practically shared. Different patterns of caring, and so configurations of masculinities and ways of doing gender, are being displayed as they engage in fathering practices which at the everyday level are less gender differentiated and in which 'being there' denotes a physical and emotional closeness. The narratives of transition which run across the book add to the 'multiplicity of stories' that make up contemporary and diverse fathering experiences (Sevenhuijsen, 2000: 19). They also reveal that more storylines are available to men as fathers. But what else does this research enable us to say about individual imaginings and practices of modern fatherhoods whilst noting the caveats in the introduction (p. 2)? That for some men and in some circumstances these are changing in ways that approximate to the caring that has been more culturally associated with ideas of femininity and maternal practice in more modern times. But that across these early months and years of new fatherhood paid work and strands of heteronormative discourses continue to shape, in sometimes dramatic and powerful ways, these men's individual choices and practices of involvement and so highlight continued constraints in women's lives. Clearly, babies and children need and deserve to be cared for in consistent ways and fathers and mothers (or significant others) need to be supported in doing this within structures and flexible mechanisms which facilitate, beyond political rhetoric, their ability to reconcile family life with paid work. The need to assess how practices of care giving are (not) valued and responsibilities around paid work conceptualised is of course a fundamental step in the process: and one that has a long association with feminist theorisations of ethics of care and responsibilities. Through focusing on the micro-politics of these men's family lives and personal relationships through the very early stages of fathering, both change and continuity have been revealed.[6] So too have these men's capacities to do emotional, hands-on caring which is remarked to be significantly different to their own fathers' style of involvement. The unfolding narratives have revealed glimpses and longer views of the men's capacities to care for their children in tender and loving ways: but in circumstances which can impede the best of intentions and clearly facilitate those more resistant to change.

[6] It is of course acknowledged that fathering relationships and ideas and practices of involvement will wend in different ways through childhood and across their children's adulthood.

References

Adkins, L. (2002) *Revisions: Gender and Sexuality in Late Modernity.* Buckingham, UK: Open University Press.

Alldred, P. and Gillies, V. (2002) Eliciting research accounts: Re/producing modern subjects? in M. Mauthner, M. Birch, J. Jessop and T. Miller (eds.), *Ethics in Qualitative Research.* London: Sage, pp. 146–65.

Allen, S.M. and Hawkins, A.J. (1999) Maternal gate-keeping: Mothers' beliefs and behaviours that inhibit greater father involvement in family work. *Journal of Marriage and the Family*, 61: 199–212.

Bailey, J. (forthcoming-a) 'A very sensible man': Imagining fatherhood in England, c. 1760–1830'. *History*, 95, 3, 319 (2010).

(forthcoming-b) Fashioning the sentimental father paper, in J. Arnold and S. Brady (eds.), *What is Masculinity? Historical Dynamics from Antiquity to the Contemporary World.* Basingstoke, UK: Palgrave Macmillan forthcoming 2011.

Baraitser, L. and Spigal, S. (2009) Editorial. *Studies in the Maternal*, 1 (1). Available at: www.mamsie.bbk.ac.uk.

Barclay, L. and Lupton, D. (1999) The experiences of new fatherhood: A socio-cultural analysis. *Journal of Advanced Nursing*, 29 (4): 1013–20.

Beck, U. and Beck-Gernsheim, E. (1995) *The Normal Chaos of Love.* Cambridge, UK: Polity Press.

Beck, U., Bonss, W. and Lau, C. (2003) The theory of reflexive modernization. Problematic, hypotheses and research programme. *Theory, Culture and Society*, 20 (2): 1–33.

Bergnéhr, D. (2007) Love and family: Discussions between Swedish men and women concerning the transition to parenthood. *Forum: Qualitative Social Research*, 8 (1). Available at: www.qualitative-research.net/index.php/fqs/article/view/210.

Birch, M. and Miller, T (2000) Inviting intimacy: The interview as therapeutic opportunity. *International Journal of Social Research Methodology*, 3 (3): 189–202.

Bjornberg, U. (1998) Family orientation among men: A process of change in Sweden, in E. Drew, R. Emerek and E. Mahon (eds.), *Women, Work and the Family in Europe.* London: Routledge, pp. 200–7.

(2002) Ideology and choice between work and care: Swedish family policy for working parents. *Critical Social Policy*, 22 (1): 33–52.

(2004) Making agreements and managing conflicts: Swedish dual-earner couples in theory and practice. *Current Sociology*, 52 (1): 33–52.

Bjornberg, U. and Kollind, A. (eds.) (1996) *Men's Family Relations*. Göteborg University: Department of Sociology.

(2005) *Individualism and Families*. Abingdon, UK: Routledge.

Bobel, C. (2002) *The Paradox of Natural Mothering*. Philadelphia: Temple University Press.

Bradley, H. (2007) *Gender*. Cambridge, UK: Polity Press.

Brandth, B. and Kvande, E. (1998) Masculinity and child care: The reconstruction of fathering. *Sociological Review*, 46 (2): 293–313.

(2003) *Fleksible fedre. Maskulinitet, arbeid, velfersstat*. Oslo Universitetsforlaget.

Brannen, J. and Moss, P. (1991) *Managing Mothers: Dual Earner Households after Maternity Leave*. London: Unwin Hyman.

Brannen, J., Moss, P. and Mooney, A. (2004) *Working and Caring over the Twentieth Century*. Basingstoke, UK: Palgrave Macmillan.

Brannen, J. and Nilsen, A. (2006) From fatherhood to fathering: transmission and change among fathers in four generation families, *Sociology*, 40 (2): 335–52.

Bray, I., Gunnell, D. and Davey Smith, D. (2006) Advanced paternal age: How old is too old? *Journal of Epidemiology and Community Health*, 60 (10): 851–3.

Broughton, T.L. and Rogers, H. (2007) *Gender and Fatherhood in the Nineteenth Century*. Basingstoke, UK: Palgrave Macmillan.

Browne, J. (2007) *The Future of Gender*. Cambridge: Cambridge University Press.

Burgess, A. (1997) *Fatherhood Reclaimed: The Making of the Modern Father*. London: Vermilion.

Butler, J. (1990) *Gender Trouble: Feminism and the Subversion of Identity*. London: Routledge.

Chodorow, N. (1978) *The Reproduction of Mothering*. Berkeley, CA: University of California Press.

Clarke, S. and Popay, J. (1998) 'I'm just a bloke who's had kids: Men and women on parenthood', in J. Popay, J. Hearn and J. Edwards (eds.), *Men, Gender Divisions and Welfare*. London: Routledge, pp. 196–230.

Collier, R. (2001) A hard time to be a father?: Reassessing the relationship between law, policy and family (practices). *Journal of Law and Society*, 28 (4): 520–45.

Coltrane, S. (1996) *Family Man: Fatherhood, Housework, and Gender Equity*. New York: Oxford University Press.

Connell, R.W. (1995) *Masculinities*. Cambridge, UK: Polity Press.

(2000) *The Men and the Boys*. Oxford, UK: Blackwell.

(2005) *Masculinities*. Cambridge, UK: Polity Press.

Connell, R.W. and Messerschmidt, J.W. (2005) Hegemonic masculinity: Rethinking the concept. *Gender and Society*, 19 (6): 829–59.

Coole, D. (1995) The gendered self, in D. Bakhurst and C. Sypnowich (eds.), *The Social Self*. London: Sage, pp. 123–39.

Crompton, R. (2007) Gender inequality and the gendered division of labour, in J. Browne (ed.), *The Future of Gender*. Cambridge: Cambridge University Press, pp. 228–50.

Davis-Floyd, Robbie E. (1992) *Birth as an American Rite of Passage*. Berkeley, CA: University of California Press.

Dermott, E. (2003) 'The intimate father': Defining parental involvement. *Sociological Research Online*, 8 (4). Available at: www.socresonline.org.uk/8/4/dermott.html.

(2008) *Intimate Fatherhood*. London: Routledge.

Deutsch, F.M. (2007) Undoing gender. *Gender & Society*, 21: 106–26.

Dienhart, A. (1998) *Reshaping Fatherhood: The Social Construction of Shared Parenting*. London: Sage.

Doucet, A. (2006) *Do Men Mother?* Toronto: University of Toronto Press.

Draper, J. (2002a) 'It's the first scientific evidence': Men's experience of pregnancy confirmation. *Journal of Advanced Nursing*, 39 (6): 563–70

(2002b) 'It was a real good show': The ultrasound scan, fathers and the power of visual knowledge. *Sociology of Health and Illness*, 24 (6): 771–95.

Duncan, S. and Edwards, R. (1999) *Lone Mothers, Paid Work and Gendered Moral Rationalities*. Basingstoke, UK: Macmillan.

Duncan, S., Edwards, R. and Alexander, C. (2010) *Teenage Parenthood: What's the Problem?* London: The Tufnell Press.

Ellingsaeter, A. and Leira, A. (eds.) (2006) *Politicising Parenthood in Scandinavia. Gender Relations and Welfare States*. Bristol, UK: Policy Press.

Elliott, A. (2001) *Concepts of the Self*. Cambridge, UK: Polity Press.

Equality and Human Rights Commission (2009) *Fathers, Family and Work: Contemporary Perspectives*. Available at: www.equalityhumanrights.com.

Fägerskiold, A. (2008) A change in life as experienced by first-time fathers. *Scandinavian Journal of Caring Science*, 22: 64–71.

Featherstone, B. (2003) Taking fathers seriously. *British Journal of Social Work*, 33: 239–54.

(2009) *Contemporary Fathering*. Bristol, UK: Policy Press.

Firestone, S. (1971) *The Dialectic of Sex*. London: Jonathan Cape.

Fisher, B. and Tronto, J. (1990) Towards a feminist theory of caring, in E. Abel and M. Nelson (eds.), *Circles of Care. Work and Identity in Women's Lives*. Albany: State University of New York Press.

Frank, A. (1995) *The Wounded Storyteller*. Chicago: University of Chicago Press.

Gaertner, B.M., Spinrad, T.L., Eisenberg, N. and Greving, K.A. (2007) Parental childrearing attitudes as correlates of father involvement during infancy. *Journal of Marriage and the Family*, 69: 962–76.

Garcia Coll, C. J., Surrey, L. and Weingarten, K. (1998) *Mothering Against the Odds: Diverse Voices of Contemporary Mothers*. New York: Guilford Press.

Gatrell, C. (2007) Whose child is it anyway? The negotiation of paternal entitlements within marriage. *The Sociological Review*, 55 (2): 352–72.

Gershuny, J., Godwin, M. and Jones, S. (1994) The domestic labour revolution: A process of lagged adaptation?, in M. Andeson, F. Bechhofer and J. Gershuny (eds.), *The Social and Political Economy of the Household*. Oxford: Oxford University Press, pp. 151–97.

Ghazi, P. (2001) Raising the next Tiger Woods is now more important than raising a happy, well-balanced child. *The Guardian*, 21 February.

Giddens, A (1991) *Modernity and Self Identity*. Cambridge, UK: Polity Press.

(1994) Institutional reflexivity and modernity, in A. Giddens, D. Held, D. Hubert, P. Seymour and J. Thompson (eds.), *The Polity Reader in Social Theory*. Cambridge, UK: Polity Press, pp. 89–94.

Gillies, V. (2007) *Marginalised Mothers: Exploring Working Class Experiences of Parenting*. Abingdon, UK: Routledge.

Gilligan, C. (1982) *In a Different Voice: Psychological Theory and Women's Development*. Cambridge, MA: Harvard University Press.

Gillis, J.R. (1997) *A World of Their Own Making: A History of Myth and Ritual in Family Life*. Oxford: Oxford University Press.

Gregory, A. and Milner, S. (2005) Fatherhood: Comparative Western perspectives. Sloan Foundation online encyclopedia on work–life interface. Available at: http://wfnetwork.be.edu/encyclopedia_entry.php.

Hafner-Burton, E. and Pollack, M.A. (2002) Mainstreaming gender in global governance. *European Journal of International Relations*, 8: 339–73.

Hakim, C. (2000) *Work–Lifestyle Choices in the Twenty-first Century: Preference Theory*. Oxford: Oxford University Press.

(2002) The politics of female diversity in the twenty-first century, in J. Browne (ed.), *The Future of Gender*. Cambridge: Cambridge University Press, pp. 191–227.

Hays, S. (1996) *The Cultural Contradictions of Motherhood*. New Haven, CT: Yale University Press.

Hearn, J. (2002) Men, fathers and the state: National and global relations, in B. Hobson (ed.), *Making Men into Fathers: Men, Masculinities and the Social Politics of Fatherhood*. Cambridge: Cambridge University Press, pp. 245–72.

Hearn, J. and Pringle, K. (2006) Men, masculinities and children: Some European perspectives. *Critical Social Policy*, 26 (2): 365–89.

Hearn, J. and Pringle, K., with members of Critical Research on Men in Europe (CROME) (2006) *European Perspectives on Men and Masculinities: National and Transnational Approaches*. Basingstoke, UK: Palgrave Macmillan.

Henwood, K. (2001) First time fathers question their role as providers. Press release. Swindon: ESRC Society Today. Available at: www.esrcsocietytoday.ac.uk/ESRCInfoCenter/PO/releases/2001/november/FIRSTTIME.aspx.

Henwood, K. and Proctor, J. (2003) The 'good father': Reading men's accounts of paternal involvement during the transition to first-time fatherhood. *British Journal of Social Psychology*, 42: 337–55.

Hill Collins, P. (1994) Shifting the centre: Race, class and feminist theorising about motherhood, in E.N. Glenn, E. Chang and L.R. Forcey (eds.), *Mothering, Ideology, Experience and Agency*. London: Routledge.

Hobson, B. (2002) *Making Men into Fathers: Men, Masculinities and the Social Politics of Fatherhood*. Cambridge: Cambridge University Press.

Hobson, B. and Morgan, D.H.J. (2002) Introduction, in B. Hobson (ed.), *Making Men into Fathers: Men, Masculinities and the Social Politics of Fatherhood*. Cambridge: Cambridge University Press, pp. 1–21.

Hochschild, A. (1989) *The Second Shift*. New York: Avon Books.

(1995) Understanding the future of fatherhood: The 'daddy hierarchy' and beyond, in M.C.P. van Dongen, G.A.B. Frinking and M.J.G. Jacobs (eds.), *Changing Fatherhood: An Interdisciplinary Perspective*. Amsterdam: Thesis, pp. 219–30.

Holloway, W. (2009) Maternal studies: The why and wherefore. *Studies in the Maternal*, 1 (1). Available at: www.mamsie.bbk.ac.uk.

Holstein, J.A. and Gubrium, J.F. (2000) *The Self We Live By: Narrative Identity in a Post-modern World*. Oxford: Oxford University Press.

Hrdy, S.B. (1999) *Mother Nature. Maternal Instincts and How They Shape the Human Species*. New York: Ballantine Books.

Jackson, S. and Scott, S. (eds.) (2002) *Gender. A Sociological Reader*. London: Routledge.

James, C. (2008) *Work–Life Balance*. London: Family and Parenting Institute.

Jamieson, L. (1998) *Intimacy: Personal Relationships in Modern Societies*. Cambridge: Cambridge University Press.

(1999) Intimacy transformed? A critical look at the 'pure relationship'. *Sociology*, 33 (3): 477–94.

Johansson, T. and Klinth, R. (2007) Caring fathers. The ideology of gender and equality and masculine positions. *Men and Masculinities*. First published online, on 9 March 2007.

Joshi, H., Makepeace, G. and Dolton, P. (2007) More or less unequal? Evidence on the pay of men and women from the British Birth Cohort Studies. *Gender, Work and Organization*, 14 (1): 37–51.

Kaganas, F. and Day Sclater, S. (2004) Contact disputes: Narrative constructions of 'good' parents. *Feminist Legal Studies*, 12: 1–27.

Kimmel, M.S., Hearn, J. and Connell, R.W. (2005) *Handbook of Studies on Men and Masculinities*. London: Sage.

Knijn, T. and Selten, P. (2002) Transformations of fatherhoods: The Netherlands, in B. Hobson (ed.), *Making Men into Fathers: Men, Masculinities and the Social Politics of Fatherhood*. Cambridge: Cambridge University Press, pp. 168–87.

Lamb, M.E., Pleck, J.H., Charnov, E.L. and Levine, J.A. (1987) A biosocial perspective on paternal involvement, in J. Lancaster, J. Altmann, A. Rossi and L. Sherrod (eds.), *Parenting across the Lifespan: Biosocial Dimensions*. New York: Aldine de Gruyter, pp. 111–42.

LaRossa, R. (1988) Fatherhood and social change. *Family Relations*, 37: 451–7.

LaRossa, R., Jaret, C., Gadgil, M. and Wynn, R.G. (2000) The changing culture of fatherhood in comic strip families: A six-decade analysis. *Journal of Marriage and Family*, 62: 375–87.

Lash, S. (1994) Reflexivity and its doubles: Structure, aesthetics, community, in U. Beck, A. Giddens and S. Lash (eds.), *Reflexive Modernization: Politics, Tradition and Aesthetics in the Modern Social Order*. Cambridge, UK: Polity Press, pp. 110–73.

Lawler, S. (2000) *Mothering the Self: Mother, Daughter, Subjects*. London: Routledge.

Letherby, G. (1994) Mother or not, mother or what? Problems of definition and identity. *Women's Studies International Forum*, 17 (5): 525–32.

Lewis, C. (2000) *A Man's Place in the Home: Fathers and Families in the UK*. York: Joseph Rowntree Foundation.

Lewis, C. and O'Brien, M. (eds.) (1987) *Reassessing Fatherhood: New Observations on Fathers*. London: Sage.

Lewis, J. (2002) The problems of fathers: Policy and behaviour in Britain, in B. Hobson (ed.), *Making Men into Fathers: Men, Masculinities and the Social Politics of Fatherhood*. Cambridge: Cambridge University Press, pp. 125–49.

Lloyd, N., O'Brien, M., Lewis, C. (2003) *Fathers in Sure Start*. London: National Evaluation of Sure Start, Birkbeck College.

Locock, L. and Alexander, J. (2006) 'Just a bystander'? Men's place in the process of fetal screening and diagnosis. *Social Science and Medicine*, 62 (6): 1349–59.

Lupton, D. (1999) *Risk*. London: Routledge.

Lupton, D. and Barclay, L. (1997) *Constructing Fatherhood: Discourses and Experiences*. London: Sage.

Mac an Ghaill, M. and Haywood, C. (2007) *Gender, Culture and Society: Contemporary Femininities and Masculinities*. Basingstoke, UK: Palgrave Macmillan.

MacIntyre, A. (1981) *After Virtue*. London: Duckworth.

Mander, R. (2004) *Men and Maternity*. London: Routledge.

Marshall, K. (2008) Fathers' use of paid parental leave. *Perspectives Labour and Income*, Cat. no. 75-001-X. Ottawa: Statistics Canada.

Marsiglio, W, Amato, P., Day, R.D. and Lamb, M.E. (2000) Scholarship on fatherhood in the 1990s and beyond. *Journal of Marriage and the Family*, 62: 1173–91.

Marsiglio, W. and Pleck, J. (2005) Fatherhood and masculinities, in S. Kimmel, J. Hearn and R.W. Connell (eds.), *Handbook of Studies on Men and Masculinities*. London: Sage, pp. 249–70.

Martin, E. (1990) Science and women's bodies: Forms of anthropological knowledge, in M. Jacobus, E. Fox Keller and S. Shuttleworth (eds.), *Body/Politics: Women and the Discourse of Science*. London: Routledge.

Masciadrelli, B.P., Pleck, J.H. and Stueve, J.L. (2006) Fathers' role model perceptions: Themes and linkages with involvement. *Men and Masculinities*, 9: 23–34.

McBride, B.A., Brown, G.L., Bost, K.K., Shin, N., Vaughn, B. and Korth, B. (2005) Paternal identity, maternal gatekeeping, and father involvement. *Family Relations*, 54: 360–72.

McMahon, A. (1999) *Taking Care of Men: Sexual Politics in the Public Mind*. Cambridge: Cambridge University Press.

McNay, L. (2000) *Gender and Agency*. Cambridge, UK: Polity Press.

McRae, S. (2003) Constraints and choices in mothers' employment careers: A consideration of Hakim's preference theory. *British Journal of Sociology*, 54 (3): 317–38.

Messerschmidt, J.W. (2009) 'Doing gender': The impact and future of a salient sociological concept. *Gender and Society*, 23 (1): 85–8.

Miller, G. (2009) Beyond the secure base: Why the maternal really matters. *Studies in the Maternal*, 1 (1). Available at: www.mamsie.bbk.ac.uk.

Miller, T. (2005) *Making Sense of Motherhood: A Narrative Approach.* Cambridge: Cambridge University Press.

(2007) '*Is this what motherhood is all about?*' Weaving experiences and discourse through transition to first-time motherhood. *Gender and Society,* 21: 337–58.

(2009) Thoughts around the maternal: A sociological viewpoint. *Studies in the Maternal,* 1 (1). Available at: www.mamsie.bbk.ac.uk.

Miller, T. and Boulton, M. (2007) Changing constructions of informed consent: Qualitative research and complex social worlds. *Social Science and Medicine,* 65 (11): 2199–211.

Miller, T. and Mann, R. (2008) Masculinities and caring across the life course: Men doing family life. Unpublished paper presented at European Sociological Association (ESA) RN 13 Interim meeting, University of Helsinki, 27–29 August 2008.

Morgan, D.H.J. (2002) Epilogue, in B. Hobson (ed.), *Making Men into Fathers: Men, Masculinities and the Social Politics of Fatherhood.* Cambridge: Cambridge University Press, pp. 273–86.

Moss, P. and Wall, K. (2007) *International Review of Leave Policies and Related Research 2007,* Employment Relations Research Series No. 80. London: Department for Business Enterprise and Regulatory Reform.

Nayak, A. and Kehily, M.J. (2006) Gender undone: Subversion, regulation and embodiment in the work of Judith Butler. *British Journal of Sociology of Education,* 27 (4): 459–72.

Oakley, A. (1972) *Sex, Gender and Society.* London: Temple-Smith.

(1974) *The Sociology of Housework.* Oxford, UK: Martin Robertson.

(1979) *Becoming a Mother.* Oxford: Martin Robertson.

O'Brien, M. (2005) Shared caring: Bringing fathers into the frame. Working Paper 18, University of East Anglia.

(2006) Fathers, family life and work: Can fathers have it all? Paper presented at the WELLCHI Network Conference 2. Centre for Globalisation and Governance, University of Hamburg.

O'Brien, M., Brandth, B. and Kvande, E. (2007) Fathers, work and family life. Global perspectives and new insights. *Community, Work and Family,* 10 (4): 375–86.

O'Brien, M. and Shemilt, I. (2003) *Working Fathers: Earning and Caring.* Manchester, UK: Equal Opportunities Commission.

Peterson, A. (2003) Research on men and masculinities: Some implications of recent theory for future work. *Men and Masculinities,* 6 (1): 54–69.

Plantin, L. (2001) *Män, familjeliv and föräldraskap* [Men, family life and parenthood]. Umeå, Sweden: Boréa Bokförlag.

(2007) *Fatherhood and Health Outcomes. The Case of Europe.* World Health Organization.

Plantin, L., Mansson, S. and Kearney, J. (2003) Talking and doing fatherhood: On fatherhood and masculinity in Sweden and Britain. *Fathering*. 1 (1): 3–26.

Pleck, J. and Levine, J. (2002) Masculinity and fatherhood: A dialogue between Jim Levine and Joseph Pleck. Sloan Work and Family Research Network, Boston College. Spring 2002, 4 (1). Available at: http://wfnetwork.bc.edu/newsletter_a.php.

Plummer, K. (1995) *Telling Sexual Stories*. London: Routledge.

Ranson, G. (2001) Man at work: Change – or no change? – in the era of the 'new father'. *Men and Masculinities*, 4: 3–26.

Ray, R. (2008) *A Detailed Look at Parental Leave Policies in 21 OECD Countries*. Washington, DC: Center for Economic and Policy Research.

Ribbens, J. (1998) Hearing my feeling voice? An autobiographical discussion of motherhood, in R. Edwards and J. Ribbens (eds.), *Feminist Dilemmas in Qualitative Research*. London: Sage.

Rich, A. (1977) *Of Woman Born*. London: Virago.

Risman, B. (2009) From doing to undoing: Gender as we know it. *Gender and Society*, 23: 81–4.

Roberts, Y. (2008) Mum is the missing word. *The Guardian*, 2 July.

Romito, P. (1997) 'Damned if you do and damned if you don't': Psychological and social constraints on motherhood in contemporary Europe, in A. Oakley and J. Mitchell (eds.), *Whose Afraid of Feminism?* London: Hamish Hamilton, pp. 162–86.

Rossi, G. (ed.) (2006) *Reconciling Family and Work: New Challenges for Social Policies in Europe*. Milan: FrancoAngeli.

Ruddick, S. (1989) *Maternal Thinking: Towards a Politics of Peace*. Boston, MA: Beacon.

(1997) The idea of fatherhood, in H.L. Nelson (ed.), *Feminism and Families*. New York: Routledge, pp. 205–20.

Sanchez, L. and Thomson, E. (1997) Becoming mothers and fathers: Parenthood, gender and the division of labor. *Gender and Society*, 11 (6): 747–72.

Scott, J.W. (1988) *Gender and the Politics of History*. New York: Columbia University Press.

Scourfield, J. and Drakeford, M. (2002) New Labour and the 'problem of men'. *Critical Social Policy*, 22 (4): 619–40.

Segal, L. (1990) *Slow Motion: Changing Men, Changing Masculinities*. London: Virago.

Segura, D.A. (1994) Working at motherhood: Chicana and Mexican immigrant mothers and employment, in E.N. Glenn, E. Chang and L.R. Forcey (eds.), *Mothering: Ideology, Experience and Agency*. London: Routledge, pp. 211–33.

Seidler, V.J. (2006) *Transforming Masculinities. Men, Cultures, Bodies, Power, Sex and Love.* London: Routledge.

(2007) Masculinities, bodies, and emotional life. *Men and Masculinities,* 10 (1): 9–21.

Sevenhuijsen, S. (2000) Caring in the third way: The relation between obligation, responsibility and care in the third way discourse. *Critical Social Policy,* 20: 5–37.

Sheller, M., and Urry, J. (2003) Mobile transformations of 'public' and 'private' life. *Theory, Culture and Society,* 20 (3): 107–25.

Shilling, C. (2003) *The Body and Social Theory* (2nd edn). London: Sage.

Smith, A.J. (2007) Working fathers in Europe: Earning and caring? CRFR Briefing Paper 30. Edinburgh: Centre for Research on Families and Relationships.

Smith, D.E. (2009) Categories are not enough. *Gender and Society,* 23: 76–80.

Social Trends (2006) (38th edn). London: Office for National Statistics.

Stanley, L. (2002) Should 'sex' really be 'gender' – or 'gender' really be 'sex'? in S. Jackson and S. Scott (eds.), *Gender. A Sociological Reader.* London: Routledge, pp. 31–41.

Stueve, J.L. and Pleck, J.H. (2003) Fathers' narratives of arranging and planning: Implications for understanding paternal responsibility. *Fathering: A Journal of Research, Theory, and Practice About Men as Fathers,* 1: 51–70.

Sullivan, O. (2000) The division of domestic labour: Twenty years of change? *Sociology,* 34: 437–56.

Torres, A., Brites, R., Haas, B. and Steiber, N. (2007) *First European Quality of Life Survey: Time Use, Work–Life Options and Preferences over the Life Course.* Dublin: European Foundation for the Improvement of Living and Working Conditions. Available at: www.eurofound.europa. eu/publications/htmlfiles/efo699.htm.

Townsend, N.W. (2002) *The Package Deal: Marriage, Work and Fatherhood in Men's Lives.* Philadelphia: Temple University Press.

Uhlmann, A.J. and Uhlmann, J.R. (2005) Embodiment below discourse: The internalized domination of the masculine perspective. *Women's Studies International Forum,* 28 (1): 93–103.

Vuori, J. (2009) Men's choices and masculine duties. Fathers in expert discussions. *Men and Masculinities,* 12 (1): 45–72.

Walby, S. (1990) *Theorising Patriarchy.* Oxford, UK: Blackwell.

Walkerdine, V. and Lucey, H. (1989) *Democracy in the Kitchen: Regulating Mothers and Socialising Daughters.* London: Virago.

Wall, G. and Arnold, S. (2007) How involved is involved fathering?: An exploration of the contemporary culture of fatherhood. *Gender and Society,* 21: 508–26.

Wall, K. (2007) Leave policy models and the articulation of work and family in Europe: A comparative perspective. Paper presented at the 8th European Sociological Association Conference, Glasgow, September 2007.

West, C. and Zimmerman, D. (1987) Doing Gender. *Gender and Society*, 1: 125–51.

Williams, F. (1998) Troubled masculinities in social policy discourses: Fatherhood, in J. Popay, J. Hearn and J. Edwards (eds.), *Men, Gender, Divisions and Welfare*. London: Routledge, pp. 63–97.

Williams, S. (2008) What is fatherhood? Searching for the reflexive father. *Sociology*, 42: 487–502.

Woodward, A.E. (2008) Too late for gender mainstreaming? Taking stock in Brussels. *Journal of European Social Policy*, 18: 289.

Websites

www.fatherhoodinstitute.org
http://nds.coi.gov.uk
http://publications.dcsf.gov.uk/eOrderingDownload/CM-7787.pdf

Index

age 30
agency 13, 40, 110, 145, 147, 159, 171–2, 173
antenatal classes 58, 60–1
   antenatal/prenatal 'appropriate' preparation 56–63
   information 58
   physical preparation of house/DIY 62–3, 157
   ultrasound scan 55, 57
anticipating motherhood and fatherhood 155–9

becoming a family 134–5
'being there' 13, 15, 56, 83, 84, 95, 111, 154, 191
birth 87–92
   anticipating the birth 64–7
   caesarean 87
   home birth 88
   hospital birth 88
   pain relief 88
birth plans 66, 87, 88
'bonding' 84, 100, 104, 119, 129, 154, 156, 158
breastfeeding 124, 147
breadwinner 7, 38, 42, 44, 47, 125, 126, 134, 179
   breadwinner discourse 125, 127, 139, 179, 190
   'modified breadwinner' 81, 144, 175

caring 12–21
   and division of labour 36
   and emotional work 109
   and paid work 98
   and time 150
   as providing 98

caring practices and new fatherhood 115, 147–54
   child-related activities 10
   elaborations of care giving 32
   home to hospital 92–5
   men and caring capacities 113, 192
   primary carer 15, 17, 158
   sharing care 84, 109, 111, 114, 148
   task- and activity-based 139

domestic responsibilities 10
   division of labour 11, 170
'domino effect' and caring responsibilities 140–3, 144, 146, 150, 171
discourses 11, 21–4
   and 'good fatherhood' 56
   and hegemonic masculinities 42, 184
   'involved fatherhood' 178
   of care 111
   of gender equality 16, 166
   of modern fatherhood 7
   of nature 112
discursive resources 85, 126, 144
dual-earner households 17

essentialism
   and biological determinism 38
   and debates 146, 154
   definition 36
   essentialist assumptions 13, 35, 112
   essentialist discourses 121
'ethic of care' 5, 19, 192

fatherhood
   anticipating fatherhood 70–5
   contemporary fatherhood 10, 11
   definition of fatherhood 6